The Indonesian Presidency
Assessing the 2024 Presidential Elections and Beyond

World Scientific Series on International Relations and Comparative Politics in Southeast Asia

Print ISSN: 2810-9910
Online ISSN: 2810-9929

Series Editor: Bilveer Singh *(National University of Singapore, Singapore)*

In view of the fast-changing developments in domestic and foreign policy confronting states in Southeast Asia, it is opportune to develop a series on International Relations and Comparative Politics in Southeast Asia. The primary purpose of the series is to invite researchers and scholars working on International Relations and Comparative Politics on the Southeast Asian region to bring out publications on topics of specific and general interests.

While there are no specific areas that are being targeted, some of the suggested topics can cover COVID-19 and the politics of Southeast Asia, rise of populism in Southeast Asia, role of the military in Southeast Asian politics, threat of radicalism and terrorism in Southeast Asia, politics within Southeast Asia, impact of US–China relations on Southeast Asia, importance of welfare politics in Southeast Asia, importance of LGBT issues in Southeast Asia, and the changing role of media in Southeast Asia.

Published:

Vol. 3 *The Indonesian Presidency:*
Assessing the 2024 Presidential Elections and Beyond
by Bilveer Singh (National University of Singapore, Singapore)

Vol. 2 *COVID-19 Pandemic and the Migrant Population in Southeast Asia:*
Vaccine, Diplomacy and Disparity
by AKM Ahsan Ullah (Universiti Brunei Darussalam, Brunei) and
Diotima Chattoraj (James Cook University, Singapore)

Vol. 1 *Myanmar's Fragmented Democracy: Transition or Illusion?*
by Felix Tan Thiam Kim (Nanyang Technological University, Singapore)

Forthcoming:

Political Change and Consolidation in Southeast Asia: The Hegemony of Institutions
Abdillah Noh (Universiti Brunei Darussalam, Brunei) and
Nadia H Yashaiya (Universiti Brunei Darussalam, Brunei)

---

*More information on this series can also be found at https://www.worldscientific.com/series/wsircpsa

World Scientific Series on International Relations and
Comparative Politics in Southeast Asia — Volume 3

The Indonesian Presidency
Assessing the 2024 Presidential Elections and Beyond

Bilveer Singh
National University of Singapore, Singapore

NEW JERSEY • LONDON • SINGAPORE • BEIJING • SHANGHAI • HONG KONG • TAIPEI • CHENNAI • TOKYO

Published by

World Scientific Publishing Co. Pte. Ltd.
5 Toh Tuck Link, Singapore 596224
USA office: 27 Warren Street, Suite 401-402, Hackensack, NJ 07601
UK office: 57 Shelton Street, Covent Garden, London WC2H 9HE

Library of Congress Control Number: 2024029682

British Library Cataloguing-in-Publication Data
A catalogue record for this book is available from the British Library.

World Scientific Series on International Relations and Comparative Politics in Southeast Asia — Vol. 3
THE INDONESIAN PRESIDENCY
Assessing the 2024 Presidential Elections and Beyond

Copyright © 2025 by World Scientific Publishing Co. Pte. Ltd.

All rights reserved. This book, or parts thereof, may not be reproduced in any form or by any means, electronic or mechanical, including photocopying, recording or any information storage and retrieval system now known or to be invented, without written permission from the publisher.

For photocopying of material in this volume, please pay a copying fee through the Copyright Clearance Center, Inc., 222 Rosewood Drive, Danvers, MA 01923, USA. In this case permission to photocopy is not required from the publisher.

ISBN 978-981-12-9689-5 (hardcover)
ISBN 978-981-12-9753-3 (paperback)
ISBN 978-981-12-9690-1 (ebook for institutions)
ISBN 978-981-12-9691-8 (ebook for individuals)

For any available supplementary material, please visit
https://www.worldscientific.com/worldscibooks/10.1142/13951#t=suppl

Desk Editors: Aanand Jayaraman/Yulin Jiang

Typeset by Stallion Press
Email: enquiries@stallionpress.com

*This book is specially dedicated to
Gurdial Kaur, Jasminder Singh, Prabhinder Singh,
Malwina Kaur, Riftiven Kaur, Karanveer Singh,
and Jasmine Kaur*

ABOUT THE AUTHOR

Bilveer Singh is a born-and-bred Singaporean. He is currently Associate Professor and Deputy Head at the Department of Political Science, National University of Singapore. He is also an Adjunct Senior Fellow at the Centre of Excellence for National Security, S. Rajaratnam School of International Studies, Nanyang Technological University, and President of the Political Science Association, Singapore. He received his M.A. and Ph.D. in International Relations from the Australian National University. He has been lecturing on issues relating to Singapore, foreign policy, and Southeast Asia, especially Indonesian politics, for nearly 45 years. He researches and publishes on comparative politics and international relations. The following are some of his works: *Is the People's Action Party Here to Stay? Analysing the Resilience of the One-Party Dominant State in Singapore*, Singapore: World Scientific, 2019; *Understanding Singapore Politics*, Singapore: World Scientific, 2017; *Quest for Political Power: Communist Subversion and Militancy in Singapore*, Singapore: Marshall Cavendish, 2015; *Politics and Governance in Singapore*, McGraw Hill Education Asia, 2012; *Papua: Geopolitics and the Quest for Nationhood*, Transaction Publishers, 2008; *The Talibanization of Southeast Asia: Losing the War on Terror to Islamist*

Extremists, Westport, CT, 2007; and *Succession Politics in Indonesia: The 1998 Presidential Elections and the Fall of Suharto*, London: Macmillan Press, 1999. He regularly lectures at the Gadjah Mada University (Yogyakarta), Sunan Kalijaga State Islamic University (Yogyakarta), and the University of Muhammadiyah (Yogyakarta).

ACKNOWLEDGEMENTS

I wish to thank the many people who assisted me in completing this book. First and foremost, my heartfelt thanks to the many Indonesian colleagues in Jakarta and Yogyakarta who helped me through their knowledge, by organizing meetings with experts, and by being prepared to hear out my arguments on various aspects of the presidential elections in Indonesia. Many of them are my long-established friends such as Professor Munir Mulkhan, Professor Zuly Qodir, Professor Sugeng Riyanto, Professor Alfitri, Professor Teuku Cut Mahmud Aziz (Poncut), Dr. Erwin Endaryanta, Mr. Ari Nurcahyo, Mr. Mohammad Jumhur Hidayat, Dr. Syahganda Nainggolan, Rendra Agusta, Kyai Hassan, Pak Azhar Sulaiman, Mas Virdika Rizky Utama, Mbak Liya Armina, and Mbak Misqola.

Second, my special thanks also go to former and current leaders, and policymakers who helped to provide special insights into and a perspective of what was going on in Indonesian politics, especially the dynamics involving political parties, political leaders, and the voters. These include Pak Wiranto, Pak Andika Perkasa, Pak Ustad Asad Ali, Pak Ansyaad Mbai, Pak Sutiyso, Ustad Irfan Awass, Dr. Sukardi Rinakit, Mr. Harry Pribadi, Major-General Rudy Rachmat Nugraha, Dr. Rakyan Adi Brata, Pak Budiman Sujatmiko, and Pak Hashim Djojohadikusumo.

Third, my special thanks, gratitude, and appreciation to the publisher, World Scientific Publishing, for dedicating themselves to publishing top-rate books inside and outside Singapore. In this regard, my heartfelt thanks go to all members of the publishing team, particularly Mr. Jiang Yulin, editor of the social sciences editorial team. I am also grateful to Maximilian Neo for acting as a research assistant for this project.

Finally, I am forever indebted and grateful for all the blessings and support I receive from my precious family members, the love and affection of my wife, Gurdial Kaur, my sons, Jasminder Singh and Prabhinder Singh, my daughters-in-law, Malwina Kaur and Riftiven Kaur, and adorable grandchildren, Karanveer Singh and Jasmine Kaur. They have always been my key source of inspiration and strength.

I, however, take complete responsibility for the views put forward and for any errors that may occur in the book.

KEY PERSONALITIES INVOLVED IN THE 2024 INDONESIAN PRESIDENTIAL ELECTIONS

Joko Widodo, Indonesia's President, 2014–2024.
Megawati Sukarnoputri, former President, daughter of Sukarno and leader of the PDI-P.
Puan Maharani, a key leader of PDI-P and daughter of Megawati.
Prabowo Subianto, Defense Minister in the Second Jokowi Cabinet, leader of Gerindra and President-elect.
Ganjar Pranowo, presidential candidate for the PDI-P.
Anies Baswedan, presidential candidate.
Andika Perkasa, former Armed Forces Chief and Deputy Head of Ganjar's campaign team.
Muhaimin Iskandar, leader of PKB and running mate of Anies Baswedan.
Amien Rais, leader of the Ummat Party.
Surya Paloh, leader of Nasdem.
Bambang Yudhoyono, Chairman, Democrat Party, and former President.
Agus Harimurti Yudhoyono, Leader of Democrat Party and son of Bambang Yudhoyono.
Hary Tanoesudibyo, leader of Perindo.

Gibran Rakabuming Raka, Mayor of Solo, son of Jokowi and running mate of Prabowo.

Mahfud MD, former Coordinating Minister for Politics, Law and Security, and running mate of Ganjar.

Kaesang Pangarep, son of Jokowi and leader of PSI.

Hasto Kristiyanto, Secretary-General, PDI-P.

CONTENTS

About the Author vii

Acknowledgements ix

Key Personalities Involved in the 2024 Indonesian Presidential Elections xi

Abbreviations xv

Glossary xxi

Introduction xxv

Chapter 1	Importance of Indonesia's 2024 Presidential Elections	1
Chapter 2	Indonesia's Political Structure and System	9
Chapter 3	The Indonesian Electoral System	23
Chapter 4	History of Indonesia's Presidents, 1945–2024	31
Chapter 5	The Key Political Parties in the 2024 Indonesian Presidential Race	53
Chapter 6	The Key Coalitions and Strategies of the Political Parties in the 2024 Presidential Contest	93

Chapter 7	The Profiles of the Key Contestants in the 2024 Indonesian Presidential Race	99
Chapter 8	Factors That Will Influence the 2024 Indonesian Presidential Election	119
Chapter 9	The 2024 Indonesian Presidential Election Playbook: Candidates, Political Parties, and Strategies to Win the Race	137
Chapter 10	The Politics and Politicking for the Presidency Prior to D-Day (February 14, 2024)	159
Chapter 11	The Results of Indonesia's 2024 Presidential and Vice Presidential Elections	187
Chapter 12	What the 2024 Indonesian Presidential Election Means for Indonesia, the Region, and the Wider World?	247

Conclusion	283
Select Bibliography	297
Index	309

ABBREVIATIONS

ABN	*Akademi Bela Negara* (National Defense Academy)
ABRI	Indonesian Armed Forces
ABS	Asian Barometer Survey
AHY	Agus Harimurti Yudhoyono
APBN	*Anggaran Pendapatan dan Belanja Negara* (National Budget)
Askeskin	Poor Community Health Insurance
ASN	State Civil Servant
BIN	Indonesian State Intelligence Agency
BOS	Schools Operational Assistance
BPK	*Badan Pemeriksa Keuangan* (National Board of Audit)
BTP	Basuki Tjahaja Purnama
CSIS	Centre for Strategic and International Studies, Indonesia
DP	Democratic Party
DPA	Supreme Advisory Council
DPD	*Dewan Perwakilan Daerah* (Regional Representative Council)

DPR	*Dewan Perwakilan Rakyat Republik Indonesia* (People's Representative Council)
DPR-GR	Mutual Cooperation People's Representative Council
FDI	Foreign Direct Investment
FPI	Islamic Defenders Front
G30S	30 September Movement
GAKARI	*Gerakan Karya Rakyat Indonesia* (Indonesian People's Working Movement)
Gerindra	*Partai Gerakan Indonesia Raya* (The Great Indonesia Movement Party)
Golkar	*Partai Golongan Karya* (The Party of Functional Groups)
HTI	*Hizbut Tahrir Indonesia*
IBRA	Indonesian Bank Restructuring Agency
IMR	Infant Mortality Rate
ITE	Electronic Information and Transactions
KAGAMA	Alumni Family of Gadjah Mada University
KIB	United Indonesia Coalition
Kino	*Kelompok Induk Organisasi* (Main Organization Groups)
KNIP	*Komite Nasional Indonesia Pusat* (Central Indonesian National Committee)
Kogasma	Commander of the Joint Task Command
Kompolnas	National Police Commission
Kopassus	Indonesian Army Special Forces
Korem	Commander of the 023 "Kawal Samudera" Military Area Command
KOPRI	*Korps Pegawai Republik Indonesia* (Employees' Corps of the Republic of Indonesia)
Korps Marinir RI	Indonesian Marine Corps

Kosgoro	*Kesatuan Organisasi Serbaguna Gotong Royong* (Mutual Cooperation Multifunction Organizations' Union)
Kostrad	Indonesian Army Strategic Reserves Command
KPK	Corruption Eradication Commission
KPU	General Elections Commission
LGBT	Lesbian, Gay, Bisexual, and Transgender
LSI	*Lembaga Survei Indonesia*
MA	Supreme Court
MARA	*Majelis Amanat Rakyat* (Peoples Mandate Council)
Masyumi	*Majelis Syuro Muslimin Indonesia* (Consultative Council of Indonesian Muslims)
MKGR	*Musyawarah Kekeluargaan Gotong Royong* (Mutual Assistance Families Association)
MMR	Maternal Mortality Rate
MPR	*Majelis Permusyawaratan Rakyat Republik Indonesia* (People's Consultative Assembly)
MPR-RI	*Majelis Permusyawaratan Rakyat Republik Indonesia* (People's Consultative Assembly)
MPRS	Provisional People's Consultative Assembly
MSME	Micro, Small, and Medium Enterprise
Nasdem	*Nasional Demokrat* (National Democrats)
NU	*Nahdlatul Ulama* (Association of Islamic Scholars)
OPM	Free Papua Movement
Ormas Hankam	*Organisasi Kemasyarakatan Pertahanan dan Keamanan* (Defense and Security Mass Organizations)
PAB	*Partai Amanat Bangsa* (People's Mandate Party)
PAN	National Mandate Party
Pangkoops Jaya	*Panglima Komando Operasi Jakarta Raya* (Operations Commander for Greater Jakarta)

Panglima TNI	Commander of the Indonesian National Armed Forces
Parmusi	Muslim Party of Indonesia
PAW	Interim Replacement
PBB	Crescent Star Party
PBR	Reform Star Party
PDI	*Partai Demokrasi Indonesia* (Indonesian Democratic Party)
PDI-P	Indonesian Democratic Party-Struggle
PDP	Democratic Renewal Party
PDS	Prosperous Peace Party
Perppu	*Peraturan Pemerintah Pengganti Undang-Undang* (Government Regulation in-lieu-of Law)
Perti	Islamic Education Movement
PK	*Partai Keadilan* (The Justice Party)
PK	Judicial Review
PKB	The National Awakening Party
PKI	*Partai Komunis Indonesia* (Indonesian Communist Party)
PKPI	Indonesian Justice and Unity Party
PKS	*Partai Keadilan Sejahteram* (Prosperous Justice Party)
PNI	*Partai Nasional Indonesia* (Indonesian Nationalist Party)
PPKI	*Panitia Persiapan Kemerdekaan Indonesia* (Preparatory Committee for Indonesian Independence)
PPP	*Partai Persatuan Pembangunan* (United Development Party)
PSI	Indonesian Solidarity Party
PSII	Islamic Association Party of Indonesia
R20	Religion 20

RIS	*Republik Indonesia Serikat* (United States of Indonesia)
RTLH	Repair of Uninhabitable Houses
RUU TPKS	Criminal Offense Bill of Sexual Abuses
SBY	Susilo Bambang Yudhoyono
Sekber Golkar	*Sekretariat Bersama Golongan Karya* (The Joint Secretariat of Functional Groups)
SK	Decree
SMRC	Saiful Mujani Research and Consulting
Soksi	*Sentral Organisasi Karyawan Swadiri Indonesia* (Central Organization of Indonesian Workers)
TNI	*Tentara Nasional Indonesia* (Indonesian National Armed Forces)
TNI-AD	Indonesian National Armed Forces-Army
TNI-AL	Indonesian National Armed Forces-Navy
TNI-AU	Indonesian National Armed Forces-Air Force
USI	United States of Indonesia
UU IKN	State Capital Act
V-Dem	Varieties of Democracy

GLOSSARY

Bawalsu	*Badan Pengawas Pemilihan Umum* is a national body that oversees elections in Indonesia.
Dalang	*Dalang* is a puppeteer in Javanese and Balinese culture, the individual responsible as the plotter of various Javanese puppetry stories, often based on the Indian epics, *Mahabharata* or *Ramayana*.
DPR	*Dewan Perwakilan Rakyat Republik Indonesia* (People's Representative Council) is the lower house of the Indonesian parliament.
Dwifungsi	This refers to the dual role of the Indonesian military in the security and socio-political arenas during the New Order under Suharto, from 1967 to 1998.
Hilirisasi	This refers to a term popularized under the Jokowi administration, depicting the process of developing the industrial base and production of raw materials in the country rather than simply being an exporter of these raw materials.

Gemoy	It refers to the moniker describing "cuteness" or "coolness," largely referring to the new image of Prabowo in the 2023–2024 Indonesian presidential campaign as a "cuddly grandfather" who danced on stage with the people.
Javanese *Wayang*	It refers to the traditional Javanese and Balinese puppetry, based on the Indian epics of *Mahabharata* and *Ramayana*, often depicting military conflicts and plots.
Keris	It is a traditional Javanese dagger, often used in rituals and ceremonies, and often believed to be embedded with spiritual powers and qualities.
KPU	The General Elections Commission that administers the country's elections.
MPR	*Majelis Permusyawarantan Rakyat Republik Indonesia* (People's Consultative Assembly) is the upper house of the Indonesian parliament.
Muhammadiyah	Literally meaning "followers of Prophet Muhammad," it is a major non-governmental organization founded in 1912 by Ahmad Dahlan in Yogyakarta.
New Order	This refers to the political system following the fall of Sukarno with the military in power under President Suharto.
NU	*Nahdatul Ulama* (Association of Islamic Scholars) is a traditional Islamic organization in Indonesia founded in 1926.
Old Order	This refers to the political system following Indonesia's independence with Sukarno as the centerpiece.
Pemilu	This refers to the general or legislative elections at the national level, as distinct from the regional level.
Pilpres	This refers to the presidential elections.

Polri	It refers to the Indonesian police force.
Projo	This refers to a nearly 7 million strong volunteer group, almost a de facto political party, that is aligned with President Jokowi and had promised to support any group or individual that would support Jokowi and his programs.
Quick Count	It is a method of verifying an election result by projecting it on a sample from polling stations.
Real Count	This refers to the manual counting of votes following an election.
Reformasi	This refers to the political order following the fall of Suharto or the New Order that was undertaking all-round reforms of the country's political system.
Tidar	This largely refers to Mount Tidar, in the vicinity of the city of Magelang, central Java, where the Indonesian military academy is located, in part to symbolize its role as the guardian of the nation's security as Mount Tidar is considered the protector of Java in legends.
TNI	*Tentara Nasional Indonesia* (Indonesian National Armed Forces) refers to the Indonesian military.
Wahyu	It translates into someone having received God's Mandate or Divine Mandate, or in the Chinese tradition, the Mandate of Heaven.

INTRODUCTION

The 2024 Indonesian presidential election was one of the most important elections in recent history due to its expected impact on society and political actors, external states, especially Indonesia's immediate neighbors, and key political and trading partners. The importance of the elections was due to the following reasons: the handover from President Jokowi to his successor; the transfer of political power from one generation to another; the consolidation of political power by the PDI-P, the leading political party since 2014, which is also the antithesis to the Suharto-led Old Order as the latter came to power by deposing President Sukarno, dubbed, leader of the Old Order, father of Megawati; the expected empowerment of Megawati, who had led the PDI-P for more than 20 years, which held dominance at the executive and legislative levels since 2014; the rise and importance of new political generations, namely, Generation Z and the Millennials; the maturing and diversification of political power and enrichment of the country's hard-won democracy; and the concern that due to increased political and social polarization, the presidential contest could lead to violence as it did in 2019, possibly leading to massive foreign interference, especially from the US and its political allies to ensure their "candidate" wins, causing concern about post-election chaos, similar to the 2019 presidential election.

Yet, many of these concerns proved unfounded, and there were also developments and outcomes that defied the expectations of political pundits, analysts, and the political actors. The campaigns for the presidential election, which was simultaneously held with the legislative election, were peaceful. Despite discontent being expressed by various political parties and actors, especially from the dominant ruling party, PDI-P, the election was successful with the country moving on with the business of government and governance rather than being concerned with what happened or was happening, including the strong win by Prabowo, backed by Jokowi, and the outright defeat of the PDI-P and its candidate, the party that had backed Jokowi in the 2014 and 2019 presidential elections.

The election also led to the victory of an almost 73-year-old president on his fourth attempt, first as a vice presidential candidate in 2009, then twice as a presidential candidate in 2014 and 2019, and finally triumphing in 2024, ironically with the endorsement and assistance of the individual who defeated him twice, namely, Jokowi. There were continuous allegations that President Jokowi was directly meddling, referred to as *cawe-cawe* in Javanese, in the presidential elections, through his office, his personal preferences, and the use of governmental apparatus to support Prabowo Subianto against his two political opponents, Anies Baswedan and Ganjar Pranowo. Jokowi's influence was important and is likely to continue as his eldest son, Gibran, was the winning vice president. Jokowi's younger son, Kaesang, was also politically active as the leader of the PSI, as was Jokowi's son-in-law, Bobby Nasution, the Mayor of Medan, Sumatra.

Jokowi's supporters, dubbed "*relawans*" or volunteers, also played an important role in supporting Prabowo and Gibran and, in particular, in winning over the all-important youth votes, as more than 57% of the voters were 40 years and below. What was also somewhat strange was the unexpected support Prabowo received from senior military and police generals, many of whom were highly critical of Prabowo in the 2014 and 2019 presidential elections, often motivated by longstanding personal differences and animosities.

Their *volte face* in the 2024 presidential elections played an important role in making Prabowo acceptable and highly electable in the eyes of the Indonesia public, especially as senior generals such as Wiranto, Susilo Bambang Yudhoyono, Agum Gumelar, Hendropriyono, and Luhut Panjaitan publicly endorsed Prabowo, making a mammoth difference in the electability of Prabowo.

The voting youth which constituted more than 57% of the electorate in 2024, played a decisive role in defeating Prabowo's political opponents. All the efforts by Prabowo's opponents to highlight his past misdemeanors and mistakes were of no avail as the younger generation, most of whom were either not born or too young to remember the past developments, chose to ignore the allegations against Prabowo and decided to back him as he was seen as good for the future of Indonesia and Indonesians, all the more with the backing of the incumbent president whose approval rating was still hovering around 80% after being in power for more than 9 years, itself an amazing achievement. What also stood out in the 2024 presidential election was the rejection of Prabowo and Jokowi's critics and opponents with a one-round resounding win in the presidential race, something that had not happened since direct presidential elections were introduced in 2004. It demonstrated the power and appeal of both Prabowo and Jokowi, making this almost an asymmetrical political race with the outcome almost determined weeks before the country voted on February 14, 2024, through various political surveys, including those that were supporting the opponents of Prabowo and Gibran that showed the latter team leading by more than 50% of voters' approval.

The 2024 presidential election also highlighted the important role played by the media, both traditional and new, and the importance of "pork-barrel" politics with promises to uplift the populace through new policies in the political, economic, socio-cultural, and technological fields as well as socialist-type policies of providing greater subsidies for health, education, and free milk and meals for school children. The 2024 presidential elections also reflected a fatigue among the electorate that was unhappy with the total politicization of almost everything by opponents of the government. Partly due to this factor, the public decisively voted in favor of the Prabowo–Gibran team as they were seen as a continuity of Jokowi and his policies that were beneficial to the public.

Simultaneously, the legislative elections also demonstrated an interesting trend, namely, a steady shift away from the PDI-P, which represented the politics of slogans and nationalism but spoke very little of substantive policies. Even though the PDI-P still emerged as the leading political party in parliament, it only received the top spot in the legislature very narrowly, and the coalition of the other political parties with Prabowo can easily outnumber the PDI-P if it chooses to be in the Opposition. Clearly, the "old ways" of the PDI-P under Megawati did not gain traction with the voters and she emerged in some ways as one of the biggest losers in the elections, especially due to her role in publicly undermining President Jokowi, which backfired and hurt her politically. It also signaled the rise of largely secular political parties such as Golkar, Gerindra, Democrats, and the National Democrats, with moderate Muslim political parties such as the PKB also improving their performance compared to the past.

Finally, and most unexpectedly, Indonesia's presidential election threw up a strongman president, Prabowo, a former special forces military general, along the lines of Putin in Russia, Xi Jinping in China, and Modi in India, signaling that the public was more concerned and focused on political, economic, and socio-cultural deliverables rather than empty political promises of democracy that tended to destabilize and polarize the country along racial, religious, and economic lines.

The Prabowo–Gibran victory was confirmed by three main methods, namely, by the Quick-Count votes by the various electorate survey agencies, by the Real-Count votes as confirmed by the KPU, and by the Constitutional Court, following challenges to the Prabowo–Gibran team, which decreed that the Prabowo–Gibran team had won and that the challenges were of no substance. Following this, while the Anies–Muhaimin team conceded defeat and congratulated Prabowo and Gibran, the Ganjar–Mahfud team, especially Ganjar, still did not concede, demonstrating the growing political distance between the PDI-P and both Jokowi and Prabowo. As the 2024 presidential election was very important, the consequences of what is likely to happen in the near future become equally significant.

First, the result was a resounding first-round win by the Prabowo–Gibran team. Second, the big question remains, largely due to his age and alleged health issues, as to how long Prabowo will remain president. Third, the other question is how Prabowo will work to craft a political coalition of those who supported him in his presidential campaign and those who opposed him, as he believes in a "united front" or "*politik rangkul*" approach to government and governance. Fourth, what role and function can be expected of political giants such as Jokowi, Wiranto, Bambang Yudhoyono, Agum Gumelar, and Luhut Panjaitan who supported Prabowo in the presidential election? Finally, it remains to be seen how the Prabowo–Gibran team will fulfill its campaign promises such as 5% annual economic growth, satisfying youth expectations, infrastructure projects such as the new political capital, the various freebies such as free milk and meals for school children, and finally positioning Indonesia correctly in an increasingly dangerous world with ongoing geopolitical challenges, the most important being the US–China rivalry.

Against this backdrop, this study is organized in a manner to shed light on the Indonesian political system, how the 2024 presidential elections were held, and the outcomes. In this endeavor, this book begins with this Introduction. In Chapter 1, the importance of the 2024 presidential elections will be discussed. Chapters 2 and 3 briefly examine the Indonesian political and electoral systems, respectively. Chapter 4 briefly talks about the Indonesian presidents from 1945 to 2024. Chapter 5 will look at the key political parties involved in the presidential elections. Chapter 6 looks at the key political coalitions and Chapter 7 profiles the key presidential contestants. Chapter 8 analyzes the factors and determinants of the 2024 presidential elections. In Chapter 9, the various aspects that will play a part in the presidential elections are discussed. In

Chapter 10, the politicking that went on prior to the voting day will be discussed. Chapters 11 and 12 examine the results of the presidential elections and the consequences of the results for Indonesia, the region, and the wider world, respectively. Finally, the Conclusion briefly examines what can be expected of Indonesia following the presidential elections.

CHAPTER 1

IMPORTANCE OF INDONESIA'S 2024 PRESIDENTIAL ELECTIONS

In accordance with the norms and regulations of the Indonesian political system implemented after the changes in the post-Suharto era in May 1998 and effectively enforced since 2004, the president is limited to serving a single 5-year term, which can be renewed once, allowing for a maximum tenure of 10 years. In contrast to previous times, the president is now elected directly by the electorate of the nation, rather than through votes in the national parliament, as was formerly the practice. Following the 2004 decision, Susilo Bambang Yudhoyono held office for a maximum period of 10 years, from 2004 to 2014. Similarly, Joko Widodo would have served for a maximum of 10 years, with his term ending in October 2024. As per the Indonesian Constitution, the Indonesian president holds a position of significant authority, serving as both the Head of State and Government, as well as the Commander-in-Chief of the Armed Forces. Since Jokowi assumed the presidency, he has also gained control over the National Police, consolidating his authority as a highly influential office bearer.

In light of this situation, the 2024 presidential elections hold importance from various angles. The significance of Indonesia in global politics is the underlying reason why the election of the country's president holds substantial consequences at the national, regional, and global levels.[1]

Firstly, it entails the direct selection of a prominent office bearer inside the nation. This would be the seventh instance in which Indonesia has undertaken this process since the downfall of the New Order administration in May 1998. It will also mark the completion of a political, economic, and socio-cultural process in which a generation has come of age in a period of peace, stability, economic expansion, and a largely transparent and democratic governmental system.

Furthermore, the individual in question holds a position of authority inside a state that holds significant influence in both regional and global political affairs. The significance of this can be observed from various perspectives and domains.

Ancient Civilization State

In the past, this region was inhabited by various Hindu, Buddhist, and Islamic kingdoms and sultanates, such as the Hindu–Buddhist Singhasari (1222–1292), Hindu–Buddhist Majapahit (1293–1527), Buddhist Srivijaya (671–1025), Muslim Demak (1475–1554), Hindu–Buddhist Mataram (716–1016), Muslim Mataram (1586–1755), and Muslim Banten (1527–1813).

Indonesia is a significant nation with a rich cultural heritage. As a result, it actively seeks to participate in regional and global matters, often desiring respect and acknowledgment from its neighboring countries. This is attributed to its perception of entitlement as a prominent regional power, stemming from its significant historical legacy, as its former emperors frequently exerted influence over other governments in the vicinity.

---

[1] Acharya, A. (2014). *Indonesia Matters: Asia Emerging Democratic Power*. Singapore: World Scientific Book; "Why Indonesia really matters". *The Australia-Indonesia Centre*, August 14, 2016; "Why Indonesia matters"? *The Economist*, November 17, 2022; and Boot, M., "Indonesia matters: The role and ambitions of a rising power". *The Washington Post*, February 20, 2023.

Geography

Indonesia holds the distinction of being the most expansive state in Southeast Asia and plays a crucial role in the broader Asia-Pacific area. Indonesia boasts a coastline that stretches for 54,716 kilometers, making it the second-longest coastline in the world behind Canada. Indonesia's extensive coastline is primarily attributed to its vast archipelago of more than 17,500 islands. Indonesia is the largest country composed of islands, situated between the Pacific and Indian Oceans. The landmass spans a vast extent of 1,913,580 square kilometers (738,837 square miles), positioning it as one of the largest countries in Asia and the 15th largest globally. Indonesia, being an archipelagic state, spans approximately 5,120 kilometers (3,181 miles) in the east–west direction and 1,760 kilometers (1,094 miles) in the north–south direction.

Demography

Demography refers to the scientific study of human populations, including their size, structure, and distribution. Currently, the population of Indonesia stands at over 280 million individuals, making it the fourth most populous country globally. Indonesia is poised to experience a shift in political leadership as the Millennial and Generation Z cohorts, which together make up over 57% of the current voting population, come of age. Indonesia possesses the largest population of young individuals globally. The population consists of 165 million individuals who are under the age of 30, while only 8% of the population is above the age of 60. Indonesia's population is expected to exceed the current population of the United States in the near future.

Religion and Belief Systems

Indonesia's belief system and set of spiritual practices are critical determinants of its behavior. It is the most populous Muslim nation, renowned for its predominantly moderate beliefs and practices.

However, the Muslim community is increasingly embracing conservative beliefs, which has significant implications at both regional and global levels. Additionally, the country also has significant Christian, Buddhist, and Hindu followers.

Democratic

After the downfall of the predominantly military-controlled New Order in May 1998, Indonesia became the largest functioning Muslim democratic state in the world, and the third-largest democracy overall, following India and the United States. This grants her credibility in global politics, particularly within the Muslim world.

Politics

The country has effectively implemented reforms, transitioning from an autocratic regime to a democratic system, while simultaneously achieving economic growth, representative pluralist democracy, and social improvements. It has become one of the key states in Asia as well as the world at large, with immense influence in the developing world and the Islamic world.

Economy

Indonesia holds much economic importance globally due to its enormous natural resources. It has a Gross Domestic Product (GDP) of US$1320 billion and a GDP per capita of US$4400. Additionally, it possesses abundant natural resources, making it one of the wealthiest nations globally, with the potential to become a prominent economic force in the coming years. Its economic influence is expanding as a result of its increasing GNP, GDP, Per Capita Income, Purchasing Power, and abundance of crucial resources, particularly nickel and cobalt. This positions it to become one of the top eight greatest economies in the near future and one of the largest marketplaces in Asia.

Strategic

Indonesia serves as a crucial link between the Asian and Pacific regions, connecting two strategically significant oceans. Additionally, it exercises authority over crucial maritime routes, including the Straits of Malacca, Straits of Sunda, Straits of Lombok, and the Makassar Straits. As an archipelagic state, it is strategically positioned to control crucial international straits that serve as passageways for essential resources. It lies in close proximity to and shares maritime borders with both China and India, two influential Asian nations with significant worldwide impact. Given the increasing geopolitical rivalry between major global powers, particularly the United States and China, it is quite likely that Indonesia's influence and importance will significantly increase in the future. Indonesia has been a prominent participant on the world stage, participating in several international organizations such as the OIC, G20, ASEAN, APEC, and EAS. Its non-aligned foreign policy as part of the Non-Aligned Movement (NAM) positions it as a significant participant and collaborator on the world stage. It engages with all major global powers without favoring any particular side, primarily through the use of its influential soft power and its ability to resolve problems.

Furthermore, apart from the significance of the presidential position and the different factors that render Indonesia crucial in regional and global politics, the 2024 presidential elections will also signify a shift from older to younger politicians. Presidential candidates and prominent politicians from previous eras, such as Prabowo Subianto, Megawati Sukarnoputri, and Airlangga, continue to be actively involved in politics. However, new individuals are also emerging, including Puan Maharani, Anies Baswedan, Sandiaga Uno, and Agus Harimurti, as well as younger figures like Gibran and Kaesang, who are also participating in politics in various capacities. The increasing number of young voters in the country, who are eligible to vote at the age of 17, raises the question of how candidates, regardless of their age, will be able to attract the attention and support of these younger voters. This is particularly important when considering the Generation Z and Millennial demographics, as well as the emergence of various issues such as identity politics related to Islam. These factors should be monitored and analyzed in order to understand the evolving voting patterns. Additionally, the Indonesian military has experienced a significant increase in its relevance and has garnered substantial credibility inside the country under the guidance of new leaders who enjoy widespread popularity among the public.

The factors that will determine the victory of the next president include leadership qualities, charisma, political party support, coalition politics, identity politics, money politics, and external interference. These factors require careful analysis and understanding. However, independent analysts agreed that the presidential elections, which took place alongside the general elections, held importance for the global community from several viewpoints. *The Guardian*, in an article titled "Five reasons why Indonesia's presidential elections matter," highlighted several factors that contributed to the significance of these elections. These include Indonesia's large-scale democracy, strong economy, vibrant society, moderate Islamic practices, and national unity.[2] The same factors will likely be relevant for the next presidential elections. *The Financial Review*, in an article titled "Five reasons why the Indonesian election matters to Australia," presented several important factors that should be taken into account. These factors include regional security, tourism and investments, the nickel industry, skilled workers, and the potential threat to democracy posed by political dynasties.[3] *The Economist* made a similar point on February 9, 2024 in an article titled "Five reasons why Indonesia's election matters."[4]

---

[2] Lamb, K. (2014). "Five reasons why Indonesia's presidential elections matters". *The Guardian*, 9 July.

[3] Connors, E. (2024). "Five reasons why the Indonesian election matters to Australia". *Financial Review*, 7 February.

[4] "Five reasons why Indonesia's election matters". *The Economist*, February 9, 2024.

Conclusion

Therefore, although numerous elections were scheduled to take place worldwide in 2024, including in the United States, Russia, and India, the election in Indonesia undoubtedly stands out as one of the most significant. This is because it was expected to have significant consequences not only within Indonesia itself but also in the Southeast Asian and Asian regions, as well as globally.

CHAPTER 2
INDONESIA'S POLITICAL STRUCTURE AND SYSTEM

The Political Structure and System of Indonesia

The Indonesian political system is influenced by various elements, including historical circumstances, necessity, and ongoing transformations that have occurred over time. The primary powers are vested in the executive, legislative, and judiciary departments of government.

Chief Executive

Indonesia's political system is a presidential representative democratic republic, where the president serves as both the head of state and head of government. The system is organized as a multi-party system.[1] The government, comprising the president, the vice president, and their ministries, exercises executive authority. The president directly appoints and dismisses ministers, each of whom is responsible for specific areas of government activity.

---

[1] Sulistyo, H. (2002). *Electoral Politics in Indonesia: A Hard Way to Democracy*. Retrieved from https://library.fes.de/pdf-files/iez/01361004.pdf.

Presidential Powers

According to the revised 1945 Constitution, the president possesses constitutional jurisdiction over the government and wields the right to appoint and dismiss ministers.[2] The president possesses the authority to submit legislative proposals to the *Dewan Perwakilan Rakyat Republik Indonesia* (DPR) or the People's Representative Council, engage in discussions with the DPR to achieve consensus on bills, establish government regulations that align with existing laws, and, in urgent situations, enact government regulations as a substitute for legislation. In terms of military affairs, the president possesses ultimate jurisdiction over the *Tentara Nasional Indonesia* (TNI) or the Indonesian National Armed Forces.

From a diplomatic standpoint, the president's authority is limited to signing treaties, overseeing prisoner rehabilitation, and appointing Judicial Committee members, all of which require the assent of the DPR. The president's authority is limited to the appointment of ambassadors and the acceptance of ambassadors from other nations, subject to the concerns of the DPR. The president possesses the authority to bestow pardons, although he/she is required to take into account the guidance provided by the Supreme Court.[3] While having the ultimate authority in selecting chief justice candidates, constitutionally the president is not to have control over the country's judiciary, which remains autonomous from both the administration and legislative branches.

The progress of democratization in Indonesia becomes evident when comparing the current powers held by the president under the Amended 1945 Constitution with previous versions of the Indonesian constitution. According to the 1950 Provisional Constitution, the president is authorized to dissolve the DPR

---

[2] *Indonesian Constitution (1945, consolidated)*. Asian Human Rights Commission. Amend. (2002). http://www.humanrights.asia/indonesian-constitution-1945-consolidated/#section-3.

[3] King, B. (2009). *A Inside Indonesia: Constitutional Tinkering: The Search for Consensus is Taking Time*. Retrieved from https://web.archive.org/web/20091029161228/http://www.insideindonesia.org/content/view/502/29.

(Democratic People's Republic) and mandate an election to take place within a period of 30 days. Additionally, the president possesses autonomous authority to designate ambassadors and approve their appointments. However, with democratization since 1998, the president no longer possesses the unilateral ability to designate ambassadors as he/she is required to consider the recommendations of the DPR. The DPR serves as a mechanism for checks and balances against the president, contrasting with the extensive powers granted to the president in the provisional 1950 Constitution, while also being responsible for passing bills and creating laws.[4]

Presidential Eligibility Criteria

According to the Revised 1945 Constitution, individuals running for president must be Indonesian citizens from birth, who have not voluntarily acquired citizenship in another country, have not committed treason against the nation, and possess the physical and mental capacity to fulfil the necessary responsibilities. In order to become a presidential candidate, individuals must receive a nomination from either a political party or a coalition of political parties. The 2017 Law No. 7 Regarding Presidential and Vice Presidential Elections provides additional details on the specific requirements that presidential candidates must meet.[5] Candidates are required to fulfil the following criteria:

1. Be conscious of God.
2. Have been a citizen of Indonesia since birth and have not voluntarily acquired citizenship of any other country.

---

[4] Friend, T. (2003). *Indonesian Destinies*. Cambridge, Massachusetts: The Belknap Press of Harvard University Press, p. 461.
[5] *Indonesian Constitution (1945, consolidated)*. Asian Human Rights Commission. Amend. (2002). http://www.humanrights.asia/indonesian-constitution-1945-consolidated/#section-3.

3. Ensure that the spouse, if applicable, possesses Indonesian citizenship.
4. The individual in question has not committed any acts of treason against the nation, nor have they been implicated in any instances of corruption or other significant criminal activities.
5. Must possess the physical and mental capacity to fulfil job responsibilities and must be free from any substance misuse.
6. Reside permanently inside the borders of the Republic of Indonesia.
7. Have disclosed their money to the Corruption Eradication Commission.
8. There is no individual or group debt that could result in a financial loss for the state.
9. Have not been adjudicated bankrupt.
10. Have never participated in any reprehensible behavior.
11. Not currently running as a candidate for legislative membership.
12. Must enroll as an eligible voter.
13. Must be officially enrolled as a taxpayer and have fulfilled tax obligations for a minimum of five consecutive years.
14. Have never before held the position of president for two consecutive terms.
15. Adhere to Pancasila, the 1945 Constitution, the Republic of Indonesia, and the official national slogan of Indonesia, *Bhinneka Tunggal Ika*, meaning "Unity in Diversity."
16. Have never received a prison sentence of 5 years or longer.
17. Must be at least 40 years old.
18. Must have completed at least a high school education or its equivalent.
19. Must not have any affiliation with the Communist Party of Indonesia, especially its mass organizations, or any active involvement in the 30 September Movement.
20. Must establish a clear and strategic vision, objective, and program for governing.

In addition, the legislation specifies that only political parties, or a coalition of political parties, that secured 20% of the seats in the DPR or 25% of the total valid votes in the preceding election are eligible to propose candidates for president and vice president. The 2017 Law and the Amended 1950 Constitution impose stricter requirements on presidential candidates compared to previous versions of the Indonesian Constitution. For instance, the original 1945 constitution only mandated that presidential candidates be of Indonesian origin, whereas the 1950 Provisional Constitution required candidates to be at least 30 years old and Indonesian citizens. In addition, candidates must not be individuals who are considered undesirable or have had their right to participate in elections revoked, and they must not be affiliated with private corporations.

Legislative

The legislative authority is held by both the government and the bicameral body known as the *Majelis Permusyawaratan Rakyat Republik Indonesia* (MPR or MPR-RI), also referred to as the People's Consultative Assembly. The MPR consists of the members of the DPR and the *Dewan Perwakilan Daerah* (DPD), also known as the Regional Representative Council. According to Indonesia's constitution, the DPD has limited authority that is focused on matters relating to regional governments. Its role is to propose and provide recommendations on bills to the DPR. As a result, the DPR has more power, privilege, and prestige due to its greater law-making capacity.[6]

---

[6] Hamzah, H., Narang, A. M., & Yusari, A. (2021). *Legal Systems in Indonesia: Overview*. Thomson Reuters Practical Law. https://uk.practicallaw.thomsonreuters.com/w-010-7310?contextData=(sc.Default).

Roles and Responsibilities of the MPR

According to Article 20A of the revised 1945 Constitution, the DPR has three primary roles: legislative, budgetary, and oversight. The legislative function of the DPR encompasses the following:

- Compiling the program *Legislasi Nasional*, often known as *Prolegnas*, which consists of a prioritized list of drafts and bills.
- Preparing and conducting discussions on the *Rancangan Undang-Undang*, which are proposed laws.
- Examining the legislative proposals submitted by the DPD, particularly those related to regional autonomy, the relationship between central and regional governance, the establishment, expansion, and consolidation of regional territories, the administration of regional resources, and the budgetary balance between the central and regional authorities.
- Conducting deliberations on legislation submitted by either the president or the DPD.
- Collaboratively enacting legislation into law alongside the president.
- Deciding whether to approve or reject the *Peraturan Pemerintah Pengganti Undang-Undang* (Perppu) or government regulation in lieu of laws implemented by the president. If the Perppu is approved, it will be officially established as a law.[7]

The budgeting function of the DPR comprises the following:

- Authorizing and enacting the *Anggaran Pendapatan dan Belanja Negara* (APBN) or National Budget recommended by the president.
- Considering the viewpoints of the DPD, particularly regarding taxes, education, and religious matters.

---

[7] *Indonesian Constitution (1945, consolidated)*. Asian Human Rights Commission. Amend. (2002). http://www.humanrights.asia/indonesian-constitution-1945-consolidated/#section-3.

- Continuing the examination of the state financial accountability reports conducted by the *Badan Pemeriksa Keuangan* (BPK), also known as the National Board of Audit.
- Authorizing the transfer of governmental assets and properties that have a significant influence on the public and the national economy.[8]

The oversight duty of the DPR encompasses the following:

- Supervising the implementation of legislation, the national budget, and governmental programs.
- Conducting discussions and monitoring the actions taken by the DPD regarding regional autonomy, the relationship between the central and regional governments, the establishment, expansion, and consolidation of regional territories, the management of regional resources, the balance of fiscal matters between the central and regional governments, the implementation of the National Budget, and matters related to taxes, education, and religious affairs.[9]

MPR's Entitlements

The 1945 Constitution ensures certain powers of the DPR, including granting the DPR the ability to properly carry out its supervisory role. The rights encompassed are as follows:

- The right to interrogate the government regarding any government policy deemed significant, strategic, and influential (Interpellation Right).
- The authority to examine accusations of violation of the laws by government policy (*Hak Angket*).

---

[8] Republic of Indonesia, Secretariat General of the DPR. (2021). *Tentang DPR: Dewan Perwakilan Rakyat.* Retrieved December 17, 2021, www.dpr.go.id (in Indonesian).
[9] *Ibid.*

- The right to express opinions (Hak Menyatakan Pendapat) is also granted regarding any government policy, extraordinary domestic or foreign events, the follow-up of the rights to question and investigate government policy, as well as the initial impeachment process of the president and/or the vice president.

MPs have individual rights that enable them to fulfil their tasks including the following items:

- The right to propose drafts and bills of laws.
- The right to interrogate the government and its officials.
- The freedom to articulate viewpoints and provide recommendations.
- The right to vote and be elected for legislative responsibilities.
- The right to defend oneself against suspected infractions of the parliamentary code of ethics.
- The right to be exempt from legal prosecution for any words, questions, and opinions expressed in the course of parliamentary duties, unless they violate the parliamentary code of ethics and code of conduct.
- Entitlement to be allocated specific formal procedures.
- Entitlement to financial and administrative benefits.
- The right to supervise the implementation of the National Budget, as well as safeguard the interests of the people and their constituency.
- The right to suggest and advocate for programs that will benefit their constituents.
- The right to advocate for and disseminate information regarding the development of a new legislation.[10]

In contrast, the rights of DPD members are considerably limited. They are only empowered to suggest regional legislation to the DPR

---

[10] Harijanti, S. D., & Lindsey, T. (2006). "Indonesia: General elections test the amended constitution and the new constitutional court". *International Journal of Constitutional Law*, 4(1), 138–150. doi:10.1093/icon/moi055.

and are required to be consulted on any regional bill put up by the DPR.

The MPR's Historical Background

Following the declaration of Indonesia's independence on August 18, 1945, the *Panitia Persiapan Kemerdekaan Indonesia* (PPKI) or Preparatory Committee for Indonesian Independence ratified a new constitution for the country. During a 6-month transition period, the new republic was governed according to the constitution by a president who was supported by a National Committee. The National Committee formed the two-chamber legislature, known as the MPR, as required by the constitution. As a result, the PPKI was disbanded on August 29, and the *Komite Nasional Indonesia Pusat* (KNIP) or Central Indonesian National Committee was formed. The KNIP, originally established to provide guidance to President Sukarno of the newly independent Indonesia, initially had a purely advisory role. However, on October 18, in response to demands for a less authoritarian and more parliamentary form of government, it was given legislative authority. Every piece of legislation, including those that established the current national policy, had to be authorized by the KNIP, specifically the Working Committee, which consisted of key members of the KNIP.[11]

The KNIP convened six sessions from 1945 to 1949 and concluded its final meeting on December 15, 1949, where members reached an agreement for the Republic of Indonesia to become a member of the United States of Indonesia (RIS). On December 27, 1949, the Dutch government relinquished control to the RIS, which consisted of 16 states and territories, including the Republic of Indonesia. According to the USI constitution, the RIS implemented a bicameral system, where the highest governing body is the senate consisting of 32 members. Each of the 16 components of the USI is

---

[11] Ricklefs, M. C. (2008) [1981]. *A History of Modern Indonesia Since c. 1300*, 4th ed. London: MacMillan, pp. 197–198.

represented by two senators.[12] Nevertheless, this structure had a brief existence; gradually, the several provinces and territories of the USI started to disintegrate and merge into the Republic, resulting in Indonesia being a unified state on August 17, 1950.

During discussions that began in May 1950, the Committee for the Preparation of the Constitution of a Unitary State reached an agreement to establish a unicameral parliament. This parliament would consist of 150 members from the RIS parliament, 46 members from the KNIP Working Committee, 13 members from the Republic of Indonesia Supreme Advisory Council, and 32 RIS senators, making a total of 241 members. The temporary constitution also mandated the formation of a Constitutional Assembly to create a lasting constitution. In 1955, this assembly was elected but was unable to reach a consensus on a new constitution. As a result, Sukarno, with the backing of the military, issued a decree on July 5, 1959 to eliminate the temporary constitution and reinstate the 1945 Constitution, thereby restoring the role of the MPR.[13]

MPR and Guided Democracy

In 1960, Sukarno disbanded the lower house, known as the DPR, due to its refusal to approve the state budget. Subsequently, he designated a Mutual Cooperation People's Representative Council (DPR-GR) and reinstated the MPR as a Provisional People's Consultative Assembly (MPRS). On September 15, the 610 members of the DPR-GR, including 94 regional representatives and 232 representatives from various sectors such as the Armed Forces and National Police, took their oaths of office. It is important to note that membership was no longer determined by the 1955 election results, but rather by the president, who had the power to appoint

---

[12] Kahin, G. M. (1952). *Nationalism and Revolution in Indonesia*. Ithaca, NY: Cornell University Press, pp. 139–140.

[13] Cribb, R. (2001). "Parlemen Indonesia, 1945–1959 (Indonesian Parliaments, 1945–1959)". In Yayasan, A.P.I. (ed.). *Panduan Parlemen Indonesia (Indonesian Parliamentary Guide)*, pp. 97–113 (in Indonesian) (n.p.).

and remove members as desired. Political adversaries were marginalized, resulting in the absence of legislative opposition. In addition, the functions and obligations of parliament were significantly reduced: Parliament had the primary purpose of assisting the administration in carrying out its policies, as demonstrated by the 9 legislations it enacted in 1960, in contrast to the 87 laws passed in 1958 and the 29 laws approved in 1959. As a result, the MPRS played a crucial role in solidifying Sukarno's position of authority. During its second General Session in 1963, the MPRS chose Sukarno as the "President for Life" with Resolution No. III/MPRS/1963. In 1965, the third General Session of the MPRS solidified Sukarno's ideological methods in governing Indonesia by including his Independence Day speeches as the basis for political and economic policy.[14]

MPR during the New Order Era

The 1966 MPR General Session initiated the formal transfer of authority from Sukarno to Suharto. After the coup attempt by the 30 September Movement organization in 1965, which was officially attributed to the Indonesian Communist Party (PKI), the DPR-GR underwent a purge, and 180 members who were either supportive of Sukarno or associated with organizations involved in the claimed coup were removed. During the session, the MPRS approved 24 resolutions. These resolutions included the removal of Sukarno as the life president, the prohibition of communism and Marxism-Leninism, the endorsement of *Supersemar* (which effectively transferred power from Sukarno to Suharto), the authorization for Suharto to form a new cabinet, and the establishment of a constitutional amendment that allowed the holder of *Supersemar* to replace a president who was unable to fulfil his/her duties, instead of the

---

[14] Kahin, G. M. (1970) [1952]. *Nationalism and Revolution in Indonesia*. Ithaca: Cornell University Press, p. 447; Ricklefs, M. C. (2008) [1981]. *A History of Modern Indonesia Since c. 1300*, 4th ed. London: Palgrave Macmillan, p. 420.

vice president. Suharto was officially designated as the interim president of Indonesia during the 1967 MPRS Special Session.[15]

In 1969, the government enacted an electoral legislation that established the composition of the DPR as consisting of 360 elected members and 100 appointed members. The military's representation grew to a total of 75 individuals. The elections in 1971 were ultimately conducted after being postponed to facilitate arrangements aimed at securing a triumph for the government's Golkar organization. After the election, the DPR-GR was renamed as the DPR. Throughout the duration of the New Order, Golkar consistently achieved overwhelming majorities in every election, enabling parliament to once again serve as a means for enacting government-proposed legislation.

MPR and the Reform Era

The 1998 Special Session (*Sidang Istimewa*) was convened as the inaugural gathering of the MPR following Suharto's relinquishment of the presidency and subsequent loss of authority in May 1998. Despite including politicians who had prospered during Suharto's rule, these MPR members were eager to dissociate themselves from Suharto and cater to the prevailing reformist attitudes in Indonesia at that time. During the extraordinary session, the MPR rescinded the president's extraordinary powers granted in the 1998 General Session and implemented a maximum of 2 5-year terms for both the president and vice president. The MPR also decided to conduct parliamentary elections in 1999, mandated a rigorous campaign against corruption, collusion, and nepotism, and repealed the resolution that had mandated the indoctrination of Pancasila to establish it as the national doctrine. The Special Session and Suharto's resignation signified the decline of the New Order regime, leading to the onset of the Reformasi era.[16]

---

[15] Hughes, J. (2002). *The End of Sukarno – A Coup That Misfired: A Purge That Ran Wild.* Singapore, Archipelago Press.

[16] Liddle, R. W. (1999). "Indonesia's democratic opening". *Government and Opposition*, 34(1), 94–116.

The 1999 General Session was the inaugural MPR with substantial reform credentials. During a subsequent reorganization, the total membership was decreased to 700 individuals, consisting of 500 members from the DPR, 135 Regional Representatives, and 65 Group Representatives. At the General Session, the MPR acknowledged the referendum in East Timor and established a task force to revise the 1945 Constitution. Furthermore, it was specified that the organization will henceforth convene yearly meetings to receive reports from the president, DPR, the Audit Board of Indonesia (BPK), the Supreme Advisory Council (DPA), and the Supreme Court. Upon receiving these annual reports, the MPR would thereafter provide recommendations regarding the appropriate course of action for the president to pursue. Abdurrahman Wahid was elected president and Megawati Sukarnoputri became vice president during the General Session.

The 2000 Annual Session furthered the process of reform. The MPR (People's Consultative Assembly) delineated the separation between the TNI (Indonesian National Armed Forces) and the National Police and clearly defined their respective responsibilities and functions. The organization also adopted resolutions concerning the strengthening of national cohesion and provided recommendations for the implementation of regional self-governance. The 2001 Special Session was convened following allegations of President Wahid's involvement in a corruption case and the DPR's assertion that his leadership had grown inept. The Special Session, originally planned for August 2001, was rescheduled to July 2001. Subsequently, Wahid was ousted from the presidency and Megawati Sukarnoputri was chosen as the new president, with Hamzah Haz assuming the position of vice president.[17]

In the 2002 Annual Session, the constitutional amendment process was extended, resulting in a total of 14 amendments. The most significant changes include the reform of the presidential election system, the elimination of the DPA, and the mandate to contribute 20% of the national budget to education. Furthermore, a recent

---

[17] Indrayana, D. (2008). *Indonesian Constitutional Reform 1999–2002: An Evaluation of Constitution-Making in Transition.* Jakarta: Kompas Book Publishing.

significant restructuring of Parliament occurred, in which regional members and group representatives, formerly part of the Regional Delegations Faction, were reassigned to the newly established DPD. As a requirement for membership in the DPD, all seats in the MPR had to be filled through direct elections. This resulted in the removal of the military, which had held 38 appointed seats in the legislature from 1999 to 2004.

The primary purpose of the 2003 Annual Session was to determine the legal validity of the resolutions previously passed by the MPR and the MPRS. Additionally, the session aimed to make decisions regarding the makeup of a Constitutional Commission. The 2003 Annual Session also delineated the MPR's forthcoming change in status, which would be implemented upon the commencement of the new president's term in 2004. Following the direct election of the president and vice president by the people, as well as the constitutional revisions implemented by the MPR between 1999 and 2002, the MPR's authority was diminished. It would cease to be the top governing body and instead have equal status with the DPR, BPK, the Supreme Court, and the Constitutional Court. The MPR would have the responsibility of organizing the inauguration ceremony for the president and vice president. Additionally, if necessary, the MPR would also handle the process of impeaching either the president or the vice president, or both. The MPR would only elect a president and vice president in the event that both posts were unoccupied.

CHAPTER 3

THE INDONESIAN ELECTORAL SYSTEM

The Indonesian electoral system adheres to six criteria: direct, general, free, confidential, honest, and fair behavior. These principles are condensed and widely disseminated as *luber-jurdil* [from *Langsung, Bebas, Jujur,* and *Adil*].[1] The initial four tenets of *Luber* were embraced by the New Order government following the 1971 election, while the final two principles of *Jurdil* were adopted in the 1999 election after the 1998 reform and subsequent political liberalization.[2] The six principles are described as follows:

- Direct (*langsung*): Voters must cast their votes independently, without any intermediaries.
- Universal (general): All eligible Indonesian citizens should have the unrestricted right to vote. Although the voting age in Indonesia is 17, the eligibility criteria for voters permit anyone

---

[1] Prokurat, S. (2014). Indonesian parliamentary and presidential elections in 2014. The electoral process and economic challenges. In: M. Sitek and M. Łęski (Eds.), *Socio-Economic Relations between Europe and Asia in the 21st Century.* Józefów: Alcide De Gasperi University of Euro Regional Economy, pp. 197–210. https://web.archive.org/web/20160922174143/http://www.proeconomics.pl/artykuly/indonesian elections.pdf.

[2] See details in "General elections in Indonesia," Wikipedia; Evans, K. R. (2003). *The History of Political Parties & General Elections in Indonesia.* Jakarta: Arise Consultancies.

with an identification card to vote. This means that anyone under 17 who is married or was married can vote, as an ID card is granted to individuals upon marriage regardless of their age.
- Free (*bebas*): Voters should have the ability to cast their vote based on their personal beliefs and without any pressure to vote for a specific candidate.
- Confidential: The voting process ensures that ballots are kept secret and the choices made by voters are only known to themselves and not anyone else.
- Honest (*kejujuran*): Voters, candidates, and election institutions must fulfil their responsibilities with utmost honesty.
- Fair (*adil*): All voters and candidates must be treated equally under the law, without any preferential or discriminatory behavior toward any specific voter or candidate.

The subsequent section provides an overview of the elections conducted from 1955 to the present.

Indirect Presidential Elections

Before 2004, the president of Indonesia was not elected directly by the Indonesian people. According to the 1945 Constitution, the election of new presidents was carried out by the members of the MPR. As a result, the elections for the MPR were conducted first, followed by the elections for the president and vice president. It is important to mention that the majority of presidential elections before 2004 had only one candidate in the running. In 1955, Sukarno was the sole nominee for the presidency, while Suharto was the only candidate nominated for the elections in 1971, 1977, 1982, 1987, 1992, and 1997. The 1999 election was the first election in which multiple candidates ran for the presidency (Table 3.1).

Direct Presidential Elections

According to revisions made to the 1945 Constitution during the 2002 MPR General Session, a candidate pair is elected into office if

Table 3.1. Indonesia's Elections from 1955 to 1999

Indonesia's 1955 General Elections for 257 DPR seats

Leader	Sidik Djojosukataro	Mohd Natsir	Abdul Hasbullah	Alimin	Others
Party	PNI	Masyumi	NU	PKI	Other parties
Seats	57	57	45	39	59
Votes	8.3 million	7.9 million	6.9 million	6.1 million	NA
% of votes	22.3	20.9	20.9	16.4	19.5

Indonesia's 1971 General Elections for 360 DPR seats out of 460

Leader	Suprapto Sukowati	Idham Chalid	Mohd Isnaeni	Mohd Syafat Mintaredia	Others
Party	Golkar	NU	PNI	Parmusi	Other Parties
Seats	236	58	20	24	122
Votes	23.6 million	10.2 million	3.7 million	2.9 million	NA
% of votes	62.8	18.6	6.9	5.3	6.4

Indonesia's 1977 General Elections for DPR 360 out of 460

Leader	Amir Murtono	Mohd Syafat Mintaredia	Mohd Sanusi Hardjadinata
Party	Golkar	PPP	PDI
Seats	232	99	29
Votes	39.7 million	18.7 million	5.5 million
% of votes	62.1	29.2	8.6

(*Continued*)

Table 3.1. (Continued)

Indonesia's 1982 General Elections for DPR 425 out of 500

Leader	Amir Murtono	Jailani Naro	Sunawar Sukowati
Party	Golkar	PPP	PDI
Seats	242	94	24
Votes	48.3 million	20.8 million	5.9 million
% of votes	64.3	27.7	7.8

Indonesia's 1987 General Elections for DPR 400 out of 500

Leader	Sudharmono	Jailani Naro	Suryadi
Party	Golkar	PPP	PDI
Seats	299	61	40
Votes	62.7 million	13.7 million	9.3 million
% of votes	73.1	15.9	10.9

Indonesia's 1992 General Elections for DPR 400 out of 500

Leader	Wahono	Ismail Hasan Metareum	Suryadi
Party	Golkar	PPP	PDI
Seats	282	62	56
Votes	66.5 million	16.6 million	14.5 million
% of votes	68.1	17.0	14.8

Indonesia's 1997 General Elections for 425 DPR seats out of 500

Leader	Harmoko	Ismail Hasan Metareum	Megawati Sukarnoputri
Party	Golkar	PPP	PDI
Seats	325	89	11
Votes	84.1 million	25.3 million	3.4 million
% of votes	74.5	22.4	3.0

Indonesia's 1999 General Elections for 362 DPR seats out of 460

Leader	Megawati	Akbar Tandjung	Matori Abdul Djalil	Hamzah Haz	Amien Rais
Party	PDIP	Golkar	PKB	PPP	PAN
Seats	153	120	51	51	34
Votes	35.6 million	23.7 million	13.3 million	11.3 million	7.5 million
% of votes	33.7	22.4	12.6	10.7	7.1

Indonesia's 1999 President and Vice-President Elections [700 members of MPR to vote]

Presidential Elections

Candidate	Abdurrahman Wahid	Megawati Sukarnoputri
Party	PKB	PDIP
Votes	373	313
% of votes	54.3	45.6

(*Continued*)

Table 3.1. (Continued)

Vice-Presidential Elections

Candidate	Megawati Sukarnoputri	Hamzah Haz
Party	PDIP	PPP
Votes	396	284
% of votes	58.2	41.7

Source: "Bab V Hasil Pemilu". General Election Commission (KPU). Retrieved from https://www.kpu.go.id/dmdocuments/modul_1d.pdf; Suryadinata, L. (2002). "The MPR Elects a President", In *Elections and Politics in Indonesia*, Singapore: ISEAS–Yusof Ishak Institute, pp. 139-160; "Kronologi Drama Voting Gus Dur-Mega", *Tempo*, 31 October 1999, p. 22. https://www.datatempo.co/MajalahTeks/detail/ARM20180612122303/kronologi-drama-voting-gus-dur-mega.

Table 3.2. Direct Presidential Elections, 2004–2019

Year	2004	2009	2014	2019
Presidential Candidate	Susilo Bambang Yudhoyono Vs Megawati Sukarnoputri	Susilo Bambang Yudhoyono Vs Megawati Sukarnoputri	Joko Widodo Vs Prabowo Subianto	Joko Widodo Vs Prabowo Subianto
Vice Presidential Candidate	Jusuf Kalla Vs Hasyim Muzadi	Boediono Vs Prabowo Subianto	Jusuf Kalla Vs Hatta Rajasa	Ma'ruf Amin Vs Sandiaga Uno
1 or 2 Rounds?	2 rounds	2 rounds	2 rounds	2 rounds
No. of Votes	69.2 million	73.8 million	70.9 million	85.6 million
% of Votes	60.6	60.8	53.1	55.5

Source: International Foundation for Electoral Systems (IFES). Election for Indonesian Presidency 2004-07-05. https://www.electionguide.org/elections/id/1936/; IFES. Election for Indonesian Presidency 2004-09-20. https://www.electionguide.org/elections/id/1938/; International Foundation for Electoral Systems (IFES). Election for Indonesian Presidency 2004-07-05; https://www.electionguide.org/elections/id/1936/; IFES. Election for Indonesian Presidency 2004-09-20; IFES. Election for Indonesian Presidency 2009-07-08. https://www.electionguide.org/elections/id/2110/; *Hasil Penghitungan Perolehan Suara Dari Setiap Propinsi dan Luar Negri Dalam Pemilu Presiden dan Wakil Presiden 2014*, General Election Commission; IFES. Election for Indonesian Presidency 2019-02-14. https://www.electionguide.org/elections/id/3105/.

they receive over 50% of the national votes and at least 20% of the votes in more than half of Indonesia's provinces. In the event that no pair obtained the necessary number of votes, the election would proceed to a second round, involving just the pairs that received the greatest and second-highest number of votes. Additional restrictions established by the General Elections Commission (KPU) stipulated that every pair of candidates must be nominated by a political party or a coalition of parties that obtained a minimum of 25% of the public vote or 20% of the seats in the DPR during the Legislative Election held in April (Table 3.2).

CHAPTER 4
HISTORY OF INDONESIA'S PRESIDENTS, 1945–2024

Indonesia has had seven presidents since declaring independence in August 1945. These presidents are Sukarno, Suharto, Habibie, Abdurrahman Wahid, Megawati, Bambang Yudhoyono, and Jokowi. A brief history of Indonesia's presidents is first presented in Table 4.1, before being explored in greater detail in the following sections.

Constitutional Democracy Period (1949 to 1958)

On August 17, 1945, Sukarno, the leader of the Indonesian independence movement against Dutch colonial rule, officially declared the independence of Indonesia. The next day, the PPKI, a group formed by the Japanese to establish the political structure of the future Indonesian state, officially appointed Sukarno as the president and Mohammad Hatta as the vice president of the newly established Republic of Indonesia. In order to achieve global recognition and meet the needs for domestic representation, a parliamentary form of government was established. Under this system, the prime minister was responsible for managing the government's daily operations, while Sukarno, as the president, held a symbolic position. Despite the promise of holding elections in January 1946 to address

Table 4.1 History of Indonesia's Presidents, 1945–2019

Name	Term of Office	Political Party	Vice-President
Sukarno 1901–1970	18 August 1945 to 12 March 1967	Independent	Mohd Hatta
Suharto 1921–2008	12 March 1967 to 21 May 1998	Golkar	Sultan Hamengkubuwono IX Adam Malik Umar Wirahadikusuma Sudharmono Try Sutrisno B.J. Habibie
B.J. Habibie 1936–2019	21 May 1998 to 20 October 1999	Golkar	Vacant
Abdurrahman Wahid 1940–2009	20 October 1999 to 23 July 2001	PKB	Megawati Sukarnoputri
Megawati Sukarnoputri 1947–present	23 July 2001 to 20 October 2004	PDI-P	Hamzah Haz
Susilo Bambang Yudhoyono 1949–present	20 October 2004 to 20 October 2014	PD	Jusuf Kalla Boediono
Joko Widodo 1961–present	20 October 2014 to 20 October 2024	PDI-P	Jusuf Kalla Ma'ruf Amin

concerns about the undemocratic nature of the newly established government, polls were postponed until 1955 due to the Indonesian National Revolution, rebellions, and domestic political instability.

The inaugural elections in Indonesia, conducted in 1955, resulted in the establishment of a fresh parliament and a constitutional assembly. The election results indicated that there was an equal level of support for four political parties: the *Partai Nasional Indonesia* (PNI) or Indonesian Nationalist Party, *Majelis Syuro Muslimin Indonesia* (Masyumi) or Consultative Council of Indonesian Muslims, *Nahdlatul Ulama* (NU) or Association of Islamic Scholars, and the PKI. However, these four parties mostly represented factions with opposing interests: the PNI and PKI advocated for secular nationalism, while *Masyumi* and the NU advocated for Islamic nationalism. Due to the absence of a dominant faction, the state of internal politics remained unstable and persistent.

Confronted with a growing chaotic political environment, Sukarno started to feel bitter about his symbolic role as president in a Western-style parliamentary democracy. Sukarno rejected the idea of implementing Western-style parliamentary democracy in Indonesia and instead advocated for a system of "guided democracy" that he believed was rooted in indigenous principles of governance. Sukarno contended that crucial matters at the village level were resolved through extensive discussions aimed at reaching a consensus, under the supervision of village elders. He advocated for the president to assume the function traditionally held by village elders, and believed that this model should be adopted by the entire nation. He suggested establishing a government that would not solely rely on political parties but also on "functional groups" consisting of the fundamental components of the nation. These organizations would collectively constitute a National Council, which would enable the expression of a national consensus under the supervision of the president.

Vice president Hatta resigned from his position in December 1956 due to his strong opposition to Sukarno's guided democracy philosophy. The issue of domestic instability was exacerbated by his retirement, especially for the non-Javanese population who saw Hatta as their spokesman in a government that was predominantly Javanese. In addition, there were regional military rebellions in the provinces of North, Central, and South Sumatra, as well as North Sulawesi, from December 1956 to March 1957. These rebellions further threatened the unity of the country, leading Sukarno to proclaim martial law on March 14, 1957. During the period of martial law, Sukarno took advantage of the situation to strengthen his control over the country. He did this by appointing and assigning loyalists who shared his views to important positions in his cabinet. Their main task was to deal with the regional commanders who opposed Sukarno's rule. Additionally, Sukarno implemented a policy of economic nationalism by nationalizing Dutch companies that had previously held significant power in the Indonesian economy.

Guided Democracy Period (1959–1965)

Sukarno, having achieved success in suppressing regional military rebellions and gaining support for his economic nationalist policies, used his increased influence to restore the original 1945 constitution through a presidential decree on July 5, 1959. He believed that this action would create a presidential system that was more suitable for implementing the principles of guided democracy. In 1960, Sukarno dissolved the parliament and established a new one in which he personally selected half of the members. Sukarno, supported by the military, dissolved the Islamic party *Masyumi*, alleging its involvement in the 1958 regional uprisings that sought to overthrow the Sukarno administration. In addition, the government and the military employed martial law powers to apprehend and incarcerate several political adversaries of Sukarno and shut down periodicals that expressed criticism toward Sukarno's policies.

As the military gained strength, Sukarno became aware of the growing necessity to offset the military's authority. Consequently, Sukarno started depending on the backing of the PKI. Sukarno regarded the PKI as the most well-structured and ideologically cohesive party in Indonesia and saw it as a valuable means to acquire additional military and financial assistance from Communist Bloc nations. In addition, Sukarno shared a sense of understanding and support for the communists' revolutionary principles, as they were in harmony with his own beliefs. In order to diminish the military's authority, Sukarno revoked martial law, which had previously granted the military extensive powers, and substituted military people in positions of prominence with individuals who were loyal to him and sympathetic to communism. As a result, the communist party grew rapidly under Sukarno's protection. By 1965, the PKI had amassed three million members, making it the most influential political organization in Indonesia. Nevertheless, the growing power of the PKI, at the expense of the military's control, created a fragile relationship between the military and the communists, as the military was concerned about the potential development of a communist state in Indonesia.

During the 30 September Movement (G30S), often referred to as a PKI coup, six army generals were abducted and killed in Jakarta on October 1, 1965. The G30S asserted, via public declarations, that the abductions were carried out with the intention of safeguarding Sukarno from a coup orchestrated by generals under the direction of the CIA. The next morning, Major General Suharto, who was in charge of the military's strategic reserve command, assumed command of the army and played a crucial role in putting an end to the attempted coup. The military's propaganda tactics effectively persuaded both domestic and Indonesian audiences that the coup was instigated by Communists. Although the PKI denied participation, the popular opinion shifted against the Communists, resulting in a widespread effort by the military and citizens to eliminate communist influences from Indonesian society, government, and armed forces. Due to the decline in the influence of the PKI following the 'coup' attempt, which was accelerated by the arrests and executions of prominent PKI members, Sukarno experienced a significant erosion of his support base.

However, Sukarno maintained the support and allegiance of significant portions of the military and the general public. Nevertheless, Sukarno's implementation of inadequate economic policies, such as the government's creation of money to fund military expenses, resulted in hyperinflation of over 600% annually from 1964 to 1965. Sukarno's economic failures resulted in a loss of public support for him. This was particularly evident when university students initiated demonstrations against the Sukarno government in January 1966. They expressed their demands for the dissolution of the PKI and measures to manage hyperinflation. On March 11, 1966, unknown military forces assembled near the parliament and thousands of students were protesting where Sukarno's entire cabinet was in emergency session. Concerned about his personal safety, Sukarno exited the conference and issued a Presidential Order called *Supersemar*. In the order, Sukarno instructed Suharto, who was serving as the Army Chief at the time, to take all actions deemed necessary to ensure the government and the revolution remained secure, tranquil, and stable, as well as to safeguard Sukarno's personal safety and authority. Following the successful transition of power from Sukarno to Suharto, Suharto officially proclaimed the PKI (Indonesian Communist Party) illegal and disbanded the party. Suharto proceeded to apprehend other senior officials who were loyal to Sukarno, accusing them of being members and supporters of the PKI. This action severely weakened Sukarno's already declining political authority and influence. Sukarno was impeached on March 12, 1967 during a session of the MPR, and Suharto was appointed as the interim president.

The *Pancasila* Democracy Period (also known as the New Order Period), 1966–1998

Suharto's rule, known as the "New Order" in contrast to Sukarno's "Old Order," was established based on two fundamental principles: the Pancasila philosophy and the *Dwifungsi* policy. Pancasila, initially formulated by Sukarno during his nationalist campaign before Indonesian independence and subsequently adopted by Suharto, comprised five principles that Sukarno believed would serve as the philosophical foundation of a sovereign Indonesia. The principles were as follows:

> *Kebangsaan Indonesia refers to the sense of Indonesian patriotism and the principle of inclusivity that encompasses all individuals residing in Indonesia.*
>
> *Internasionalisme or Internationalism that prioritizes fairness and the moral excellence of humanity.*
>
> *Musyawarah Mufakat is a kind of representative democracy that emphasizes deliberative consensus. In this system, there is no ethnic domination, and each member of the council has equal voting power.*
>
> *Social welfare is based on the principles of the welfare state and emphasizes the concept of popular socialism.*

Ketuhanan yang Maha Esa refers to a concept of divinity that represents the ultimate unity. This formulation can be interpreted as encompassing both monotheism and pantheism, thereby accommodating all of Indonesia's major faiths.

According to Suharto, the New Order regime was established based on Pancasila democracy, which aimed to achieve a balance between individual and societal interests and prevent the oppression of the weak by the strong, whether through economic or political means. Pancasila played a crucial role in creating a socio-religious society that strongly rejected poverty, backwardness, conflicts, exploitation, capitalism, feudalism, dictatorship, colonialism, and imperialism. However, despite its seemingly noble principles, the vague wording of Pancasila was often exploited by Suharto's government to justify their actions by labelling their opponents as "anti-Pancasila."

The New Order regime was characterized by the implementation of the *Dwifungsi* ("Dual Function") policy, which granted the military an active role in all aspects of the Indonesian government, economy, and society. This policy allowed military officers to hold seats in the MPR and occupy important positions in the government. Suharto utilized this opportunity to place military loyalists in political positions, thereby strengthening his power and influence.

In response to the demands of civilian politicians for elections, Suharto's government created a set of laws in November 1969. These laws established the structure and responsibilities of parliament, as well as the process for electing presidents. The legislation established a parliament called the MPR, which had the authority to elect presidents. The MPR consisted of two bodies: the DPR, which was the house of representatives, and regional representatives. Out of the 460 members of the DPR, the government directly appointed 100, while the remaining seats were allocated to political organizations based on the outcome of the general election. This system ensured that the government had significant control over legislative matters, particularly the appointment of presidents.

In order to participate in the elections, Suharto recognized the necessity of aligning himself with a political party. In 1969, Suharto assumed control of Golkar, an obscure military-run federation of non-governmental organizations, and utilized it as his means of running for office. The first general election took place on July 3, 1971, with ten participants including Golkar, four Islamic parties, and five nationalist and Christian parties. Golkar campaigned on a non-ideological platform focused on "development," and with official government support and subtle intimidation tactics, managed to secure 62.8% of the popular vote. In the March 1973 general session, the recently elected MPR promptly reappointed Suharto for a second term in office, with Sultan Hamengkubuwono IX serving as vice president.

In order to exert greater control over electoral processes, the government under Suharto's leadership compelled the four Islamic parties to amalgamate into the *Partai Persatuan Pembangunan* (PPP), also known as the United Development Party, while the five non-Islamic parties were coerced to merge into the *Partai Demokrasi Indonesia* (PDI), or the Indonesian Democratic Party. In order to prevent the emergence of strong opposition from these parties, the government exerted control over their leadership and implemented a "recall" procedure to oust vocal legislators from their positions. The Pancasila Democracy system enabled Golkar to achieve overwhelming majorities in the MPR during the elections of 1978, 1983, 1988, 1993, and 1997, resulting in Suharto's uncontested reelection in each of these elections.

Although the New Order administration had considerable success in fostering economic growth and ensuring stability in domestic politics, this prosperity was accompanied by a simultaneous surge in corruption, collusion, and nepotism. Suharto's self-enriching impulses were the most troublesome aspect. Companies led by Suharto's family, for instance, were given profitable government contracts and shielded from market competition through monopolies. The family members of Suharto were granted complimentary shares in 1251 of Indonesia's most profitable local enterprises, while foreign-owned corporations were incentivized to form strategic alliances with the companies owned by Suharto's family. The combination of the severe economic decline of Indonesia during the 1997 Asian financial crisis and Suharto's family and associates being exempt from the strict economic reform measures imposed by the International Monetary Fund resulted in growing political tension and a rapid loss of public confidence in Suharto's leadership.

Due to Suharto's cronyism and widespread nepotism, which were seen as the main causes of the country's growing economic and political problems, influential political figures started to openly criticize his rule, which had been confirmed in the 1997 election. In 1998, university students initiated countrywide protests, which escalated into widespread rioting, looting, and violence throughout Jakarta and other urban areas following the deaths of four demonstrators on May 12, 1998.

On May 16, 1998, a large number of university students gathered on the grounds and roof of the parliament building, demanding the resignation of Suharto. In view of the increasing protests in Jakarta and other major cities, Suharto proposed to resign and overhaul his government. However, several of his political friends declined to participate in the suggested new cabinet. In response to waning support from both the public and his political allies, Suharto declared his resignation on May 21, 1998. Following this, the vice president assumed office. B.J. Habibie took up the role of the presidency in conformity with the provisions of the constitution.

Reformasi Period or the Post-Suharto Period (May 1998 to Present)

Habibie

Following Suharto's resignation and Habibie's assumption of the presidency, Habibie declared the establishment of the Development Reform Cabinet, which resulted in the removal of several highly contentious members from Suharto's Seventh Development Cabinet. However, a majority of the members of the Development Reform Cabinet were ministers and military officers who had previously served in Suharto's Seventh Development Cabinet. The only exception was Hamzah Haz, a member of the United Development Party, who held the position of Minister for Investment in Habibie's administration. Nevertheless, Hamzah stepped down from his position in May 1999 in order to assume leadership of the PPP for the 1999 elections.

The Development Reform Cabinet implemented several significant reforming measures. Shortly after being appointed, Habibie promptly requested his relatives to step down from their government positions and pledged to hold an early election. In order to ensure the independence of the governor of the central bank and the attorney general from executive control, Habibie made the decision to exclude them from the cabinet. During his presidency, Habibie successfully granted the governor of the central bank autonomous power, while maintaining control over the attorney general.

The Habibie administration implemented a number of significant political reforms that enhanced competitiveness and freedom of expression. Upon assuming office, Habibie's administration promptly released political detainees who had been apprehended by the previous New Order regime. Additionally, in June 1998, they enacted the Political Parties Law, which abolished the Suharto-era limitations on political parties, including the mandate for parties to adhere to Pancasila as their guiding ideology. As a result, there was a rapid increase in the number of political parties vying for power in the 1999 legislative election. In addition, the Habibie administration enacted the Regional Autonomy Law, which decentralized the government of Indonesia and granted provinces greater autonomy in administering their respective territories. The law also led to the introduction of indirect elections for mayors and regents and granted local legislatures the power to hold these executives responsible. However, the implementation of this law was delayed until after Habibie's administration. The press saw increased freedom during Habibie's leadership. Furthermore, Habibie promptly made a firm commitment to conducting democratic elections, although the specific timeline was initially unclear. In December 1998, Habibie introduced political reform legislation that was approved by the legislature and MPR. These laws scheduled elections for December 1999, decreased the military's representation in parliament, and prohibited political engagement by government servants.

Although Habibie achieved some degree of success in democratizing many elements of Indonesia and stabilizing the Indonesian economy during the Asian Financial Crisis, he was not reelected in the 1999 parliamentary elections. The main reasons for Habibie's electoral failure may be attributed to two things, the first of which was his unpopular choice to initiate a referendum regarding the future of East Timor. Although the Timorese independence movements had been advocating for a referendum in the region for a while, Habibie initially opposed the idea of East Timorese independence. However, he did propose granting East Timor special autonomy. As the demand for East Timorese independence grew and tensions rose, there was increasing international pressure on the Indonesian government and Habibie to find a resolution. For instance, John Howard, the Prime Minister of Australia, suggested in a letter to Habibie in late 1998 to adopt the approach used by France in settling the demands for independence in New Caledonia. This approach involved granting autonomy initially and then promising a referendum in the future. In order to prevent the perception that Indonesia had control over East Timor as a colony, Habibie made a sudden announcement that a referendum would take place in East Timor. The referendum would give the people the option to choose between special autonomy and independence. Notably, this decision was made without consulting the leaders of the Indonesian armed forces (ABRI).

The referendum took place on August 30, 1999, and the people of East Timor decisively opted for independence. The 1999 East Timorese crisis was ignited by this event, during which pro-Indonesia forces caused significant casualties and forced many people to flee their homes. During the crisis, divisions within Habibie's cabinet were evident. On September 10, General Wiranto reportedly made a threat to carry out a military coup if Habibie permitted the entry of peacekeeping forces. As a result, Habibie decided to retract his decision. On September 12, however, Habibie agreed to the deployment of a peacekeeping force authorized by the United Nations in order to stop the ongoing violence. Subsequently, East Timor underwent a period of United Nations rule and achieved independence in May 2002. The loss of the East Timorese territory had a significant negative impact on Habibie's popularity and political alliances, and it is one of the main reasons why his reelection attempt failed. Habibie's political reputation suffered even more due to the 1999 Bank Bali scandal. Investigations uncovered that Golkar officials and Habibie's assistants had conspired with the Indonesian Bank Restructuring Agency (IBRA) to pressure Bank Bali into paying an unlawful commission. Some of this money was then used to support Habibie's campaign for reelection.

Abdurrahman Wahid

Abdurrahman Wahid assumed the presidency after winning the 1999 legislative elections. The newly revised constitution stipulated that the next president would be elected by the members of the MPR during a joint session. As a result, although the Indonesian Democratic Party Struggle (PDI-P) received the most number votes from the public, its candidate for president, Megawati Sukarnoputri, did not win the election and instead became the vice president.

Wahid's initial cabinet, known as the National Unity Cabinet, was a coalition cabinet with members from multiple political parties, including the PDI-P, PKB, Golkar, PPP, PAN, and Justice Party (PK). The Cabinet also included representatives from non-partisans and the Indonesian Armed Forces (TNI), previously known as ABRI. Subsequently, Wahid implemented two administrative changes. The initial administrative reform involved the elimination of the Ministry of Information, which served as the primary tool for media control under the Suharto administration. The subsequent administrative reform entailed the dissolution of the Ministry of Welfare, which had become corrupt and engaged in extortion during the Suharto regime. Wahid's efforts to address corruption were intensified during his second year as president. In April 2000, Wahid accused Minister of Industry and Trade Jusuf Kalla and Minister of

State-Owned Enterprises Laksamana Sukardi of corruption, although he did not provide any supporting evidence, and subsequently removed them from his cabinet. In February 2000, Wahid also demanded the resignation of General Wiranto, who was serving as the Coordinating Minister of Politics and Security. These actions strained Wahid's relationships with the respective political parties of Wiranto, namely, Golkar and the PDI-P.

Many of Wahid's efforts to bring about reforms and liberalize Indonesia's socio-political climate were met with strong opposition from both the political elite and the general population. In March 2000, Wahid proposed the lifting of the 1966 MPRS decision that prohibited Marxism-Leninism. Wahid also endeavored to build trade links with Israel, which provoked the anger of numerous Indonesian Muslim groups. The departure of the then Coordinating Minister of People's Welfare, Hamzah Haz, in November was mostly due to his dissatisfaction with Wahid's conciliatory approach toward Israel.

During his presidency, Wahid's relationship with the Indonesian military also worsened. Upon assuming the presidency, Wahid aimed to transform the military and reduce its influence in politics. As a result, in March 2000, Wahid appointed Agus Wirahadikusumah, who held similar beliefs, as the Commander of the Indonesian Army Strategic Reserves Command (Kostrad). In July 2000, Agus initiated a disclosure of scandals within Kostrad. As a result, elements of the Indonesian military, under the influence of Megawati, started exerting pressure on Wahid to dismiss Agus. Wahid succumbed to the pressure first but subsequently devised a plan to have Agus named as the Army Chief of Staff. However, this decision was met with threats of retirement from high-ranking military officers, leading Wahid to once again yield to the pressure. In July 2000, it became known that the military was providing weapons to *Laskar Jihad*, a radical Islamic militia, to support Muslims in their conflict with Christians in Maluku. This revelation further worsened Wahid's already strained relationship with the military, despite his explicit order for them to prevent Laskar Jihad from going to Maluku.

Wahid's ability to lead Indonesia as president was further undermined by his involvement in two significant scandals. These scandals included the misappropriation of US$4 million from the pension fund of the State Logistics Agency and allegations that Wahid had withheld a US$2 million donation from the Sultan of Brunei intended to aid Aceh. Due to ongoing mistakes, Wahid was ultimately impeached on July 23, 2001 by the MPR, and Megawati Sukarnoputri, the daughter of Sukarno, took over as president.

Megawati Sukarnoputri

During Megawati's tenure, the ongoing process of democratic change, which had been initiated by Habibie and Wahid, persisted, but it progressed at a sluggish and unpredictable pace. Megawati assumed a predominantly symbolic position and infrequently interceded in governmental affairs. During her time in office, the Mutual Assistance Cabinet held the main responsibility for running the country.

Although the ascension of an influential figure who opposed the Suharto dictatorship to the presidency was originally met with widespread approval, it quickly became evident that her tenure was characterized by indecisiveness, a lack of strong ideological orientation, and a reputation for failing to take action on significant policy matters. As a result, although the economy had achieved stability and saw some improvement after the 1997 Financial Crisis, unemployment and poverty rates remained elevated by 2004. Following Suharto's downfall, the military, previously tarnished, managed to reclaim a significant amount of power, and corruption continued to be widespread. An advantageous consequence of Megawati's cautious implementation of reforms and deliberate avoidance of conflicts was the establishment of stability in the process of democratization, leading to a gradual achievement of equilibrium among the legislative, executive, and military branches.

During this period, the Indonesian Constitution was revised to include provisions for the direct election of a president and the imposition of a two-term limit on the president. However, Megawati was unsuccessful in securing a second term in the 2004 elections. Megawati frequently lagged behind in the opinion polls, partly because Muslim voters favored male candidates and also owing to her underwhelming record in office.

Susilo Bambang Yudhoyono

Susilo Bambang Yudhoyono assumed the presidency after winning the 2004 elections and was officially inaugurated on October 20, 2004. The main focus of Yudhoyono's tenure was his economic reforms. One notable achievement was his leadership in securing a free trade deal with Japan in late 2007. Yudhoyono additionally provided more monies to reduce poverty and implemented cash transfers to mitigate the impact of inflation on the less affluent sectors of Indonesian society. The *Bantuan Langsung Tunai*, or cash transfers, were conducted in Indonesia from October 2005 to December 2006, aiming to reach 19.2 million impoverished households. The program was implemented again in 2008. The program faced significant criticism due to its contribution to government debt and its discouragement of individual work, ultimately hindering long-term sustainable economic growth. However, the program significantly bolstered Yudhoyono's popularity, particularly in election years. Yudhoyono's primary emphasis on addressing the difficulties faced by the impoverished was also extended to the domains of education and healthcare. In January 2005, Yudhoyono initiated the Poor Community Health Insurance (*Askeskin*), a program specifically aimed at providing the underprivileged with improved healthcare accessibility. In July 2005, Yudhoyono initiated the Schools Operational Assistance (BOS) program, which provides financial aid to schools on the condition that they reduce or eliminate fees, thus enhancing educational opportunities for the underprivileged. Yudhoyono also initiated the launch of the Book BOS in June 2006, a program that offers financial assistance to underprivileged individuals for the acquisition of educational books.

An enduring issue throughout Yudhoyono's presidency was the distribution of authority between him and his vice president, Jusuf Kalla. The Democratic Party, led by Yudhoyono, together with its coalition allies, had a smaller number of deputies compared to Golkar and the PDI-P, who served as the opposition in parliament. Upon assuming the position of chairman of Golkar in December 2004, Kalla's influence in parliament surpassed that of the president due to which Yudhoyono faced a significant change in power dynamics. One instance of this was after the 2004 Indian Ocean tsunami, when Kalla, without consulting Yudhoyono, gathered ministers and issued a vice presidential decree to initiate the rehabilitation of Aceh. Yudhoyono, nonetheless, asserted that he was the one who issued the instructions for Kalla to proceed. Several other examples illustrating the delicate power balance between Kalla and Yudhoyono exist. One such instance occurred when Yudhoyono travelled to New York to participate in the annual United Nations Summit in September 2005. Despite leaving Kalla in charge during his absence, Yudhoyono still held a video conference from New York to receive reports from ministers. In 2009, Yudhoyono secured a second term as president by defeating the challenge from Megawati–Prabowo and Wiranto–Kalla.

Joko Widodo

In 2014, Yudhoyono, who was legally prohibited from seeking a third term, was replaced by Joko Widodo, commonly known as Jokowi. Jokowi was reelected in the 2019 election and, according to the constitution, is disqualified from running for the presidency in the 2024 elections. Significantly, Jokowi was the first Indonesian president who did not come from a privileged political or military lineage.

The legacy of Jokowi is complex and has many different aspects. Jokowi has received praise for his initiatives in reducing poverty in Indonesia. These include the redistribution of land to the impoverished in 2016 by formalizing land ownership, the implementation of the Indonesian health card (*Kartu Indonesia Sehat*) to establish a universal healthcare system, the introduction of the Smart Indonesia Card (Kartu Indonesia Pintar) to enhance school enrolment and achieve universal education, and the implementation of a cash transfer program (Program *Keluarga Harapan*) for those in need. These initiatives have resulted in a reduction in Indonesia's Gini coefficient of wealth disparity from 40 in 2013 to 38.2, marking the first substantial dip in Indonesia's inequality levels in 15 years. It is important to mention that these programs have not resulted in any financial burden. Indonesia's public debt, which is less than 40% of its Gross Domestic Product, is considered modest compared to global standards.

In addition, Jokowi has utilized his popularity to implement challenging reforms aimed at enhancing competitiveness in the economy, such as the restructuring of inflexible labor regulations and the removal of fuel subsidies. As an illustration, in 2018, Widodo implemented a new regulation that permitted foreign workers to work in Indonesia without the need for Indonesian language proficiency. Additionally, in 2020, the Omnibus Law on Job Creation was enacted with the aim of stimulating investment and streamlining bureaucratic procedures that had previously impeded foreign investment. However, these initiatives faced strong resistance from local organizations, including labor unions.

However, Jokowi's devotion to infrastructure development is particularly noteworthy. Throughout his presidency, the government has formulated strategies to construct extensive road networks throughout Indonesia and establish intercity railroads to enhance both interregional and intraregional connectivity. The metro train network in Jakarta has experienced significant and rapid growth. Additionally, between 2015 and 2018, almost 700 kilometers of toll roads were constructed, which is a remarkable accomplishment compared to the just 220 kilometers of roads created in Indonesia during the previous 10 years. Jokowi's reforms have contributed to the enhancement of Indonesia's position on the World Bank's Doing Business index, which evaluates the business and investment environment in nations, ascending from 120th in 2014 to 73rd in 2020.

Nevertheless, Jokowi has faced criticism for his role in Indonesia's decline in democratic standards. The democratic regression in Indonesia is backed by statistical evidence. The Varieties of Democracy (V-Dem) Deliberative Democracy Index, which combines indicators measuring both electoral and non-electoral aspects of democracy, shows that Indonesia reached its peak of democracy in 2006 and has since experienced a decline with some fluctuations. In 2018, the democratic quality of Indonesia experienced a decline, reaching its lowest point since the year 2000. Although various indexes, such as Freedom House and the Economist Intelligence Unit Democracy Index, may have slightly different criteria, they all indicate a similar pattern: Indonesian democracy currently surpasses the minimum requirements for an electoral democracy but falls considerably short of the democratic standards it achieved around 10 years ago, in the mid-to-late 2000s.

Two elements contribute to the problem of democratic regression: Jokowi's dependence on his political coalition and his utilization of illiberal tactics to consolidate political authority. Due to the absence of strong family, corporate, or military ties, Jokowi aimed to secure political backing by establishing a wide-ranging alliance. The fundamental issue with this approach, however, is that by appointing a diverse group of influential individuals to his cabinet and forming a sizable coalition in parliament, Jokowi compromised his capacity to advocate for substantial democratic reforms. Despite his early pledge of democratic reforms, Jokowi instead formed alliances with conservative people and forces in order to strengthen his political coalition. Despite promising to appoint a cabinet mainly composed of professionals, Widodo's selection of 38 ministers and 12 vice ministers on October 23, 2019 can be seen as a way of repaying political allies and campaign funders who supported him in defeating Prabowo Subianto during the campaign. This can be likened to a form of debt repayment, or *hutang budi*. Out of the 50 appointees, 21 are affiliated with political parties, including Airlangga Hartarto from the Golkar Party, Megawati Sukarnoputri from the PDI-P, and Surya Paloh from the National Democratic Party (Nasdem). The rest of President Widodo's cabinet consists mainly of wealthy individuals like Erick Thohir and Nadiem Makarim, as well as retired military officers who were supportive of his campaign. Only a select group of well-known experts in technology were chosen for cabinet positions, including Finance Minister Sri Mulyani Indrawati and Pratikno, the former president of Gadjah Mada University, who is one of the president's most trusted advisors. Specifically, the unusually large size of his cabinet reflects Widodo's intention to reward people who played a crucial role in his successful reelection campaign.

The presence of political groups aligned with the winning coalition in Jokowi's cabinet means that the leaders of his alliance will still have influence over Indonesian politics, which limits the effectiveness of any significant reforms that Widodo may attempt to implement. The appointment of Yassona Laoly, a hardliner from the PDI-P party, as Minister of Law and Human Rights in Indonesia, has had detrimental effects on democracy and individual freedoms. Laoly has been instrumental in proposing revisions to the Indonesian criminal code that would result in severe penalties for those found guilty of "defaming" the president, parliament, and other state institutions. Additionally, these revisions would criminalize almost all forms of pre-marital sexual relations. Widodo's decision to appoint Nadiem Maskarim, the founder of Gojek, as Minister of Education and Culture, has been deemed ineffective. Despite Maskarim's inclination toward reform, his proposed changes to Indonesia's education system and support for entrepreneurs in e-commerce and creative industries have faced strong opposition from long-established bureaucrats who have tightly controlled the education sector for many years. In a broader sense, the selection of individuals from groups that are inherently competitive and have different ideologies and priorities is considered to be detrimental to Widodo's ambitious reform plans. This is because the likelihood of bureaucratic conflicts arising from conflicting interests between different ministries will hinder the ability to reach a consensus on consistent and coordinated policies.

A matter of concern is Widodo's deliberate fostering of strong relationships with military personnel, and their ongoing significance and participation in the decision-making procedures related to governing the nation. Former military generals who were part of President Widodo's first-term administrations, including his close ally Luhut Pandjaitan, who is now the coordinating Minister of Maritime Affairs and Investment, and Moeldoko, the Presidential

Chief of Staff, have been kept in their positions. Police General Tito Karnavian, who formerly served as the head of the National Police, has been designated as the new Minister of Home Affairs. Additionally, Fachrul Razi, a retired general with previous experience in the intelligence agency, has been chosen as the new Minister of Religious Affairs. Specifically, Luhut's decision to replace the technocrat Tom Lembong with himself as the senior minister responsible for handling new foreign direct investment (FDI) has given him more power over the profitable oil, gas, and mining sectors. These are industries from which his company, PT Toba Sejahtera Group, would directly benefit.

In a broader sense, the ongoing rise in the presence of military personnel has resulted in a corresponding surge in military participation in civilian matters. Prior to the 2019 elections, it was reported that Jokowi directed military commands at the village level to actively endorse his policies and suppress efforts by opposition actors to disseminate false information about him and his government. Furthermore, his bid for reelection entailed the activation of bureaucratic establishments, including public servants, governors, district administrators, and village chiefs, to garner backing for Jokowi. Consequently, the changes that previously prohibited officers from having civilian positions have gradually been weakened, reflecting the influence of the *Dwifungsi* concept, which was a key aspect of Suharto's New Order administration. The utilization of bureaucratic mobilization, along with the manipulation of legal and security systems for political motives, poses a significant risk to the progress that Indonesia painstakingly achieved during the Reformasi era.

This issue is exacerbated by the growing limitation of civil liberties, such as freedom of speech and organization, under Jokowi's administration. The government has increasingly utilized the Criminal Code, the 1965 Blasphemy Law, and the 2008 Law on Electronic Information and Transactions (ITE) to prohibit defamatory or insulting statements, including those that incite hatred toward religious, racial, or ethnic groups. These measures are aimed at suppressing and controlling criticism from citizens, opposition figures, and anti-corruption activists. Government entities, including as the police, had been using the ITE law more frequently in the period leading up to the 2019 presidential elections. They had targeted anti-Jokowi activists who were active in the "*Ganti Presiden*" or "Change the President" campaign. In addition, as a response to an overall increase in sectarian activism, Jokowi implemented a Regulation in Lieu of Law (*Perppu*) that grants the government the authority to dissolve any organization it perceives as a danger to Pancasila, the officially endorsed philosophy of the state. This law, along with the 2013 Law on Societal Organizations, prohibits organizations from engaging in activities that contradict Pancasila, thereby enabling the banning of groups that pose a threat to Jokowi's administration, such as *Hizbut Tahrir Indonesia* (HTI), a radical yet nonviolent Islamist group. Although the actions have garnered backing from numerous Indonesians due to the undemocratic and illiberal characteristics of the targeted parties like the HTI, these measures themselves are illiberal and pose a threat to the delicate democracy that has been established in the last 10 years.

Indonesia's response to COVID-19 faced significant criticism due to its lack of effectiveness. The administration's response was characterized by a lack of promptness, inconsistency, and a fundamental lack of realism. Prominent figures within the administration made statements emphasizing the efficacy of prayer rather than implementing practical measures. Additionally, Jokowi himself appeared hesitant to take decisive actions that may have been unpopular but necessary to effectively address the pandemic. An evident instance of the Jokowi administration's failure was their unwavering claim that Indonesia had no instances of COVID-19 during the initial stages of the pandemic.

In Summary

Indonesia's first president, Sukarno earned his political feathers as a fighter for the country's independence, uniting various nationalist forces and ultimately succeeding in compelling the Dutch colonialists to surrender their more than 350 years colonial possession.

However, due to the times of his life and the various ideologies that pervaded in the early decades of the 19th century, Sukarno was largely anti-capitalist and wanted to chart an independent destiny for his country, leading him to clash with the West, especially the United States in the post-Second World War Cold War between the so-called 'East' vs 'West'. He was eventually deposed following the still much-debated 'communist coup' that brought the Indonesian military to power with the backing of the West, especially the US.

Suharto, the distinguished military leader, who was involved in Indonesia's anti-colonial struggles as well as in leading various combat operations in Aceh, Malukus and West New Guinea, (present-day Papua), eventually what brought him to power was his role as military leader in crushing the PKI, then a powerful political force as well as its political guardian, Sukarno. While Sukarno has been dubbed as the 'father' of Indonesia's independence, alongside, Mohammad Hatta, Suharto is more known for bring political stability and economic growth to Indonesia, albeit, also described as an authoritarian leader. If Sukarno was president for slightly more than 20 years, then Suharto was president for slightly more than 30 years, until he was brought down by Western-supported 'people's power' revolution.

Since then, following the May 1998 'revolution', Indonesia entered what is known as the 'reformasi' or reform period, with the public given greater say in most political activities, with Indonesia emerging as the third largest democracy in the world, albeit, also known for its instability, especially following the fall of Suharto in 1998 until the election of Bambang Yudhoyono in 2004. Following Suharto, Habibie, Abdurrahman Wahid, Megawati Sukarnoputri, Bambang Yudhoyono and Joko Widodo were the country's presidents.

CHAPTER 5

THE KEY POLITICAL PARTIES IN THE 2024 INDONESIAN PRESIDENTIAL RACE

Technically, 18 political parties qualified to participate in the general elections, claiming to have a voice and right to nominate a presidential candidate, either from their own parties or by endorsing someone else, including an independent candidate. However, there were only a number of key political parties that were critical in this regard.

Indonesian Democratic Party of Struggle (PDI-P)

The PDI-P was founded by Megawati Sukarnoputri, president of Indonesia from 2001 to 2004 and daughter of Sukarno, the first president of Indonesia, who has led the party since its founding in 1999. Megawati was forced out from the leadership of the PDI by the government of Indonesia under Suharto in 1996. Megawati formed the PDI-P in 1999 after Suharto resigned and restrictions on political parties were lifted. Notably, the PDI-P is a member of the Council of Asian Liberals and Democrats, a regional organization of liberal democratic political parties in Asia, and Progressive Alliance, an international political organization of social democratic and progressive political parties founded on May 22, 2013 in Leipzig, Germany.

Party platform

The PDI-P's ideology is based on the official Indonesian national philosophy, Pancasila. According to its website, the party strives to realize the aims contained in the preamble to the 1945 Constitution in the form of a just and prosperous society and to bring about an Indonesia that is socially and politically sovereign, economically self-sufficient, and Indonesian in character and culture. At the party's fourth congress in 2015, the PDI-P issued a seven-point statement entitled "Realizing Great Indonesia, an Indonesia that is Truly Independent," in which it committed itself to overseeing the program of the central government and ensuring it keeps its campaign promises, while reinforcing its position as a political force, underlining its support for the poor, and battling structural poverty.

Electoral history

Since its founding in 1999, the PDI-P has remained one of the major players in the Indonesian political scene, consistently obtaining a significant portion of votes in legislative elections. Driven by reformist sentiments amidst the electorate, the PDI-P emerged with the largest share of the votes at 33% in the 1999 legislative elections, albeit failing to attain absolute majority in the MPR. By 2004, however, the reformist sentiments that had aided the PDI-P in its 1999 legislative elections victory had died down, as many were disappointed with what the reform process had achieved thus far and were disillusioned with Megawati's presidency: This was reflected in the 2004 legislative election, where the PDI-P obtained only 18.5% of the total vote. The PDI-P nominated Megawati as its presidential candidate for the 2004 presidential election: Megawati selected Nahdatul Ulama chairman Hasyim Muzadi as her running mate, expecting that she would appeal to nationalist sentiments while Hasyim would appeal to Islamist voters. Contrary to expectations, however, the pair came second to Susilo Bambang Yudhoyono and Jusuf Kalla in the first round of elections. To improve their chances in the runoff, the PDI-P formed a coalition called the "Nationhood

Coalition" with the PPP, Golkar, the Reform Star Party (PBR), and the Prosperous Peace Party (PDS), but were ultimately defeated by Susilo Bambang Yudhoyono and Jusuf Kalla. Since Kalla was elected as Golkar's chairman, it defected to the government's side, leaving the PDI-P as the only major opposition party in the DPR.

Given the PDI-P's less than optimal performance in the 2004 legislative elections, during the second PDI-P Congress held in 2005, a faction of the PDI-P called for a change in the party leadership if it won the 2009 legislative elections; naming themselves the Renewal of PDI-P Movement, these members eventually defected to form the Democratic Renewal Party (PDP) after Megawati was reelected to the chairpersonship for a third term.

In the 2009 legislative election, the PDI-P came in third with 14% of the votes and had 95 seats in the DPR. Megawati was chosen as the presidential candidate, this time forming a coalition with the Great Indonesia Movement Party, with Prabowo Subianto as her running mate. The pair, however, lost to Susilo Bambang Yudhoyono, with Boediono as vice president, with 26.6% of the vote. In March 2014, the party nominated Jakarta governor Joko Widodo as its presidential candidate, with Jusuf Kalla as his running mate. The pairing won with 53.15% of the vote, and the PDI-P returned as the largest party in the DPR, winning nearly 19% of the vote. In April 2019, incumbent president Joko Widodo was the party's presidential candidate running for a second term, with Ma'ruf Amin as his running mate. Widodo successfully won a second term with 55.5% of the vote. The PDI-P remained the largest party in the DPR, winning 19.33% of the vote.

The PDI-P is currently the largest political party in Indonesia, and the party of Joko Widodo. Five PDI-P politicians serve as ministers in Jokowi's cabinet, and the party has 128 seats in the national parliament, which exceeds the threshold of 115 seats needed to nominate a presidential candidate under Indonesia's election laws. The PDI-P is hence the only political party that has the ability to nominate a presidential candidate for the 2024 presidential elections, without the need to form a political coalition with other parties. Additionally, the PDI-P is electorally strong in the key battleground

Table 5.1. PDI-P's Strength in the Legislative Elections

Election	Total Seats Won	Total Votes	Share of Votes (%)
1999	153/500	35,689,073	33.74
2004	109/550	21,026,629	18.53
2009	95/560	14,600,091	14.03
2014	109/560	23,681,471	18.95
2019	128/575	27,053,961	19.33
2024	110/575	25,387,279	16.72

Table 5.2. PDI-P and Presidential Election Results

Election	Candidate	Running Mate	Outcome
2004	Megawati Sukarnoputri	Hasyim Muzadi	Lost
2009	Megawati Sukarnoputri	Prabowo Subianto	Lost
2014	Joko Widodo	Jusuf Kalla	Elected
2019	Joko Widodo	Ma'ruf Amin	Elected
2024	Ganjar Pranowo	Mahfud MD	Lost

Source: IFES Election Guide | Elections: Indonesia Presidential July 5, 2004. (n.d.). See https://www.electionguide.org/elections/id/1936/; IFES Election Guide | Elections: Indonesia Presidential (Round 2) September 20, 2004. (n.d.). See https://www.electionguide.org/elections/id/1938/; IFES Election GuideElections: Indonesia Pres July 8, 2009. (n.d.). See https://www.electionguide.org/elections/id/2110/; IFES Election Guide | Elections: Indonesia President 2014. (n.d.). See https://www.electionguide.org/elections/id/2405/; IFES Election Guide | Elections: Indonesia President 2019. (n.d.). Retrieved October 24, 2023, from https://www.electionguide.org/elections/id/3105/.

provinces of Central Java and East Java, home to more than 70 million Indonesians, as well as the Outer Island provinces of Bali, East Nusa Tenggara, and Papua. Given its power and influence, the PDI-P is undoubtedly one of the key political parties for the 2024 presidential elections (Tables 5.1 and 5.2)

Golkar

The *Partai Golongan Karya* (Golkar) or the Party of Functional Groups is a political party in Indonesia. Golkar was the ruling political group from 1971 to 1999, under presidents Suharto and B.J. Habibie. It subsequently joined the ruling coalitions under presidents Abdurrahman Wahid, Megawati Sukarnoputri, and Susilo Bambang Yudhoyono. When President Joko Widodo of the Indonesian Democratic Party of Struggle was elected in 2014, Golkar initially joined an opposition coalition led by former general Prabowo Subianto, but in 2016 it switched allegiance to Widodo's government.

Guided democracy period

Golkar was founded as the *Sekretariat Bersama Golongan Karya* (Sekber Golkar) or the Joint Secretariat of Functional Groups in 1964. In 1959, President Sukarno introduced his concept of Guided Democracy, in which so-called functional groups would play a role in government in the place of political parties. The Indonesian National Armed Forces supported its creation, believing that these groups would balance the growing strength of the PKI. In 1960, Sukarno awarded sectoral groups such as teachers, the Armed Forces, the Indonesian National Police, workers, and artists seats in the Mutual Cooperation People's Representative Council. As some of the members of these functional groups were linked to political parties, this gave political influence to the National Armed Forces. The TNI then established an anti-PKI trade union, the *Sentral Organisasi Karyawan Swadiri Indonesia* (Soksi) or the Central Organization of Indonesian Workers, and used this as the core of an Armed Forces-led Sekber Golkar, which was officially established on October 20, 1964. By 1968, there were almost 250 organizations under the Sekber umbrella. On November 22, 1969, they were organized into seven main organizations, or *Kelompok Induk Organisasi* (Kino), namely, Soksi, Kosgoro (Union of Mutual Cooperation Multifunction Organizations), MKGR (Mutual Assistance Families Association), *Gerakan Karya Rakyat* (People's Working Movement), *Ormas Hankam* (Defense and Security Mass Organizations), *Professi* (professional organizations), and *Gerakan Pembangunan* (Development Movement). The Joint

Secretariat was one of those organizations mobilized against the PKI in the aftermath of the failure of the 30 September Movement in 1965.

New order

It was only during the Suharto era that Golkar became a political organization, and it participated for the first time in national elections in 1971 as a federation of functional groups. In March 1968, General Suharto was officially elected by the MPR as Indonesia's second president. Because of his military background, Suharto was not affiliated to any political party and had never expressed much interest in party politics. He, however, needed to align himself with a political party if he were to be elected for a second term as president. While he had originally shown interest in aligning with the PNI, the party of his predecessor, Sukarno, Suharto wished to distance himself from the old regime. Suharto hence chose to align himself with Golkar, and ordered his closest associate, Ali Murtopo, to transform Golkar into an electoral machine. Under Murtopo, and with Suharto's supervision, Golkar was turned from a federation of NGOs into a political party. Under Suharto, Golkar continued to portray itself as a non-ideological entity, without favoritism or political agendas. It promised to focus on "economic development" and "stability" rather than a specific ideological goal. Golkar also began identifying itself with the government, encouraging civil servants to vote for it as a sign of loyalty to the government.

Murtopo claimed that workers were a functional group, which by rights ought to be subsumed under Golkar: "Thus all unions were united into a single body answerable to the state. The population was no longer there to be mobilized by political parties," rather, the people were the "floating mass" or the "ignorant mass" who needed firm guidance so they would not be lured into politics. In order to "Golkar-ize" the nation, Murtopo sometimes used the military and gangs of young thugs to eliminate political competition.

Golkar declared on February 4, 1970 that it would participate in the 1971 legislative elections, where it won 62% of the votes and an overwhelming majority in the DPR. Since the members of the DPR also doubled as members of the MPR, Suharto was easily reelected to a second term as president in March 1973. Strengthened by his reelection, Suharto quickly began tightening his grip on Golkar. Control was increased in October 1973 with the implementation of a less democratic and more centralized system headed by a chairman. In October 1978, after his reelection to a third term, Suharto further consolidated his control of Golkar by appointing himself chairman of the executive board or Ketua Dewan Pembina, a position whose authority supersedes that of even the party chairman. From this position, Suharto assumed supreme power in Golkar, while leaving the day-to-day running of Golkar to the chairman. Notably, Golkar was also dominated by the Armed Forces. Out of its four chairmen during the New Order, three had a military background as officers. It was only in the last years of Suharto's rule that Harmoko, a civilian, was elected as Golkar chairman.

Golkar continued to dominate Indonesian politics well beyond the 1971 legislative elections. In subsequent New Order legislative elections, Golkar won 62% (1977), 64% (1982), 73% (1987), 68% (1992), and 74% (1997) of the votes. Golkar's dominance was so absolute that for most of the Suharto era, Indonesia was effectively a one-party state. Suharto was able to pass his bills without any meaningful opposition and was able to form a Cabinet which consisted only of Golkar appointees. After 1973, Suharto banned all political parties but the PDI and the PPP. These two parties were nominally permitted to contest the reign of Golkar; in reality, however, Golkar permitted only a semblance of competition. Elections were "exercises in controlled aggression" and were ritualized performances of "choice," in which local authorities were to obey directives about Golkar's electoral results in their area. A system of rewards, punishments, and violence meted out by thugs helped to guarantee cooperation across the archipelago, and the perpetual reelection of Golkar. Resultantly, claims of electoral fraud and intimidation were lodged against Golkar by the PDI and the PPP, in particular after the 1977 and 1997 legislative elections, albeit to little avail.

During the New Order, Golkar was formally divided into seven (eight after 1971) organizations, called *Kelompok Induk Organisasi* (KINO) or Main Organization Groups. These were the Trikarya, consisting of *Sentral Organisasi Karyawan Swadiri Indonesia* (SOKSI) or Central Indonesian Workers' Organization (CIWO); *Kesatuan Organisasi Serbaguna Gotong Royong* (KOSGORO) or Mutual Cooperation Multifunction Organizations' Union; *Musyawarah Kekeluargaan Gotong Royong* (MKGR) or Mutual Assistance Families' Association; *Gerakan Karya Rakyat Indonesia* (GAKARI) or Indonesian People's Working Movement (IPWM); *Organisasi Kemasyarakatan Pertahanan dan Keamanan* (Ormas Hankam) or the Defense and Security Mass Organizations (DSMOs); Professional organizations (*Golongan Profesi*); and the Development Movement (Gerakan Pembangunan). The eighth organization is the *Korps Pegawai Republik Indonesia* (KOPRI) or Employees' Corps of the Republic of Indonesia, which was established by Presidential decree in 1971.

The membership in Golkar during this era was also de facto divided into three factions, which worked closely together to gain consensus and whose leaders represented the core leadership of Golkar. The first was the ABRI faction. This consisted of members of the ABRI, who under Suharto played a dominant role in political affairs. This faction was headed by the ABRI Commander and was commonly known as the A faction. The Ormas Hankam was, as a general rule, supportive of the Armed Forces faction. It provided much of the military representation in the People's Consultative Assembly. The second was the Bureaucrat or *Birokrat* faction. This consisted of KOPRI members, who were de jure all civil servants; non-civil servant public officers; employees of state-, provincial-, and municipal-owned enterprises; and ABRI members employed by the government. This faction was headed by the Home Affairs Minister and was commonly known as the B faction.

The third was the Groups or *Utusan Golongan* faction, which consisted of Golkar members who were neither armed forces service personnel nor part of the bureaucracy. This faction was headed by the Golkar chairman and was commonly known as the G faction. It was made up of members of the other organizations that were part of the party.

Reformasi period

Golkar did not officially become a political party until 1999, when it was required to become one in order to contest elections. Upon Suharto's fall from power in May 1998, Golkar quickly sought to adapt and reform itself. In July 1998, a Special National Congress was held to elect the next chairman of Golkar. Attended by both pro-Suharto and anti-Suharto groups, the Special National Congress was the first time that a Golkar chairman was elected democratically rather than appointed by the chairman of the executive board. Akbar Tanjung emerged as the new chairman of Golkar after beating Army General Edi Sudrajat. Under Akbar, the executive board was abolished and replaced by an advisory board which had considerably less authority.

Party platform

Under chairman Aburizal Bakrie, Golkar produced a blueprint known as "Vision Indonesia 2045: A Prosperous Nation" with the aim of making Indonesia a developed nation by the centenary of the country's independence in 2045. The plan comprises three stages, each lasting a decade. The key strategies in the vision involve developing Indonesia from the villages, strengthening the role of the state, quality economic growth, equalizing incomes, ensuring even development in all areas, quality education and healthcare, strengthening communities, sustained economic development, upholding the law and human rights, and industrial development based on technology and revitalization of agriculture and trade.

The first decade would lay the foundations for a developed nation, the second would accelerate development, and the final decade would see Indonesia become a developed nation. Each stage would have targets for indicators such as economic growth, GDP, and levels of unemployment and poverty.

Electoral history

Golkar lost its first democratic legislative election in 1999 to Megawati Sukarnoputri's PDI-P. Golkar won 22.46% of the votes and was the runner-up in the legislative elections, but was nonetheless still able to secure the election of Akbar Tanjung as Head of the DPR. For the 1999 Presidential elections, Golkar had joined the Central Axis, a political coalition put together by MPR chairman Amien Rais, to nominate and successfully secure the election of Abdurrahman Wahid as president. Golkar was rewarded for its support of Wahid by having its members appointed to ministerial positions in Wahid's cabinet.

Much like those who had supported Wahid, however, Golkar grew increasingly disillusioned with Wahid. This was further compounded by the sacking of Jusuf Kalla, then Minister of Industries and Trade, in April 2000 by Wahid. When Golkar inquired as to why this was done, Wahid alleged it was because of corruption. Resultantly, Golkar, along with its Central Axis allies, held an MPR Special Session in July 2001 to replace President Wahid with Megawati.

By 2004, the reformist sentiments that had led the PDI-P to victory in the 1999 legislative elections had died down. Many Indonesians were disappointed with what Reformasi had achieved thus far and were also disillusioned with Megawati's presidency. This discontent enabled Golkar to emerge victorious in the 2004 legislative elections with 21% of the votes. Golkar, however, had five potential presidential candidates for the 2004 presidential elections; resultantly, it held a national convention in April 2004 to decide who would become Golkar's candidate for president. These five potential candidates were Akbar Tanjung, General Wiranto, Lieutenant-General Prabowo, Aburizal Bakrie, and Surya Paloh. Akbar won the first round of elections but Wiranto emerged as the winner in the second round. Wiranto chose Solahuddin Wahid as his running mate, but ultimately lost to Susilo Bambang Yudhoyono and Jusuf Kalla in the first round of elections. Golkar's electoral failure prompted allegations of disunity within the party with Akbar not fully supporting Wiranto after losing the nomination.

In August 2004, Golkar formed a national coalition with the PDI-P, PPP, PBR, and PDS to back Megawati. However, further infighting arose: Fahmi Idris led a group of Golkar members in defecting and throwing their support behind Yudhoyono and Kalla. At the presidential runoff in September 2004, Yudhoyono emerged victorious over Megawati to become Indonesia's sixth president. Jusuf Kalla, who had left Golkar in April 2004, became vice president.

Although Yudhoyono had overwhelmingly won the presidency, he was still weak in the DPR, since his own Democratic Party had only won 7% in the legislative elections. Faced with the prospect of an opposition comprising of Golkar and the PDI-P, Yudhoyono gave Kalla permission to run for the Golkar chairmanship. On December 19, 2004, Kalla became the new Golkar chairman with over 50% of the votes, defeating the incumbent Akbar, who had expected to win a second term. Kalla's new appointment as chairman of Golkar significantly strengthened Yudhoyono's government in Parliament and left the PDI-P as the only major opposition party in the DPR.

In the 2009 legislative elections, Golkar obtained 14.45% of the votes, equivalent to 106 of the 560 seats in the DPR. Golkar fielded Kalla as its presidential candidate for the 2009 presidential elections, paired with Wiranto, but the pair only obtained 12.41% of the total votes. In the 2014 legislative elections, Golkar won 14.75% of the votes, equivalent to 91 of the 560 seats in the DPR. Golkar joined Prabowo's political coalition for the 2014 presidential election, but Prabowo and Hatta eventually lost to Jokowi. Golkar initially joined an opposition coalition led by former general Prabowo Subianto, but in 2016 switched its allegiance to Widodo's government. In the

Table 5.3. Golkar and Legislative Election Results

Election	Total Seats Won	Total Votes	Share of Votes (%)	Party Leader
1971	236/360	34,348,673	62.80	Suprapto Sukowati
1977	232/360	39,750,096	62.11	Amir Murtono
1982	242/360	48,334,724	64.34	Amir Murtono
1987	299/400	62,783,680	73.11	Sudharmono
1992	282/400	66,599,331	68.10	Wahono
1997	325/400	84,187,907	74.51	Harmoko
1999	120/500	23,741,749	22.46	Akbar Tandjung
2004	128/550	24,480,757	21.58	Akbar Tandjung
2009	106/560	15,037,757	14.45	Jusuf Kalla
2014	91/560	18,432,312	14.75	Aburizal Bakrie
2019	85/575	17,229,789	12.31	Airlangga Hartarto
2024	102/575	23,208,654	15.29	Airlangga Hartarto

Source: "Bab V Hasil Pemilu". General Election Commission (KPU). Retrieved from https://www.kpu.go.id/dmdocuments/modul_1d.pdf; IFES Election Guide | Country Profile: Indonesia. (n.d.). Retrieved October 24, 2023, from https://www.electionguide.org/countries/id/102/; Nathalia, T. (2019). *Jokowi wins re-election, PDI-P wins most seats*, Jakarta Globe. Retrieved October 24, 2023, from https://jakartaglobe.id/context/jokowi-wins-reelection-pdip-wins-most-seats.

Table 5.4. Golkar and Presidential Election Results

Election	Pres. Candidate	Running Mate	Share of Votes	Outcome
2004	Wiranto	Salahuddin Wahid	22.15%	Lost
2009	Jusuf Kalla	Wiranto	12.41%	Lost
2014	Prabowo Subianto	Hatta Rajasa	46.85%	Lost
2019	Joko Widodo	Ma'ruf Amin	55.50%	Elected
2024	Prabowo Subianto	Gibran	58.6%	Elected

Source: IFES Election Guide | Country Profile: Indonesia. (n.d.). Retrieved October 24, 2023, from https://www.electionguide.org/countries/id/102/.

2019 legislative elections, Golkar obtained 12.31% of the votes and currently hold 85 of the 575 seats in the DPR. Golkar was a member of Jokowi's political coalition in his ultimately successful bid for a second term (Tables 5.3 and 5.4).

The Nasdem Party (Partai Nasdem)

The Nasdem Party originated from a youth-oriented non-governmental organization (NGO) called Nasional Demokrat (National Democrats), which was established by Surya Paloh, the owner of the media conglomerate Media Group, and Hamengkubuwono X, the sultan of Yogyakarta, in 2010. The NGO received significant media coverage from Surya Paloh's media outlets. However, in 2011, Hamengkubuwono decided to leave the organization due to dissatisfaction with its transformation into a political party. Shortly after, Surya Paloh formed the Nasdem Party and appointed Patrice Rio Capella, a former politician from the National Mandate Party (PAN), as its inaugural chairman.

The party was officially established on July 26, 2011, although it had registered with the Ministry of Law and Human Rights in March. During the party's first convention in January 2013, Surya Paloh was appointed as the party chairman for the term from 2013 to 2018. At the same convention, he was given full authority to determine the party's strategy and policies in order to win the 2014 election. However, later in the same month, one of the other founders and financial backers, media tycoon Hary Tanoesoedibjo, who is the founder of the Media Nusantara Citra media group, abruptly left the party in protest against Surya Paloh's appointment. Hary then joined the People's Conscience Party, led by former general Wiranto, and became their vice presidential candidate.

The Nasdem Party stands out from other political parties in Indonesia by having its own formalized and specialized cadre education and training facility called *Akademi Bela Negara Nasional Demokrat* (ABN Nasdem) or the National Defense Academy of National Democrats. ABN Nasdem is a political corporate university that follows the curriculum of the National Resilience Institute, which is the primary national leadership education and training facility in Indonesia. The academy was established by Surya Paloh and IGK Manila and was officially inaugurated by Joko Widodo on July 16, 2017.

Political agenda

According to the information on its website, the party's policies are as follows: satisfy the requirements of individuals; denounce democracy that unnecessarily complicates governance without yielding widespread wealth and that only results in a regular rotation of power without generating exemplary leaders; establish a well-developed democratic system; establish a democratic system that relies on capable individuals who are tasked with creating a promising future; reestablish the principles of the Indonesian Republic; endorse the constitutional requirement to establish a successful country founded on the principles of economic democracy, a state governed by the rule of law that highly values human rights, and a nation that acknowledges and respects variety; and establish a nation characterized by fairness, wealth, and independence by initiating a Movement for Change aimed at revitalizing Indonesia.

Political track record

In late 2013, the Nasdem Party applied to participate in the 2014 elections. On January 7, 2014, the KPU announced that Nasdem was the only new party that met all the requirements. It competed alongside 12 other national parties and received 6.72% of the votes, securing 36 out of the 560 seats in the MPR as part of Widodo's coalition. In the 2019 legislative elections, Nasdem once again participated as part of Widodo's political coalition and received 9.05% of the total votes, winning 59 out of the 575 seats in the MPR.

However, during the election campaign, the party leader, Surya Paloh, faced criticism from the Indonesian Broadcasting Commission for excessively promoting the party through his news network, MetroTV. In June 2021, the party faced public backlash when one of its members, the parliament speaker of Tolikara Regency in Papua, was accused of providing money and weapons to armed groups associated with the Free Papua Movement. The party, however, denied these allegations (Tables 5.5 and 5.6).

Table 5.5. Nasdem and Legislative Election Results

Election	Total Seats Won	Share of Votes (%)	Party Leader
2014	36/560	6.72	Surya Paloh
2019	59/575	9.05	Surya Paloh
2024	69/575	9.66	Surya Paloh

Sources: IFES Election Guide | Country Profile: Indonesia. (n.d.). Retrieved October 24, 2023, from https://www.electionguide.org/countries/id/102/; Info Publik Pemilu 2019. (n.d.). Retrieved October 24, 2023, from https://pemilu2019.kpu.go.id/#/dprri/rekapitulasi/.

Table 5.6. Nasdem and Presidential Election Results

Election	Candidate	Running Mate	First Round (Total Votes)	Outcome
2014	Joko Widodo	Jusuf Kalla	70,997,833	Elected
2019	Joko Widodo	Ma'ruf Amin	85,607,362	Elected
2024	Anies Baswedan	Muhaimin Iskandar	40,971,906	Lost

Source: IFES Election Guide | Country Profile: Indonesia. (n.d.). Retrieved October 24, 2023, from https://www.electionguide.org/countries/id/102/.

Greater Indonesia Movement Party (Gerindra)

The Partai Gerakan Indonesia Raya (Gerindra), also known as the Great Indonesia Movement Party, is a political party in Indonesia. It was established in 2008 and is led by former general Prabowo Subianto. Gerindra is currently the third-largest party in the House of Representatives, with 78 seats. Although it initially positioned itself as an opposition party, it joined President Joko Widodo's Onward Indonesia Cabinet in 2019, despite Prabowo having contested against Widodo in the 2014 and 2019 presidential elections.

After finishing in the last place in Golkar's presidential convention on April 21, 2004, Prabowo became a member of Golkar's Advisory Board until he resigned on July 12, 2008. Gerindra was established on February 6, 2008 based on the suggestion of Prabowo's younger brother, Hashim Djojohadikusumo, who financially supported the party's prime-time TV advertising campaign.

Prabowo was appointed as the chairman of the party's Founding Board. Gerindra's provincial-level election teams were established in February 2009. The party claimed to have approximately 15 million members, with its support base spanning across Java, Sumatra, Kalimantan, and Sulawesi. PBR was merged into Gerindra in February 2011, and Prabowo was appointed as the general chairman on September 20, 2014 after the death of Gerindra Chairman Suhardi on August 28, 2014.

Political agenda

Gerindra espouses a populist and nationalist economic agenda that primarily caters to the lower middle class, including farmers and fishermen. However, it is worth noting that the party's supporters in the 2014 general election were predominantly urban residents. In November 2019, Fadli Zon, the deputy chairman of Gerindra, unequivocally stated the party's opposition to individuals who identified as lesbian, gay, bisexual, or transgender (LGBT). Gerindra's official Twitter account expressed the same sentiment.

Political track record

Gerindra garnered 4.5% of the vote in its inaugural election, the 2009 legislative election, resulting in 26 seats in the People's Representative Council. In the subsequent national legislative election on April 9, 2014, the party's vote share surged to 11.8%, positioning it as the third most popular party in Indonesia. Gerindra nearly tripled its seat count from 26 in 2009 to 73 in 2014. In 2019, Gerindra secured 12.57% of the votes, which translated to 78 out of the 575 seats in the DPR. Notably, Gerindra consistently nominated Prabowo as its candidate in all three presidential elections since its establishment — as a vice presidential candidate in 2009 and as a presidential candidate in 2014 and 2019 — yet he was unsuccessful in all three elections (Tables 5.7 and 5.8).

Table 5.7. Gerindra and Legislative Election Results

Election	Total Seats Won	Total Votes	Share of Votes (%)	Party Leader
2009	26/560	4,642,795	4.46	Prabowo Subianto
2014	73/560	14,760,371	11.81	Prabowo Subianto
2019	78/575	17,594,839	12.57	Prabowo Subianto
2024	86/575	20,071,708	13.22	Prahowo Subianto

Source: IFES Election Guide | Country Profile: Indonesia. (n.d.). Retrieved October 24, 2023, from https://www.electionguide.org/countries/id/102/; Info Publik Pemilu 2019. (n.d.). Retrieved October 24, 2023, from https://pemilu2019.kpu.go.id/#/dprri/rekapitulasi/.

Table 5.8. Gerindra and Presidential Election Results

Election	Candidate	Running Mate	First Round (Total Votes)	Share of Votes (%)	Outcome
2009	Megawati Sukarnoputri	Prabowo Subianto	32,548,105	26.79	Lost
2014	Prabowo Subianto	Hatta Rajasa	62,576,444	46.85	Lost
2019	Prabowo Subianto	Sandiaga Uno	68,650,239	44.50	Lost
2024	Prabowo Subianto	Gibran	96,214,691	58.6	Won

Source: IFES Election Guide | Country Profile: Indonesia. (n.d.). Retrieved October 24, 2023, from https://www.electionguide.org/countries/id/102.

Partai Kebangkitan Bangsa (National Awakening Party)

The National Awakening Party, also referred to as PKB, is an Islamic political party in Indonesia. It is characterized as a nationalist Muslim party that advocates for inclusive and nationalist values while adhering to the Pancasila philosophy. The party is presently under the leadership of Muhaimin Iskandar.

The PKB was established on May 11, 1998 by traditionalist religious Muslim scholars (Indonesian: Kyai), who were members of the

NU and shared a common view on several problems facing Indonesia that they deemed to be critical. They developed an official statement, which was to be delivered to President Suharto. Before they were able to deliver the statement, however, Suharto resigned on May 21, 1998. The PKB was subsequently founded on May 30, 1998 by these religious scholars based on the NU's political aspirations and was helmed by Kyai Cholil Bisri. The party's name was chosen by a "Standing Committee" consisting of 11 people, with Bisri as chairman, Gus Yusuf Muhammad as secretary, and regional representatives of the NU, on July 4, 1998. Upon its founding, the PKB consisted of 72 people, representing the age of the NU organization, consisting of the Standing Committee Team (11), the Lajnah Assistance Team (14), Team NU (5), the NU Assistance Team (7), and two Representatives from each of the 27 regions (27 × 2). The 72 founders signed the party's manifesto. Subsequent to this, however, the PBNU, the Pengurus Besar Nahdlatul Ulama or the Central Board of Nahdlatul Ulama, decided that only five people could become the party's declaratory. Those five were Kyai Munasir Ali, Kyai Ilyas Ruchiyat, Kyai Muchid Muzadi, KH A. Mustofa Bisri, and KH Abddurahman Wahid, who was the chairman of the PBNU. The 72 original signatories were hence erased by the PBNU.

The party's primary support lies in Java Island and is derived from the constituency that previously backed the conservative Muslim organization NU. The PKB distinguishes itself from the NU by endorsing the involvement of Islam in governance, but it does not share the older organization's endorsement of an overtly Islamic republic.

Political agenda

As per the party's website, the party's policies include the following: enhance the democratic system in order to enhance the economic well-being of individuals residing in rural areas; enhance the safeguarding measures for agriculturalists and seafarers; facilitate the expedited progress of underprivileged areas; promote the prosperity of laborers; and enhance the participation of women in key industries.

Electoral support

In the 1999 elections, the National Awakening Party received 12.61% of the votes. In the 2004 elections, the party obtained 10.57% (11,989,564) of the votes and secured 52 seats in the People's Representative Council. However, in the 2009 legislative election, the party only managed to win 4.9% of the votes and 28 seats in the legislature. In the 2014 and 2019 legislative elections, the party garnered 9.04% and 9.69% of the vote share, respectively, resulting in 47 out of 560 seats in the MPR in 2014 and 58 out of 575 seats in 2019 (Tables 5.9 and 5.10).

Table 5.9. PKB and Legislative Election Results

Election	Total Seats Won	Total Votes	Share of Votes (%)	Election Leader
1999	51/500	13,336,982	12.61	Matori Abdul Djalil
2004	52/550	11,989,564	10.57	Alwi Shihab
2009	28/560	5,146,302	4.94	Muhaimin Iskandar
2014	47/560	11,298,957	9.04	Muhaimin Iskandar
2019	58/575	13,570,097	9.69	Muhaimin Iskandar
2024	68/575	16,115,655	10.62	Muhaimin Iskandar

Source: IBP, Inc. (2015). *Indonesia Electoral, Political Parties Laws and Regulations Handbook*, p. 58.

Table 5.10. PKB and Presidential Election Results

Election	Candidate	Running Mate	First Round (Total Votes)	Share of Votes (%)	Outcome
2004	Susilo Bambang Yudhoyono	Jusuf Kalla	39,838,184	33.57	Runoff
2009	Susilo Bambang Yudhoyono	Boediono	73,874,562	60.80	Elected
2014	Joko Widodo	Jusuf Kalla	70,997,833	53.15	Elected
2019	Joko Widodo	Ma'ruf Amin	85,607,362	55.50	Elected
2024	Anies Baswedan	Muhaimin Iskandar	40,971,906	24.95	Lost

Source: IBP, Inc. (2015). *Indonesian Electoral, Political Parties Laws and Regulations Handbook*, p. 58.

The Prosperous Justice Party (PKS)

The *Partai Keadilan Sejahtera* (PKS), also known as the Prosperous Justice Party, is an Islamist political party in Indonesia. It originated from an influential Islamic movement called *Jemaah Tarbiyah*, which had a significant presence on university campuses during the 1980s and 1990s. The activists of *Jemaah Tarbiyah* established the *Partai Keadilan* (PK), or the Justice Party, on July 20, 1998, with Nurmahmudi Ismail as its first president. However, the Justice Party failed to meet the required 2% electoral threshold in the 1999 election, which was necessary for it to participate in the 2004 election. As a result, it was reconstituted as the Prosperous Justice Party in April 2002.

The PKS gained popularity between the 1999 and 2004 legislative elections due to its strong stance against political corruption. However, this reputation was tarnished as some influential party members, including former PKS president Lutfi Hasan Ishaaq, were accused of involvement in corruption cases. Ishaaq was arrested in 2013 by the Corruption Eradication Commission on charges of graft.

The party is closely associated with Islamic teachings: Several of its founders attended schools related to the Egypt-based Muslim Brotherhood, and the party has called for Islam to play a central role in public life and provided political support to Indonesian Islamist movements such as the Islamic Defenders Front and 212 Movement. Today, it is considered a nationalist Islamist party that conforms with the Pancasila doctrine but does not promote the mandatory implementation of Sharia or require Indonesia's Muslims to follow Islamic law. Many of its campaigns are based on conservative religious teachings, such as opposition to the selling of pornography and strict punishments for violations of narcotics laws. The organization has staged rallies supporting Hamas in its conflict with Israel and against the influence of the United States both in the Middle East and Indonesia. Notably, the PKS has also been involved in several relief and reconstruction projects, such as in Aceh after the 2004 Indian Ocean Tsunami.

Over time, the political party has faced ongoing internal conflicts, particularly between two groups that can be categorized as pragmatists and idealists. The pragmatist faction mainly consists of younger, secular-educated officials, while the idealist faction is composed of older officials who often studied in Middle Eastern institutes. Recently, the party lost popularity among the public, and some individuals have even been calling for its dissolution due to controversial actions taken by the party. These actions included rejecting the State Capital Act (UU IKN) of 2021, which involves relocating the capital of Indonesia from Jakarta to Nusantara in East Kalimantan, and supporting the Criminal Offence Bill of Sexual Abuses (RUU TPKS) of 2022, which imposes prison sentences for forced marriage, sharing non-consensual sexual content, and other sexual offences. Additionally, the party's support for declaring Suharto as a National Hero in 2008 also contributed to its decline in popularity.

Political agenda

The party aims to establish a civil society characterized by justice, prosperity, and dignity. The purpose of this organization is as follows: implement pioneering reforms in the political system, government, bureaucracy, judicial system, and military with a strong commitment to enhancing democracy; alleviate poverty, decrease unemployment, and enhance the overall well-being of society by implementing a comprehensive approach that aims to equalize incomes, foster high value-added economic growth, and ensure sustainable development; and promote equitable access to education by offering a wide range of possibilities to all individuals in Indonesia.

Electoral support

During the 2004 legislative elections, the Prosperous Justice Party (PKS) obtained 7.3% of the popular vote and secured 45 out of 550 seats, positioning itself as the seventh-largest party in parliament. This marked a significant increase from the 1.4% it received in 1999. Furthermore, the PKS leader, Hidayat Nur Wahid, was elected as the speaker of the People's Consultative Assembly. The party garnered

Table 5.11. PKS and Legislative Election Results

Election	Total Seats Won	Total Votes	Share of Votes (%)	Party Leader
1999	7/500	1,436,565	1.36	Nur Mahmudi Ismail
2004	45/550	8,325,020	7.34	Hidayat Nur Wahid
2009	57/560	8,204,946	7.88	Tifatul Sembiring
2014	40/560	8,480,204	6.79	Anis Matta
2019	50/575	11,493,663	8.21	Sohibul Iman
2024	53/575	12,781,353	8.42	Ahmad Syaikhu

Source: IBP, Inc. (2015). *Indonesia Electoral, Political Parties Laws and Regulations Handbook*, p. 61.

Table 5.12. PKS and Presidential Election Results

Election	Candidate	Running Mate	First Round (Total Votes)	Share of Votes (%)	Outcome
2004	Amien Rais	Siswono Yudo husodo	17,392,931	14.66	Eliminated
2009	Susilo Bambang Yudhoyono	Boediono	73,874,562	60.80	Elected
2014	Prabowo Subianto	Hatta Rajasa	62,576,444	46.85	Lost
2019	Prabowo Subianto	Sandiaga Uno	68,650,239	44.50	Lost
2024	Anies Baswedan	Iskandar Muhaimin	40,971,906	24.95	Lost

Source: IFES Election Guide | Country Profile: Indonesia. (n.d.). Retrieved October 24, 2023, from https://www.electionguide.org/countries/id/102/.

its strongest support in major urban centers, particularly Jakarta, where it won the largest number of seats in 2004. In the 2009 elections, PKS ranked fourth, experiencing a rise in its vote share to 7.88% and gaining an additional 12 legislative seats. Subsequently, PKS achieved 6.79% and 8.21% of the total vote share in the 2014 and 2019 elections, respectively, resulting in the party securing 40 out of 560 seats in the MPR in 2014 and 50 out of 575 seats in the MPR in 2019 (Tables 5.11 and 5.12).

The National Mandate Party (PAN)

The Partai Amanat Nasional (PAN), also known as the National Mandate Party, is an Indonesian political party that is based on the teachings of Islam. It was established during the Indonesian Revolution by the modernist faction of Muslim society, which included Amien Rais, the chairman of the Muhammadiyah organization. The PAN is characterized as a nationalist Muslim party and is committed to upholding the Pancasila doctrine.

On May 14, 1998, around 50 political figures including Goenawan Mohammad, Faisal Basri, and Amien Rais established an organization called *Majelis Amanat Rakyat* (MARA) or the Peoples Mandate Council, open to anybody who wanted to listen to and express opinions. MARA was intended to be a strong forum that was respected by those in power, to allow the populace to voice their opinions to political elites, who MARA leaders felt had become overtly arrogant and deaf to the will of the people. The founding of the PAN was only initiated upon the downfall of the Suharto regime in 1998 when many new parties were being established: While some of these parties wanted Amien Rais and other members of MARA to join them, others, such as the leader of the Crescent Star Party, Yusril Ihza Mahendra, prompted Amien Rais to establish a party. Resultantly, Amien Rais announced the establishment of a new party to be called the Partai Amanat Bangsa (PAB) or the People's Mandate Party on July 27, 1998. This was changed to the current name after a lengthy voting process. The new party had its roots in the principles of religious morality, humanity, and prosperity.

The PAN national congress held in Kendari, Southeast Sulawesi, on February 11, 2020 was disrupted by violence as party members engaged in a physical altercation, throwing chairs at each other. The dispute arose from disagreements over the selection of candidates to lead the party. One PAN member sustained a fractured leg during the chaotic incident. According to reports, individuals with violent tendencies were present at the congress to support Mulfachri Harahap's bid for party leadership. Zulkifli, the PAN leader, was reelected at the congress with 331 votes, while Mulfachri received 225 votes.

Political agenda

The PAN party welcomes individuals from all sectors of society, irrespective of their gender, ethnicity, or religious background. As stated on the party's official website, the PAN is committed to achieving popular sovereignty, social justice, and an improved quality of life for the Indonesian people. Its ultimate goal is to establish a prosperous, developed, independent, and dignified nation. Additionally, the PAN aims to promote transparent and effective governance that safeguards the welfare of all citizens and fosters prosperity. The party also aspires to contribute to the establishment of a global order based on independence, lasting peace, and social justice, while ensuring that Indonesia is esteemed in the international community.

Electoral support

In the 1999 elections, the PAN party secured 7.12% of the vote and obtained 34 seats in the legislature. Subsequently, the party played a crucial role in forming a central alliance of Islamic political parties in the People's Consultative Assembly. This alliance played a significant role in ensuring the victory of Abdurrahman Wahid over Megawati Sukarnoputri in the presidential election. However, the PAN's support for Abdurrahman Wahid was short-lived. Less than a year after officially endorsing him at its inaugural congress in Yogyakarta in February 2000, the party withdrew its support, citing concerns about the nation's condition and the state of Indonesia. Shortly after, Abdurrahman Wahid was ousted from office and replaced by Megawati Sukarnoputri.

In the 2004 elections, the party aimed to secure 15% of the vote. To boost his chances of becoming president, Amien Rais conducted a series of nationwide visits. He also expressed his opinion that a retired military officer should be his vice president. However, in the legislative election, the party only received 6.4% of the popular vote and won 53 out of 550 legislative seats. In the presidential election, Amien Rais ran with Siswono Yudo Husodo as his running mate, but they only managed to secure 15% of the vote.

In the 2009 legislative election, the party secured 6% of the vote and obtained 46 seats in the People's Representative Council, placing fifth. Despite a decline in influence and popularity, the party aimed to achieve a minimum of 10% of the vote in 2014. However, the PAN only managed to win 7.59% of the vote in the legislative election. Shortly after the election, the PAN announced Hatta Rajasa, the party leader, as the vice presidential candidate to run alongside Prabowo Subianto. Nevertheless, they were ultimately defeated by Jokowi and Jusuf Kalla. In the 2019 legislative elections, the PAN obtained 6.84% of the vote share, resulting in 44 out of the 575 seats in the MPR (Tables 5.13 and 5.14).

Table 5.13. PAN and Legislative Election Results

Election	Total Seats Won	Total Votes	Share of Votes (%)	Party Leader
1999	34/500	7,528,956	7.12	Amien Rais
2004	53/550	7,303,324	6.44	Amien Rais
2009	46/560	6,273,462	6.01	Sutrisno Bachir
2014	49/560	9,481,621	7.59	Hatta Rajasa
2019	44/575	9,572,623	6.84	Zulkifli Hasan
2024	48/575	10,984,003	7.24	Zulkifli Hasan

Source: IBP, Inc. (2015). *Indonesia Electoral, Political Parties Laws and Regulations Handbook*, p. 62.

Table 5.14. PAN and Presidential Election Results

Election	Pres. Candidate	Running Mate	Total Votes	Share of Votes (%)	Outcome
2004	Amien Rais	Siswono Yudo Husodo	17,392,931	14.66	Lost
2009	Susilo Bambang Yudhoyono	Boediono	73,874,562	60.80	Elected
2014	Prabowo Subianto	Hatta Rajasa	62,576,444	46.85	Lost
2019	Prabowo Subianto	Sandiaga Uno	68,650,239	44.50	Lost
2024	Prabowo Subianto	Gibran	96,214,691	58.6	Won

Source: IFES Election Guide | Country Profile: Indonesia. (n.d.). Retrieved October 24, 2023, from https://www.electionguide.org/countries/id/102/.

Democratic Party

The Democratic Party (Indonesian: *Partai Demokrat*) is a center to center-right political party in Indonesia. It was created on September 9, 2001 and is ideologically based on the Indonesian philosophy of Pancasila. The 2001 Special Session of the People's Consultative Assembly which impeached Wahid and elected Megawati as president of Indonesia resulted in a vacancy in the position of vice president. Susilo Bambang Yudhoyono was one candidate who competed for the vice presidency, but ultimately lost out to Hamzah Haz. Yudhoyono's supporters saw his participation in the vice presidential election as a sign of his popularity and recognized Yudhoyono's potential as a possible leader for Indonesia. One of these supporters, Vence Rumangkang, approached Yudhoyono with the idea of forming a political party to help shore up support for the 2004 presidential elections, to which Yudhoyono agreed.

Between August 12 and August 19, 2001, Rumangkang began holding a series of meetings to discuss the formation of the party while holding consultations with Yudhoyono, who was now serving as the Coordinating Minister for Politics and Security. Yudhoyono personally led the meeting on August 19, and on August 20, 2001, the basic outline of the party was finalized. On September 9, 2001 (Yudhoyono's 52nd birthday), the formation of the Democratic Party was officially declared, and on September 10, 2001, it was registered at the Ministry of Law and Human Rights. The party also elected Subur Budhisantoso as party chairman.

Internal conflict arose within the Democratic Party in 2021. On March 5, 2021, an extraordinary congress held by some of the Democratic Party members elected Moeldoko as the new General Chairman of the party, despite the results of the 2020 Democratic Party Congress that elected Agus Harimurti Yudhoyono as the General Chairman until 2025. The result of the extraordinary congress was heavily opposed by former General Chairman Susilo Bambang Yudhoyono, who argued that the extraordinary congress was unlawful as such sessions have to be held at the request of the upper house of the party, and none of the upper house members of the party had requested any extraordinary congress. Yudhoyono also stated that the extraordinary congress had to be requested by at least two-thirds of the party's regional representative council, and none of the regional representative council had requested the extraordinary congress. Reflectively, Agus Harimurti Yudhoyono claimed that the election of Moeldoko was illegal, and reinforced his claim as the legitimate leader of the party. On March 31, 2021, the government ruled that the result of the extraordinary congress was illegitimate, thereby confirming Agus Yudhoyono's position as legitimate chairman of the Democratic Party.

Party platform

As per the party's website, the Democratic Party's goal is for Indonesia to become a developed country in the 21st Century, an Emerging Economy by 2030, and a Strong Country by 2045. The party's ambition for itself is to become a political party that is strong, possesses integrity and capacity; is relevant and adaptive to the times; is consistent with the values, ideals, and platform of the party's struggle in defending peace, justice, welfare, democracy, and environmental sustainability; is united with the people and continues to fight for the interests and aspirations of the people; and maintains its identity as a nationalist-religious party, an open party, a center party, a pluralist party, and a pro-little people's party.

Electoral history

In the 2004 legislative elections, the Democratic Party won 7.5% of votes and won 55 out of 560 seats in the People's Representative Council and finished in the fifth place overall. The party nominated Yudhoyono as its presidential candidate with Jusuf Kalla as the vice presidential candidate for the 2004 presidential election, with the support of the Crescent Star Party (PBB) and Indonesian Justice and Unity Party (PKPI). Yudhoyono and Kalla won the first round of elections in July 2004 with 33.6% of the votes and would go on to win 60.1% in the runoffs, thereby securing Yudhoyono's election as president. In May 2005, the party held its first party congress, during which Hadi Utomo was elected as chairman. Nevertheless, the highest authority in the party remained with Yudhoyono, who was elected chairman of the Advisory Board (Dewan Pembina).

The party came first in the 2009 legislative election with 20.9% of the votes, making it the largest party in the People's Representative Council, with 150 seats, just over one-quarter of the total. The party again nominated Yudhoyono, now the incumbent, for the 2009 presidential election. Yudhoyono won the election with former Governor of Bank Indonesia, Boediono, as the vice presidential candidate, with a total tally of 60.8% in the first round, beating former president Megawati Sukarnoputri and incumbent vice president Jusuf Kalla. On March 30, 2013, the party held an extraordinary congress after the resignation of chairman Anas Urbaningrum to fill the chairmanship. Yudhoyono ran unopposed and was unanimously elected after no other party member opted to run.

For the 2014 legislative election, the party set a target of 15% of the national vote, less than its 2009 share. One reason the party expected its vote share to fall was that Susilo Bambang Yudhoyono would not be able to run for president, having served the two terms allowed in the constitution. However, the party won only 10.19%, losing over half of its seats in the legislature. For the 2019 legislative election, the party initially set a target of 15% but later changed the target to 10% of the national vote. The party managed to gain 7.77% of the vote, thereby attaining only 54 seats in the legislature. On March 15, 2020, Agus Harimurti Yudhoyono, after serving as the Commander of the Joint Task Command (Kogasma) during the 2019 General Election, was elected to be the new General Chairman of the Party, replacing his father as the chairman (Tables 5.15 and 5.16).

Table 5.15. Democratic Party and Legislative Election Results

Election	Total Seats Won	Total Votes	Share of Votes (%)	Party Leader
2004	55/550	8,455,225	7.45	Susilo Bambang Yudhoyono
2009	150/560	21,703,137	20.85	Susilo Bambang Yudhoyono
2014	61/560	12,728,913	10.19	Susilo Bambang Yudhoyono
2019	54/575	10,876,507	7.77	Susilo Bambang Yudhoyono
2024	44/575	11,283,160	7.43	Agus Yudhoyono

Source: IBP, Inc. (2015). *Indonesia Electoral, Political Parties Laws and Regulations Handbook*, p. 52.

Table 5.16. Democratic Party and Presidential Election Results

Election	Candidate	Running Mate	First Round (Total Votes)	Share of Votes (%)	Outcome
2004	Susilo Bambang Yudhoyono	Jusuf Kalla	39,838,184	33.57	Runoff
2009	Susilo Bambang Yudhoyono	Boediono	73,874,562	60.80	Elected
2014	Prabowo Subianto	Hatta Rajasa	62,576,444	46.85	Lost
2019	Prabowo Subianto	Sandiaga Uno	68,650,239	44.50	Lost
2024	Prabowo Subianto	Gibran	96,214,691	58.6	Won

Source: IFES Election Guide | Country Profile: Indonesia. (n.d.). Retrieved October 24, 2023, from https://www.electionguide.org/countries/id/102/.

United Development Party

The *Partai Persatuan Pembangunan* (PPP) or the United Development Party, sometimes translated as Development Unity Party, is an Islam-based political party in Indonesia. Today, the PPP is considered a nationalist Islamist party which conforms with the Pancasila doctrine and no longer upholds Sharia as the main goal. The party was led by Suryadharma Ali until 2014 when he was prosecuted for corruption. From 2014 to 2016, the party was split in a dispute over its chairmanship. In April 2016, Muhammad Romahurmuziy was declared the new chairman after a reconciliation congress.

The PPP was formed in 1973 as the result of a merger between several Islam-based parties, assuming the role of an umbrella party for Muslims. Ten political parties participated in the 1971 legislative elections, a number that President Suharto considered to be too many. Suharto wished that political parties be reduced to just two or three and that the parties should be grouped based on their programs. The PPP was hence formed from a merger of the four Islamic Parties in the DPR in 1973: Termed the United Development Faction, the coalition consisted of the Nahdatul Ulama (NU), the Muslim Party of Indonesia (Parmusi), the Islamic Association Party of Indonesia (PSII), and the Islamic Education Movement (Perti). With encouragement by the government, officials from all four parties had meetings with each other and after finding some common ground, merged the four Islamic parties into the United Development Party on January 5, 1973. Despite this formal merging of the parties, internal PPP politics under the Suharto government were dominated by the differing priorities of the original groups that formed the party.

In the mid-1970s, popular support for Suharto's regime was rapidly waning. When Suharto seized power with a bloody military coup in 1965 and ousted President Sukarno, the Islamic groups supported Suharto and aided in persecuting his political opponents. But as the regime had become corrupt and even more authoritarian, this alliance began to crumble. As the 1977 legislative elections approached, many people began to seek other options to vote for aside from the government-backed Golkar.

Worried that the PPP might win the elections, Suharto played on the fears of the people by having the military arrest a group of people who claimed to be associated with the Jihad Commando (*Komando Jihad*). Many among the populace became worried that to vote for the PPP and its Islamic leaning would mean expressing support for the Jihad Commando; faced with an increasingly authoritarian government, many of the PPP supporters defected from the party. Golkar would go on to win the legislative elections with 62%, with the PPP coming second with 27% of the votes.

The PPP, however, did not sit back and accept defeat. At the 1978 MPR General Session, PPP member Chalid Mawardi launched a scathing criticism of Suharto's regime. Mawardi accused the government of being anti-Muslim, complained about the government's violent crackdown on dissent, and alleged that the 1977 Legislative Election was won because of electoral fraud. The PPP members also conducted a mass walkout when Suharto referred to religions as "streams of beliefs." Gradually, the PPP cemented for itself a status as the strongest opposition party. In 1984, however, the NU, under its Chairman, Abdurrahman Wahid withdrew from the PPP, severely weakening it. The PPP vote share fell from almost 28% in the 1982 legislative elections to 16% in the 1987 legislative elections, and the PPP was also forced by the government to replace its ideology of Islam with the national ideology of Pancasila and stop using Islamic symbols. As a result, the party replaced its logo showing the Kabah shrine in Mecca with a star.

At the 1988 MPR General Session, Jailani Naro, the PPP chairman, was nominated as vice president. Suharto, who had been elected to the presidency for a fifth term at the aforementioned General Session, intervened. He cited a decision that the MPR made in 1973 that one of the criteria for a vice president was that he should be able to work with the president. Suharto also conducted discussions with Naro and convinced him to withdraw the nomination. Naro's nomination was unprecedented in the New Order as both Suharto and his vice presidents had always been elected unopposed. The problem this time was Suharto's choice for vice president — Sudharmono; many within ABRI did not like Sudharmono because he was a military attorney, instead of a field officer. Seeing a gap to exploit, Naro nominated himself, possibly with the private support of ABRI, who in public had shown support for Sudharmono.

For the duration of Suharto's administration, the PPP persisted as the second-biggest party out of the three authorized in the New

Order. In May 1998, after the collapse of Suharto's government, the PPP returned to its Islamic ideology and positioned itself for the 1999 parliamentary elections.

Party platform

The party's vision is to bring about a nation that is just, prosperous, moral, and democratic, that upholds the law, that respects human rights, and that holds in high esteem the dignity of mankind and social justice based on the values of Islam. The party believes that religion (Islam) has an important role to play as a moral guide and inspiration in the life of the nation. It is committed to improving the quality of democracy in Indonesia and respects freedom of expression, opinion, and organization, the realization of good governance, and the endeavor to preserve the unitary Republic of Indonesia based on Pancasila and the 1945 Constitution. It supports the concept of a people-based economic system, economic justice, the creation of jobs, the eradication of poverty, state control of sectors of the economy that have a controlling influence on the lives of the majority, a major role for state-owned companies, and economic independence.

Electoral history

The PPP won 11% of the vote in the 1999 legislative elections. In the 1999 MPR General Session, the PPP was part of the Central Axis, a political coalition of Muslim parties that was formed by the MPR Chairman, Amien Rais, to counter the dominance of Megawati Sukarnoputri's PDI-P. The PDI-P had won the legislative election and Megawati was expected to win the presidency. However, the MPR was still at this stage responsible for electing the president and vice president, and the Muslim parties in the Central Axis did not want a female president. Instead, they nominated and successfully secured the election of Abdurrahman Wahid as president. In the vice presidential election, PPP Chairman Hamzah Haz ran against Megawati and was defeated.

The PPP was the first of Wahid's political allies to become disillusioned with him. The PPP's main problem with Wahid was his visit to Israel and the suggestion that he was willing to reestablish diplomatic relations with the nation. Hamzah, who served in Wahid's Cabinet as Coordinating Minister for People's Welfare, immediately resigned from his position just a month after Wahid had appointed him to it. Many other Wahid allies would follow, and in July 2001, the PPP would join in removing Wahid from the presidency and naming Megawati as the president. Hamzah was then elected as vice president after defeating Susilo Bambang Yudhoyono and Akbar Tanjung in the vice presidential election.

The PPP won 8.1% of the vote in the 2004 legislative elections, a decrease from its 10.7% share of the vote in 1999, but enough to retain its place as the third-best represented party in the legislature, behind the PDI-P and Golkar. The PPP originally did not have a presidential candidate in mind for the 2004 presidential elections. It had expected that Hamzah would be picked as Megawati's running mate and continue the Megawati/Hamzah President/Vice President partnership. Megawati, however, chose NU Chairman Hasyim Muzadi as her running mate. Nonetheless, the PPP still expected Hamzah Haz to be picked as a vice presidential candidate. A day before the registration of the presidential/vice presidential candidates was closed, Hamzah was nominated as the PPP's presidential candidate. His running mate was Agum Gumelar, who served as Minister of Transportation in Megawati's cabinet. Hamzah's presidential run was unsuccessful as he received only 3.1% of the vote and came fifth.

In August 2004, the PPP announced that it was forming a national coalition with the PDI-P, Golkar, PBR, and the Prosperous Peace Party to back Megawati to win the presidential runoff against Susilo Bambang Yudhoyono. Yudhoyono, however, would emerge victorious and the PPP would defect from the national coalition to Yudhoyono's camp. The PPP was rewarded with cabinet places. The PPP held its 6th National Congress in Jakarta from January 30 to February 3, 2007. On the last day of the Congress, Suryadharma Ali emerged as the new PPP Chairman to replace Hamzah. Suryadharma

Table 5.17. PPP and Legislative Election Results

Election	Total Seats Won	Total Votes	Share of Votes (%)	Party Leader
1971	94/360	14,833,942	27.11	Muhammad Syafaat Mintaredja
1977	99/360	18,743,491	29.29	Muhammad Syafaat Mintaredja
1982	94/360	20,871,880	27.78	Jailani Naro
1987	61/400	13,701,428	15.97	Jailani Naro
1992	62/400	16,624,647	17.01	Ismail Hasan Metareum
1997	89/400	25,340,028	22.43	Ismail Hasan Metareum
1999	58/500	11,329,905	10.71	Hamzah Haz
2004	58/550	9,248,764	8.15	Hamzah Haz
2009	38/560	5,544,332	5.32	Suryadharma Ali
2014	39/560	8,157,488	6.53	Suryadharma Ali
2019	19/575	6,323,147	4.52	Suharso Monoarfa
2024	0/575	5,878,777	3.87	Muhammad Mardiono

Note: The total votes for the PPP in 1971 are the total votes for the NU, Perti, PSII, and Parmusi, which were fused into the PPP in 1973.
Source: Info Publik Pemilu 2019. (n.d.). Retrieved October 24, 2023, from https://pemilu2019.kpu.go.id/#/dprri/rekapitulasi/.

served as Minister of Cooperatives and State and Medium Enterprises in President Yudhoyono's cabinet and announced that he would continue as minister while concurrently holding the position of PPP Chairman.

The party came sixth in the 2009 legislative election with 5.3% of the vote, winning 38 seats in the People's Representative Council. Throughout the election, the party obtained much of its support base from older generations of Muslim men throughout rural and urban areas, both inside and outside Java. In the 2014 legislative election, the party attained 6.53% of the vote, winning 39 seats in the MPR. The PPP was part of Prabowo and Hatta's political coalition, which eventually lost to Widodo and Jusuf Kalla. In the 2019 legislative election, the party attained 4.52% of the vote share, winning 19 seats in the MPR. The PPP joined Jokowi's political coalition for the 2019 presidential elections and emerged victorious over Prabowo and Sandiaga Uno (Tables 5.17 and 5.18).

Table 5.18. PPP and Presidential Election Results

Election	Pres. Candidate	Running Mate	First Round (Total Votes)	Share of Votes (%)	Outcome
2004	Hamzah Haz	Agum Gumelar	3,569,861	3.01	Eliminated
2009	Susilo Bambang Yudhoyono	Boediono	73,874,562	60.80	Elected
2014	Prabowo Subianto	Hatta Rajasa	62,576,444	46.85	Lost
2019	Joko Widodo	Ma'ruf Amin	85,607,362	55.50	Elected
2024	Anies Baswedan	Muhaimin Iskandar	40,971,906	24.95	Lost

Source: IFES Election Guide | Elections: Indonesia Leg Apr 9, 2009. (n.d.). Retrieved October 24, 2023, from https://www.electionguide.org/elections/id/443/.

TNI

One organization that can make a comeback, or minimally exert undue influence during the 2024 Presidential Elections, is the *Tentara Nasional Indonesia* (TNI) or the Indonesian Armed Forces. The TNI consists of the Army (TNI-AD), Navy (TNI-AL), and Air Force (TNI-AU), and the President of Indonesia is the commander-in-chief of the Armed Forces. In 2021, it comprised approximately 395,500 military personnel, including the Indonesian Marine Corps (*Korps Marinir RI*), which is a branch of the Navy.

The Indonesian Armed Forces were formed during the Indonesian National Revolution, when they undertook a guerrilla war along with informal militia. As a result of this, and the need to maintain internal security, the Armed Forces including the Army, Navy, and Air Force are organized along territorial lines, aimed at defeating the internal enemies of the state and potential external invaders. During the New Order, the role of the Indonesian military drastically expanded: The TNI had a pervasive presence in state affairs, including mandated seats in politics, management of state-owned enterprises, control of information and media, and a militarized approach to internal security. This was legitimated under the doctrine of *dwifungsi*, which stipulated that the military held a dual function in the provision of security, as in the traditional role of the military, and in the day-to-day running of the country in political, economic, and administrative areas. *Dwifungsi* was abolished after Suharto stepped down in May 1998, and the military subsequently exited politics. After the New Order, the transition to democracy was popularly known in Indonesia as reformasi ("reformation"), during which public trust in institutions such as the parliament and courts was painstakingly rebuilt and corruption rooted out, while the military and police underwent limited structural and cultural reforms. Formal legislative changes have moved the military out from politics and into a more traditional security role. During the administration of Susilo Bambang Yudhoyono, a focus on external activities such as peacekeeping helped to further this shift in identity.

Return of dwifungsi?

The mindset that the military is the "guardian of the nation," however, remains pervasive in the TNI, particularly among the older officers. The military's territorial structure, which was never reformed after 1998, and community service program, where soldiers undertake activities like teaching in classrooms, entrench the military's identity as "people's army" in the eyes of both the public and itself. While the dismantling of the territorial command system, which functioned as a means of gathering intelligence against potential insurrections in the past, has been debated after reformasi, albeit to little success, Jokowi has instead increased his reliance upon this system, leveraging upon it as a source of labor. Between 2014 and 2017, the Jakarta-based Centre for Strategic and International Studies (CSIS Indonesia) found that the military and defense ministry signed 133 deals with ministries and other groups for not just basic military training in some cases but also recruiting soldiers as teachers and for rural development projects. While such a strategy redresses logistical shortfalls and benefits poorer communities in remote areas, it further encourages the dominance of the TNI in civilian life by virtue of the number of personnel required and

related wages, as well as maintaining a close rapport between the military and the people.

Additionally, many in the military, both active and retired officers, continue to believe they are more capable than civilians in both military and civilian roles. According to these officers, technocrats such as former president B.J. Habibie, who was seen as responsible for the "loss" of East Timor, are not to be trusted. While this mindset is not as pervasive among younger officers, the consistent presence of older officers in influential, non-military positions signals to both the military and the Indonesian public that this state of affairs is "normal." In some ways, it resembles the New Order's culture of military omnipresence, albeit in a contemporary democratic context.

These factors have been further reinforced under the Jokowi administration, where the domestic functions and political prominence of the armed forces have flourished. Today, Indonesian civil–military relations are overwhelmingly characterized by the continuity of prominent figures from former president Suharto's 1967–1998 New Order regime who remain in or have been appointed by Jokowi to influential positions, such as ministers and advisors, and by intergenerational connections to the New Order. For instance, the former head of the state intelligence agency (BIN), retired General A.M. Hendropriyono, is the father-in-law of the former Army and Armed Forces chief, Andika Perkasa. Meanwhile, Luhut's son-in-law, then Major General Maruli Simanjuntak, who was appointed head of the Presidential Security Force in 2018, later became Commander of Kostrad and then the Army Chief. The effect of this is the entrenchment of the influence of key figures and a continuation of narrow interests and values in the upper echelons of the military hierarchy.

As a result of the military's omnipresence, particularly in cabinet roles, retired officers have a platform to disseminate their beliefs and values more vocally under Jokowi. While not all of these values undermine state or democratic institutions, muting public debate on the army-led communist purges of 1965–1966 curtails freedom of speech and circumvents attempts at accountability. According to the military, Indonesia must remain vigilant against "latent" threats of communism, justifying a continued internal security role. This is exemplified by the military and police-led confiscation of books in 2018 and public statements by military leaders about the persistence of a communist threat in contemporary Indonesia, which demonstrates the continued ability of the military to control public discourse. Jokowi willingly reinforces the military's narrative when politically convenient. During the military's 73rd birthday celebrations in 2018, the president played to his audience at the Armed Forces Headquarters, warning of the threat posed by the legacies of 1965. Despite promising during his 2014 campaign and again in 2019 to address unresolved human rights issues including the 1965 killings, his administration has produced few results.

Societal perceptions

Another significant factor that can prompt the resurgence of military presence amidst Indonesia's political climate is a societal perception of the importance of democracy and their expectations for civil–military relations. New research conducted in Indonesia has shown that democracy enjoys support as an abstract concept, but Indonesians are not necessarily wedded to liberal values. According to the Asian Barometer Survey (ABS) 2016, 70% of respondents said democracy is always preferable, with only 16% claiming authoritarianism to be preferable. However, additional questions reveal a more nuanced picture. Of those surveyed, only 8% said "democracy more important than economic development," showing that, under certain conditions of hardship, almost all Indonesians might be willing to forgo democratic rights in return for the promise of economic prosperity. These societal perceptions are important, particularly as the COVID-19 pandemic continued to put further pressure on the economy and health system of the country until the pandemic was declared over even though its negative impacts continues in the country.

Looking more specifically at the military's role in governance, the ABS 2016 found that 38% of Indonesians surveyed "strongly agree" or "agree" that "the Army should come in to govern the country," second only to 54% in Thailand. The figure is down from 43% in 2011 but still represents a significant portion of those surveyed. Despite a history of military rule, various national surveys conducted across Indonesia over the past 5 years have shown consistently high levels of public trust in the military, over other institutions including the president and the popular Corruption Eradication Commission (KPK). The military scored an approval rating of 70.7% in a recent study that polled community satisfaction with government bodies during the first 100 days of Jokowi's second term.

CHAPTER 6

THE KEY COALITIONS AND STRATEGIES OF THE POLITICAL PARTIES IN THE 2024 PRESIDENTIAL CONTEST

The 2024 Presidential Election had three main contenders: Prabowo Subianto, Ganjar Pranowo, and Anies Baswedan. According to a study conducted by Lembaga Survei Indonesia (LSI) and published on October 4, 2023, 34% of the 1,206 respondents indicated their intention to vote for Prabowo. The proportions of individuals selecting Ganjar and Anies were 30.4% and 22%, respectively, while 13% either did not provide a response or expressed uncertainty. Prabowo and Ganjar have consistently been the frontrunners in pre-election polling.

Prabowo Subianto

Prabowo leads the Great Indonesia Movement (Gerindra) party, which officially supported him as its presidential nominee in August 2022. Prabowo declared his candidature for the 2024 election, choosing Mr. Gibran Rakabuming Raka, the eldest son of President Joko Widodo, as his vice presidential candidate. Similarly to his father, Gibran is a member of the ruling PDI-P party. Before Gibran announced his campaign, there were rumors of a potential alliance between Gibran and Prabowo. In response, the PDI-P party emphasized the importance of party loyalty among its members.

Gibran's nomination was made public subsequent to a contentious decision by the Constitutional Court on October 16, 2023. The ruling upheld the minimum age requirement of 40 for presidential and vice presidential candidates in Indonesia, but exempted elected regional leaders from this age restriction. This paved the door for Gibran, the current mayor of Surakarta city, who celebrated his 36th birthday on October 1, 2023, to be eligible for candidature. Hundreds of Indonesians took to the streets in protest following the court verdict, expressing their opposition to what they perceive as undemocratic measures that facilitated the establishment of political dynasties. Jokowi explicitly stated that he would refrain from making any comments on the findings in order to avoid being perceived as meddling with the power of the judiciary. Furthermore, he emphasized that the selection of presidential and vice presidential candidates is solely determined by political parties. The verdict was notably issued by a panel of nine judges, with Chief Justice Anwar Usman, who is Jokowi's brother-in-law, leading the group. The ruling was a response to multiple requests for judicial review, which advocated for a reduction in the age limit. One of these requests was made by the Indonesian Solidarity Party, a political party focused on youth issues, led by Kaesang Pangarep, the youngest son of Mr. Widodo. This party has criticized the age limit for being discriminatory.

Prabowo receives backing from the Indonesia Onward Coalition, which includes his own party Gerindra, Indonesia's oldest party Golkar, the National Mandate Party, the Democratic Party, and four minor parties that do not hold seats in the House of Representatives. Prabowo has garnered the most substantial political backing among the current presidential candidates, making him the nominee with the highest level of support. On August 28, 2023, Prabowo officially renamed his electoral alliance as the "Onward Indonesia Coalition" in response to Jokowi's Onward Indonesia Cabinet. He said that his

alliance represented "team Jokowi" in an effort to position himself as Jokowi's legitimate successor.

Jokowi had allegedly been clandestinely mobilizing assistance for Prabowo, despite outward indications that he planned to endorse the PDI-P candidate Ganjar. Both Prabowo and Ganjar expressed their intention to maintain Jokowi's economic policies, ensuring the continuation of key initiatives such as relocating the capital from Jakarta and fostering the growth of the trillion-dollar electric car sector. On October 15, 2023, Projo, the biggest informal volunteer network of Jokowi supporters, declared their support for Prabowo. According to Projo chief Budi Aric Setiadi, Jokowi provided them with some criteria for his future successor and they inferred that the president was referring to Prabowo Subianto. This assertion of endorsement from Jokowi was further corroborated by reports indicating that Jokowi had separately summoned the leaders of Golkar and the National Mandate Party to instruct them to back Prabowo, despite Golkar's previous inclination to proclaim support for Ganjar. Jokowi had provided assistance to Ganjar by mobilizing teams and volunteer organizations to contribute to his campaign, as reported by four sources. In September, the president made an appearance at a nationwide PDI-P event, where he exhorted Ganjar to begin preparing for his future leadership of the country. "I quietly spoke to him, 'Once you are officially sworn into office — specifically, the day following your inauguration — it is imperative that you prioritise the establishment of food self-sufficiency.' Do not prolong the duration," Jokowi stated. There were rumors suggesting that Jokowi's decision to endorse Prabowo may have been influenced by growing conflicts between Jokowi and PDI-P chief Megawati.

Political observers highlighted three key elements that contributed to Prabowo's current success in the polls, despite his previous unsuccessful bids in the last three presidential elections. Prabowo increased his chances of winning by presenting himself as a potential successor to Jokowi, which garnered substantial backing from Jokowi's followers. The inclusion of Jokowi's son as Prabowo's running companion undoubtedly highlighted this aspect, providing evidence of Prabowo's candidature as Jokowi's successor. Furthermore, Prabowo successfully restored his public reputation by displaying a more composed and affable demeanor, while also exhibiting a reduced tendency for outbursts. Moreover, he endeavored to appeal to young people and actively involve his critics, particularly activist organizations. Prabowo's impressive performance as defense minister and his skill in harnessing Indonesian nationalism also struck a chord with voters. However, his recent contentious "peace proposal" to address the Ukraine conflict at the 2023 Shangri-La Dialogue and his announcement of an unauthorized procurement budget in June 2021 reveal a persistent tendency toward boldness, which could harm his candidature if not properly addressed.

Ganjar Pranowo

On October 18, 2023, Mahfud MD, Indonesia's security minister, was selected as Ganjar's running partner. Additionally, Dr. Mahfud was a member of the Nahdatul Ulama (NU), which is Indonesia's largest and most powerful Islamic organization. He garnered substantial public support by addressing the government's efforts to combat corruption and the misconduct of rogue government and law enforcement personnel. Having held many positions, including defense minister from 2000 to 2001 under President Abdurrahman Wahid and chief justice of the Constitutional Court from 2008 to 2013, he is an experienced senior technocrat. Mahfud was formerly a candidate for the position of vice president in the 2019 election, serving as Mr. Widodo's running mate. He was excluded at the final moment after influential members of the PDI-P and its coalition partners selected Mr. Ma'ruf Amin, a higher-ranking leader of the NU who currently holds the position of vice president. The Ganjar–Mahfud ticket received support from the PDI-P, the United Development Party (PPP), Perindo, and Hanura. Only the PDI-P and PPP held seats in the national Parliament, but the other two parties were only represented at the province, regency, and city levels.

Anies Baswedan

Anies received backing from the Coalition for Change and Unity, initially comprising the Democratic Party, the Prosperous Justice Party (PKS), and the National Democratic Party (Nasdem). Subsequently, the Democratic Party declared its departure from the coalition and aligned with Prabowo's coalition, while the PKB opted to leave Prabowo and join the Coalition for Change and Unity.

Muhaimin Iskandar, commonly referred to as Cak Imin, was officially declared as Anies's vice presidential candidate in September 2023. Cak Imin is the head of the National Awakening Party (PKB). As a result, the PKB immediately withdrew from Prabowo's coalition, although it had previously supported his candidature since August 2022. According to reports, Cak Imin was attempting to secure this job under Prabowo since 2022, but was unsuccessful. Surya Paloh, the chairman of Nasdem, facilitated the appointment of Cak Imin. Cak Iman held the position of deputy speaker of the People's Representative Council starting in 2019 and previously served as the labor minister from 2009 to 2014. He is a distant relative of Abdurrahman Wahid, well known as Gus Dur, a highly esteemed former president and religious figure. He possesses influential connections inside the Nahdatul Ulama and was anticipated to attract votes for the Anies ticket, using his support base in East Java.

The choice of Cak Imin, however, caused divisions within Anies's coalition. The Democratic Party withdrew from the coalition, alleging that Anies had previously guaranteed them that his vice president would be Agus Harimurti Yudhoyono, the son of former president Susilo Bambang Yudhoyono, who is also the chairman of the party. However, the withdrawal of the Democrats is unlikely to have an impact on Anies's candidature. This is because his coalition still has control over 38.56% of the seats in the House of Representatives (DPR) and can easily nominate him and Cak Imin. Nevertheless, the PKS had openly conveyed its dissatisfaction with the selection of Cak Imin as Anies's running mate. The PKS expressed dissatisfaction with the fact that the PKB's inclusion was unilaterally imposed by Surya Paloh. However, the PKS had limited options due to its public opposition to Jokowi's government, which supports both alternative camps, particularly Prabowo's.

The inclusion of the PKB in Anies's alliance brought about more structural problems, particularly between the PKB and PKS. The PKB, historically associated with the Nahdatul Ulama (NU), represented the traditional or indigenous factions of Islamic ideology, while the PKS represented the more rigid, conservative, and modernist factions within Indonesian Islam. In the past, these two factions existed together in the Masjumi Party throughout the 1950s but later separated and were hostile toward each other. Although collaboration between these parties is feasible among high-ranking members, it could be a potential obstacle to cooperation at the grassroots level for the alliance.

CHAPTER 7

THE PROFILES OF THE KEY CONTESTANTS IN THE 2024 INDONESIAN PRESIDENTIAL RACE

Before the official selection of candidates for the presidential and vice presidential elections, there were multiple political candidates proposed by different political parties, as well as some independent candidates who received support from certain political parties. Outlined in the following are several prominent candidate biographies for the 2024 presidential and vice presidential elections.

Puan Maharani

Puan Maharani Nakshatra Kusyala Devi, born on September 6, 1973, is an Indonesian politician currently holding the position of speaker in the DPR, which is Indonesia's lower house, for the period of 2019–2024. She holds the distinction of being the first woman and the third-youngest individual (at the age of 46 when she assumed office) to permanently hold the position. Prior to her current position, she held the role of Coordinating Minister for Human Development and Cultural Affairs from 2014 to 2019. She made history as the first female and youngest coordinating minister, assuming office at the age of 41.

She is a member of the PDI-P and was initially elected to the People's Representative Council in 2009. She held the position of leader of the party's group from 2012 till she was chosen as a minister in 2014. She was among a group of eight women chosen as ministers, and she held the unique position of being the sole female coordinating minister. In the 2019 election, she was once again elected to the People's Representative Council. Puan is the youngest offspring and sole female child of the previous president and current leader of the PDI-P party, Megawati Sukarnoputri. She is also the granddaughter of Sukarno, the first president of Indonesia. Taufiq Kiemas, Puan Maharani's father, was also a politician who held the position of speaker of the People's Consultative Assembly from 2009 until his passing in 2013. Following Suharto's downfall in 1998, Puan entered the realm of politics due to her mother's prominent role in the national political arena. Throughout Megawati's 3-year administration from 2001 to 2004, Puan frequently accompanied her mother on both domestic and international official tours as well as independently organizing social gatherings.

In 2008, Megawati endorsed Puan, who was then the leader of PDI-P's public and women's empowerment division, as her potential successor during her campaign for the 2008 gubernatorial elections in Ngawi, East Java. Subsequently, Puan contested the 2009 elections in Central Java's election district 5, encompassing Surakarta, Sukoharjo, Klaten, and Boyolali, and emerged victorious with a total of 242,504 votes, which ranked as the second-highest among all parliamentary candidates nationwide. In her initial tenure, she assumed the role of leader of the PDI-P faction starting in 2012, taking over from Tjahjo Kumolo (who subsequently became the Minister of Home Affairs). She was designated to the DPR's 6th commission, which focused on investment and small and medium-sized enterprises (SMEs). During this period, she voiced opposition to a program of increasing fuel prices in 2013. Puan was briefly considered as a potential PDI-P presidential contender for the 2014 elections and as a potential vice presidential candidate for Joko Widodo.

In the 2014 legislative elections, she garnered a total of 326,927 votes, once again securing the second-highest number of votes across the entire country.

Disputes or disagreements that have caused public debate or disagreement

After Jokowi won the 2014 presidential election against Prabowo Subianto, Puan was chosen as a cabinet member. However, her appointment was met with controversy due to her lack of expertise and the perception of her mother's political influence. Alfia Reziani, who replaced Puan as a parliamentarian, took up her position in parliament, was not sworn in until 2016. Puan asserted her achievements during her term, citing the increasing Human Development Index (HDI) as well as the declining poverty and Gini ratio figures. She was the sole coordinating minister who managed to retain her position during two cabinet reshuffles during Jokowi's initial term, leading the media to label her as "untouchable." Puan's tenure as coordinating minister, however, was tarnished by two significant events. On August 24, 2016, Puan, in her role as Coordinating Minister for Human Development and Culture, inaugurated a website, revolusimental.go.id, with the purpose of promoting President Joko Widodo's initiative for a "mental revolution" in Indonesia. The ministry had obtained a budget allocation of Rp149 billion in 2015, which led to criticism when the website became inaccessible two days after its introduction. Authorities asserted that the website had been compromised by hackers, resulting in a financial loss of Rp200 million. According to reports, certain portions of the website's script code were borrowed from barackobama.com, which is a website run by fans of Barack Obama. The initial website was constructed using a theme sourced from the open-source platform, and was hosted on a server that was shared with other websites. The website underwent subsequent redevelopment, but it faced criticism for its excessive expenditure and lack of substantial content.

While serving as Coordinating Minister, Puan was implicated in a corruption scandal. On March 22, 2018, Setya Novanto, the former House of Representatives speaker who was on trial for corruption, testified that Puan received a bribe of US$500,000 from businessman Made Oka Masagung. This bribe was related to an electronic identity card program during her time as a legislator when she held the position of chairwoman of the PDI-P faction in the House of Representatives. Puan acknowledged her acquaintance with Made Oka, but refuted any involvement in discussing the e-ID case with him. Made Oka, who received a 10-year prison sentence for his involvement in the e-ID bribery case, refuted allegations of providing funds to lawmakers, claiming a lack of recollection regarding any encounters with them. Indonesia Corruption Watch urged the KPK to verify the truthfulness of the accusation against Puan. Chairman Agus Rahardjo of the Corruption Eradication Commission (KPK) dismissed Setya's statement as mere rhetoric and stated that Puan would not be subjected to questioning unless concrete proof had been discovered.

After the April 2019 general election in Indonesia, when preliminary results showed that PDI-P had obtained the greatest number of votes, Puan was expected to become the Speaker of the House for the 2019–2024 term. This would make her the first woman to hold this position. Furthermore, she expressed her intention to potentially pursue a presidential candidature in the year 2024. She received a total of 404,034 votes for her council ticket, which is the highest number of votes among all the legislative candidates in the country. On October 1, 2019, she was designated as the Speaker, making her the first female occupant of the role. Puan's term as Speaker, however, has been tarnished by multiple issues. One such example is when Puan violently silenced Benny Kabur Harman, a legislator from the Democratic Party, by turning off his microphone during the ratification of the Omnibus Law on Job Creation. Puan maintained that she had the power as Speaker to take such action and stated that she had received instructions from the Deputy Speaker, Azis, in order to ensure the continuation of parliamentary procedures. Subsequently, Partai Demokrat withdrew from the ratification process. In addition, Puan disregarded interruptions by other parliamentarians during the confirmation hearing of General

Andika Perkasa, abruptly ending the discussion without acknowledging the request for interruption. Puan also dismissed another interruption from Partai Keadilan Sejahtera during the ratification of the Law on State Capital, arguing that since the majority of the party had already agreed to pass the law, the dissenting party should only be given a chance to speak after the bill is ratified.

Ganjar Pranowo

Ganjar Pranowo, born on October 28, 1968, held the position of Governor of Central Java from August 23, 2013. He is a current member of the Indonesian Democratic Party of Struggle and has served as a member of the People's Representative Council representing the PDI-P faction from 2004 to 2009 and from 2009 to 2013. Furthermore, Ganjar held the position of General Chairperson of KAGAMA (Alumni Family of Gadjah Mada University) from 2014 to 2019.

Pranowo moved to Jakarta after completing his master's degree in Political Science from the Faculty of Social and Political Sciences at Universitas Indonesia. He began his career in the oil and gas industry, working as a human resource development consultant for firms including PT Prakarsa Pramandita, PT Prastawana Karya Samitra, and PT Semeru Realindo Inti. Pranowo, who was a part of the Gerakan Mahasiswa Nasional Indonesia (GMNI) or Indonesian National Student Movement during his undergraduate years, developed a deep admiration for Sukarno and eventually became a sympathizer of the PDI.

Pranowo ultimately became a member of the PDI and officially identified himself as a PDI cadre in 1996. The PDI-P was formed by Megawati Sukarnoputri as a result of internal ideological conflict between Suryadi and Megawati's supporters who advocated for the Bung Karno (Sukarno) ideology. Pranowo left the PDI and joined Megawati at the PDI-P after witnessing the July 27, 1996 incident. During this event, the New Order regime, led by Suharto, instructed a group of police officers and soldiers dressed as civilians to attack the PDI headquarters. This was in response to allegations that the

PDI-P was encouraging protests in support of their candidate, Megawati Sukarnoputri. Megawati was leading a movement against Suharto's oppressive measures to restrict election freedom. He subsequently pursued a political career through the PDI-P under the leadership of Megawati Sukarnoputri.

The People's Representative Council

Pranowo initially contested for a position in the People's Representative Council in 2004. Although Pranowo did not win the election, he was offered the opportunity to serve as an interim replacement (PAW) for Jakob Tabing. Tabing, who represented the Central Java 7 constituency, had been appointed by President Megawati to become ambassador to South Korea. Pranowo served as a member of the DPR from 2004 to 2009. During this period, he was part of the Fourth Commission of the People's Representative Council. This commission was responsible for overseeing matters related to agriculture, environmental affairs, forestry, and maritime affairs. Furthermore, he was designated as the chairman of a special committee, a member of the legislative body of the DPR, and chairman of the special committee on the MPR, DPR, DPD, and DPRD in the DPR. In 2009, Pranowo was reelected for a second term. During this term, Ganjar was given the opportunity to lead legislative council members by being appointed as the head of the Special Committee responsible for handling the MD3 Bill. Given his industry skills, the management of the PDI-P appointed him to the Second Commission, responsible for overseeing home affairs, local autonomy, public service, bureaucratic reform, elections, land affairs, and agrarian reform. Pranowo achieved considerable recognition through his appointments, notably for his role as a member of the Special Committee for Inquiry Rights for Century Bank and as Deputy Chairman of Commission II of the DPR.

The individual holding the highest executive position in the province of Central Java is referred to as the Governor. During his tenure in the DPR, Ganjar garnered recognition as a prominent leader for his substantial influence in managing governmental matters. As a result of this experience, he made the choice to campaign for the position of Governor of Central Java in 2013, with Heru Sudtmoko as his partner. The campaign motto for the Pranowo–Heru campaign was "mboten korupsi, mboten ngapusi" which translates to "no corruption, no lying." Ganjar was inaugurated as governor on August 23, 2013 by the Minister of Home Affairs, Gamawan Fauzi, after winning the election with 48.82% of the vote. In 2018, Pranowo sought reelection alongside Taj Yasin Maimoen, who was a member of the Central Java DPRD from 2014 to 2019. Maimoen represented the PPP faction and the four Central Java Electoral Districts (Pati, Rembang, Grobogan, and Blora regencies) as Pranowo's running mate. Pranowo was reelected with 58.78% of the vote, which was lower than anticipated. This translated to a total of 10,362,694 votes. It is worth mentioning that Pranowo lost in the Brebes, Tegal, Purbalingga, and Kebumen regencies, which were previously considered strongholds for the PDI-P.

Due to his extensive tenure in the legislature, Ganjar had amassed sufficient expertise in governance and leadership, enabling him to successfully revamp Central Java during his two consecutive terms as governor from 2013 to 2023. He shifted his focus to enhancing community programs, rehabilitating infrastructure, implementing free education, capitalizing on coffee cultivation, and various other initiatives. Under Ganjar's leadership, he implemented a reform in financing loans from Bank Jateng for Micro, Small, and Medium Enterprises (MSMEs) through the KUR Mitra 25 product, which carries an annual interest rate of 7%. Additionally, the Mitra 02 product was introduced with an interest rate of 2%. Both loans are offered without the requirement of collateral or administrative costs. Upon its introduction, the loan interest rate was the most minimal in Indonesia. Presently, this approach has been adopted by various local administrations across the nation and has received commendation from President Joko Widodo.

Pranowo successfully implemented measures to combat widespread corruption in Central Java. His efforts were acknowledged by the Corruption Eradication Commission, which awarded the Provincial Government of Central Java, under Pranowo's leadership, for consistently reporting incidents of corruption and bribery in 2015. Ganjar's commendation was a result of his unwavering commitment to regulating the distribution of gratuities among both governors and officials of the Central Java provincial government. Pranowo implemented a policy that mandated all state civil servants (ASN) in the Central Java Provincial Government, totaling over 40,000 individuals, contribute to zakat. This policy is based on PP No. 14 of 2014, Presidential Instruction No. 3 of 2014, and a request made by the Governor of Central Java, Ganjar Pranowo. Every month, 2.5% of the income of each ASN, amounting to around IDR 1.6 billion, is gathered and allocated for disaster relief, rehabilitation of uninhabitable dwellings (RTLH), education and Islamic boarding schools, mosques, the health sector, and other purposes.

In 2016, Ganjar initiated a program aimed at establishing disaster-resilient villages in Central Java. The objective was to ensure that all 2204 villages in the region, which are susceptible to disasters, would achieve disaster resilience by 2018. Pranowo played a crucial role in establishing 100 autonomous villages, primarily in regions with the capacity to develop into tourist attractions and provide valuable natural resources for the advancement of the community. Ganjar proposed the development of a state-of-the-art hospital at MAJT (Central Java Grand Mosque) in the healthcare industry. Furthermore, Ganjar Pranowo introduced the "Jateng Gayeng Nginceng Wong Meteng" program at the beginning of his term. This initiative aimed to decrease the elevated Maternal Mortality Rate (MMR) and Infant Mortality Rate (IMR) in Central Java by closely monitoring the health and dietary intake of expectant mothers. During his reign, Pranowo implemented the utilization of farmer cards. These cards, which include information about the farmer's identity, land area, plant type, and fertilizer requirements, provide cardholders with access to subsidized fertilizers. This system eliminates instances of crime and abuse of authority, where subsidized fertilizers were distributed or sold for profit without justification. Significantly, President Jokowi praised this program and it was implemented nationwide.

However, Ganjar's performance as governor is not entirely flawless. Following Ganjar's observation of Department of Transportation agents engaging in unlawful extortion during an unannounced inspection at the Subah weighbridge on April 27, 2014, Ganjar implemented a policy to shut down all weighbridges in Central Java. Although there was no subsequent official assessment of the responsibilities and roles of the staff stationed at each weighbridge after its closure, the Supreme Audit Agency claimed that the closing of the weighbridge resulted in a loss of Rp.10.118 billion in revenue for Central Java. Ganjar's actions were condemned as a capricious exertion of authority and detrimental to the province.

Ganjar was also involved in the Indonesian Cement dispute litigation from 2015 to 2017. Since 2015, the inhabitants of Rembang have endeavored to oppose the establishment of a cement manufacturing facility in the Kendeng mountains through legal proceedings and organized protests. In 2017, the series of protests reached their peak when farmers from Kendeng gathered in front of Istana Negara in Jakarta. As a form of protest against the newly issued environmental permit for PT Semen Indonesia, which was signed by Pranowo, the farmers symbolically placed their feet on cement blocks. Following the Supreme Court's decision on August 2, 2016, the Kendeng residents' lawsuit to revoke the cement factory permit was successful. The court's Judicial Review decision invalidated the Decree regarding the Environmental Permit for Mining Activities issued to PT Semen Gresik in Rembang Regency. Although the PK ruling banned the extraction of minerals and oil from underground water sources in the Kendeng mountain region, Ganjar issued an "addendum" decree on November 9, 2016, which renamed PT Semen Gersik Tbk PT Semen Indonesia Tbk. Granjar said that the court did not issue an injunction for the firm to halt its operations, thereby permitting the formation of the Semen Indonesia factory. In response to significant public outcry, Governor Ganjar revoked the environmental permit for the construction of the facility by issuing a decree on January 17, 2017, which nullified his previous addition. He opted to delay the establishment of the Semen Indonesia factory in Rembang until a permit decree was granted in accordance with the PK MA judgment. However, eventually, a new permit was reissued on February 23, 2017, albeit with a minor alteration to the territory. Ganjar's actions have been criticized as authoritarian and neglectful of his duty to comply with the law and court rulings.

Although the nomination of Ganjar by the PDI-P is still doubtful, other political parties have shown their support for his candidature for the presidency. Ganjar has been nominated by the Indonesian Solidarity Party (PSI) as their candidate for the 2024 presidential election, despite not being affiliated with the party. Although the PSI lacks representation in the MPR, it possesses a substantial number of voters nationwide, which could be of significant importance. PSI Chairwoman Grace Natalie stated that the party unanimously believes that Ganjar is the most qualified individual to carry on the progress initiated by Mr. Jokowi in building a great nation for Indonesia. Natalie also emphasized that Ganjar shares PSI's dedication to promoting diversity and fostering national development. Furthermore, she emphasized that Ganjar comprehends the ambitions of the younger generation, who form PSI's primary demographic of supporters.

Prabowo Subianto Djojohadikusumo

Prabowo Subianto Djojohadikusumo, born on October 17, 1951, is an Indonesian politician, entrepreneur, and former army lieutenant general. He now holds the position of Minister of Defense in the Republic of Indonesia. He is the son of Sumitro Djojohadikusumo, an economist who formerly held positions as President Suharto's minister for the economy and minister for science and technology. Additionally, he was formerly married to Titiek Suharto, the second daughter of the late President Suharto.

Professional experience in the Armed Forces

Prabowo completed his studies at the Indonesian Military Academy in 1974 and thereafter joined the Special Forces (Kopassus). He remained in this role until he was appointed as chief of Kostrad in 1998. Nevertheless, his military tenure was marred by numerous accusations of human rights violations. In the early 1990s, Prabowo, as the commander of Kopassus, endeavored to suppress the East Timorese independence movement by mobilizing troops to assault cities and villages, as well as instructing and guiding militias. In 1996, Prabowo spearheaded the Mapenduma Operation in Papua with the objective of ensuring the liberation of 11 scientific researchers who had been abducted by the Free Papua Movement (OPM). After the hostage transfer, Kopassus, led by Prabowo, initiated a retaliatory operation, targeting communities believed to be supportive of OPM. In one particular event at Geselema village, the military attacked the locals using a military helicopter that was camouflaged as a Red Cross chopper.

Prabowo's most notable violation of human rights took place prior to and during the May 1998 riots, which happened within three months of his appointment as the leader of Kostrad. Preceding the riots, military forces under the authority of Prabowo abducted and subjected a minimum of nine activists to torture in an effort to ascertain their political engagements. Prabowo was also implicated in orchestrating the abductions of an additional 13 activists (all of whom are still unaccounted for) from February 1997 to May 1998.

During the initial day of the riots, Prabowo requested that Wiranto, the commander of the Indonesian National Armed Forces, allow him to deploy his Strategic Reserve units from outside Jakarta to assist in restoring order in the city. After Wiranto refused, Prabowo utilized his connections in his previous unit, Kopassus, and instructed Kopassus soldiers to accompany young criminals from southern Sumatra to the capital. He also encouraged Indonesians to join him in combating "traitors to the nation," which further provoked and intensified the riots. Following the riots and Habibie's inauguration as president, an investigation by ABRI was initiated to examine Prabowo's involvement in the riots. Prabowo admitted to being responsible for the abduction of the activists and was subsequently dismissed from military duty in August. Subsequent inquiries into the May riots uncovered that the unrest in Jakarta stemmed from an internal power struggle among the military elite vying to succeed Suharto. Prabowo, who was the commander of the Strategic Reserve, was widely considered to have wanted to succeed his father-in-law and craved the position of commander of the Armed Forces, which was held by General Wiranto, who was favored to succeed Suharto. In collaboration with Major General Sjafrie Sjamsoeddin, Panglima Komando Operasi Jakarta Raya (Pangkoops Jaya) or Operations Commander for Greater Jakarta, Prabowo sought to intimidate government opponents and demonstrate that Wiranto was an ineffective leader incapable of maintaining order.

Following his military release, Prabowo entered into his brother Hashim Djojohadikusumo's enterprise and they together acquired Kiani Kertas, a company involved in paper pulp and plantation operations located in Mangkajang, East Kalimantan. Currently, the Nusantara Group, led by Prabowo, has dominion over 27 enterprises both within Indonesia and internationally. These include Nusantara Energy, which deals with the extraction of oil, natural gas, and coal, Tidar Kerinci Agung, which specializes in palm oil plantations, and Jaladri Nusantara, which operates in the fishing business. Prabowo is affiliated with several non-governmental organizations, including the Indonesian Farmer's Association, the Indonesian Traditional Market Traders Association, and the Indonesian Pencak Silat Association. Prabowo held the position of president of the Indonesian Pencak Silat Association in 2004, 2008, and 2014.

Political career

Prabowo has been politically active since the 1990s. During Suharto's reign, Prabowo and his brother actively suppressed journalists and political opponents. Prabowo, holding the rank of lieutenant colonel, sent an invitation to Gus Dur to visit his battalion headquarters in 1992. During this meeting, Prabowo cautioned Gus Dur to focus solely on religious matters and refrain from involvement in politics. Prabowo further warned that if Gus Dur persisted in opposing the president, he would suffer consequences. Subsequently, he advised the intellectual Nurcholish Madjid (Cak Nur) to step down from the KIPP, the election monitoring unit established by Goenawan

Mohamad, which was criticized by armed forces commander Feisal Tanjung as being "clearly unconstitutional." In 2004, Prabowo was among five people competing for the position of Golkar party's presidential candidate. Nevertheless, he garnered the fewest votes, a mere 39, and was subsequently eliminated in the initial round. Wiranto became victorious in the second round of voting.

During the beginning of 2008, Prabowo's close group of advisors, notably Fadli Zon, founded Gerindra, a political party that selected Prabowo as their candidate for the presidential race in the 2009 elections. Despite securing only 26 seats out of 560 in the Indonesian parliament, the party did not possess the necessary majority. Consequently, Prabowo decided to run as the vice presidential candidate for Megawati Sukarnoputri. The duo, commonly known as Mega–Pro in the Indonesian media, garnered 27% of the vote but were defeated by Susilo Bambang Yudhoyono and his running mate, economist Boediono. He participated in the 2014 presidential election but decided to drop out of the campaign on the day the KPU was scheduled to disclose the official results, due to the fact that most of the preliminary rapid counts indicated that Jokowi was leading. Prabowo cited Indonesia's failure to uphold democracy as the reason for his withdrawal, pointing to the structured and systematic cheating. He said that he and Hatta were using their constitutional right to reject the presidential election and deem it unconstitutional. During his live statement, he insinuated that he would contest the results in the Constitutional Court. However, his assertion was ultimately dismissed by the Indonesian Constitutional Court on August 21, 2014.

In 2019, Prabowo made another unsuccessful bid for the presidency, partnering with Sandiaga Uno as his running mate and receiving support from Gerindra, PKS, PAN, the Democratic Party, and Berkarya Party. After the election, independent organizations authorized by the government conducted "quick counts" at polling stations. These counts suggested that Widodo had won by a margin of approximately 10%. However, Prabowo disputed the results and claimed victory, asserting that a count conducted by his side showed he received 62% of the vote. His baseless assertions of extensive cheating incited his followers to organize demonstrations in Jakarta, leading to violent disturbances that resulted in the deaths of eight individuals and injuries to 737 others. In June 2019, the Constitutional Court unanimously dismissed Prabowo's appeal challenging the election outcome.

Prabowo assumed the position of Indonesia's Minister of Defense on October 23, 2019, following his appointment by President Joko Widodo. Prabowo's tenure as Minister of Defense was moderately successful. Although he faced criticism for not taking strong action against Chinese vessels violating Indonesia's Exclusive Economic Zone, a recent poll conducted by Indo Barometer in early 2022 indicated that Prabowo was the most popular minister in President Jokowi's cabinet.

Gerindra Party declared on October 10, 2021, that Prabowo would participate in the upcoming Indonesian presidential election in 2024. Prabowo initially planned to allow other politicians the chance to become president and potentially wanted to move on from his own presidential bid on June 1, 2022. However, on August 12, 2022, he revealed that he had accepted the nomination from Gerindra to compete in the 2024 Indonesia presidential election. One specific worry was the possible influence that Prabowo could have on Indonesia's democratic reforms if he was elected successfully. Prabowo consistently expressed his belief that Indonesia's democratic reforms have been an error. He advocated for a concentration of power in Jakarta, similar to the political paradigm of the Suharto dictatorship since he believed it would be more beneficial for the country. Several other politicians have voiced similar opinions regarding the excessive decentralization and broad democracy in Indonesian politics. They have expressed their backing for a shift toward centralizing power in the capital. If Prabowo becomes president, there is a possibility that he may take steps to abolish regional and local elections. These elections have given Indonesians more power and have made local politicians more accountable.

The potential regression of democracy that may occur if Prabowo is elected is exacerbated by his style of politics. Prabowo's previous political campaigns have promoted the notion that he possesses the ability to single-handedly resolve issues, resembling the autocratic populist governments (such as Rodrigo Duterte and Thaksin Shinawatra) that were once prevalent in Southeast Asia. Prabowo's connections to organizations engaged in the vilification and assault of religious minorities, as well as his track record of human rights violations, indicate a possible regression in democracy if he were to be elected.

Airlangga Hartarto

Airlangga Hartarto is an Indonesian statesman and entrepreneur. He currently holds the position of Coordinating Minister for Economic Affairs in President Joko Widodo's Onward Indonesia Cabinet. He was appointed to this role on October 23, 2019. Additionally, he serves as the chairman of the Golkar Party. Airlangga was born in Surabaya, the capital of East Java, on October 1, 1962. Hartarto Sastrosoenarto, an engineer and politician, held ministerial positions under former president Suharto for a span of 15 years, from 1983 to 1998. Airlangga became a member of the Golkar Party in 1998. In 2004, he joined the House of Representatives as a member of Golkar. From 2004 to 2009, he held the position of deputy treasurer in Golkar. During his second tenure as a legislator from 2009 to 2014, he held the position of Chairman for House Commission VI, which focused on matters related to industry, trade, investment, and state-owned businesses. During this period, he implemented the 2014 Industry Law. During his third tenure as a legislator, which began in 2014, he was a member of House Commission VII, which focused on mineral resources, environment, research, and technology. In April 2015, he was reassigned to Commission X, which focused on education, tourism, creative economy, culture, sports, and youth. In January 2016, he joined Commission XI, which focused on financial problems.

President Joko Widodo nominated him as the industry minister on July 27, 2016. On December 13, 2017, he was chosen as the new chairman of Golkar, taking over from Setya Novanto, who had been apprehended and was facing trial for suspected corruption. In 2019,

Airlangga resumed his position as the Coordinating Minister of Economic Affairs in Jokowi's Onward Indonesia Cabinet. In addition to his political endeavors, Airlangga is also a distinguished entrepreneur. Airlangga has engaged in several enterprises spanning a wide range of industries, including the distribution of fertilizers, paper packaging, and construction machinery. Airlangga is the primary owner of PT Graha Curah Niaga, a company that distributes fertilizer. Additionally, he holds the positions of President Commissioner and Chairman at PT Fajar Surya Wisesa, a paper packaging factory that he co-founded with Winarko Sulistyo in 1988. In addition, he held the position of President Director at PT Jakarta Prima Cranes in 1991 and served as Chairman of PT Ciptadana Sekuritas, an asset management organization, in 1994.

Anies Rasyid Baswedan

Anies Rasyid Baswedan, born on May 7, 1969, is an Indonesian scholar, advocate, and statesman holding the position of Governor of Jakarta since 2017, representing himself as an independent candidate. Anies was formerly engaged in student activism and worked as a political analyst before joining the public sector. Anies, a Fulbright Scholar, obtained a master's degree in Public Administration with a focus on international security and economic policy from the University of Maryland School of Public Policy. During his time there, he was recognized as a William P. Cole III Fellow. He later pursued his Ph.D. in political science at Northern Illinois University, where he was honored as a Gerald S. Maryanov Fellow. After coming back to Indonesia, Anies was designated as the rector of Paramadina University, a privately owned institution located in Jakarta. Anies, at the age of 38, became the youngest rector of a university in Indonesia. He founded the Paramadina Fellowship and incorporated anti-corruption education into the main curriculum. Anies gained national recognition in 2009 on founding the Indonesia Mengajar (Indonesia Teaching) Foundation. This program selects, trains, and assigns university graduates to teach around the country for 1 year. The program was created in order to address the disparity in the educational standards in Indonesia, especially the lower quality in the impoverished and rural regions of the archipelago. Anies held the leadership position until 2013, at which point he voluntarily stepped down in order to focus on his political aspirations.

Minister of Education and Culture

Politically, Anies initially pursued an independent path in the early stages of his career. He served as the official spokesperson for the "Team of Eight" during the first debate of the 2009 presidential election. This team was appointed by President Yudhoyono to manage the well-known public conflict between the Corruption Eradication Commission and the National Police. The conflict resulted in two of the commissioners facing criminal charges. In December 2011, Anies participated in a panel tasked with choosing potential members of the General Election Commission. In 2010, Anies, together with notable individuals like Hamengkubuwono X of Yogyakarta and former Muhammadiyah chairman Ahmad Syafi'i Maarif, established Nasdem, a large-scale organization. He departed shortly after Nasdem was declared a political party led by media tycoon Surya Paloh. Nasdem successfully secured legislative seats in the 2014 legislative election and thereafter joined the Widodo alliance.

Anies became an official spokesman for the Joko Widodo presidential campaign in 2014. It is reported that Widodo, who graduated from the same university as Anies, believed that Anies's presence would attract votes from Indonesian youth. After Widodo's victory was announced by the General Elections Commission on July 22, 2014, Anies was chosen as the deputy for the presidential transition office. This office was responsible for preparing the cabinet before Widodo and Kalla were officially appointed as President and Vice President, respectively. Anies was elected as the leading candidate for the position of Minister of Education and Culture. He was then officially sworn in on October 27, 2014 as a member of President Joko Widodo's working cabinet. As minister, he delayed the implementation of the 2013 Curriculum, reverted back to the previous 2006 Curriculum, transformed the National Exam from a graduation requirement to a tool for assessing the quality of regional education, introduced the National Examination Integrity Index to gauge the integrity of students in each province, and implemented a Teacher Competency Test and Teacher Certification Program to enhance teacher competence. Anies was substituted by Muhadjir Effendy, the Chancellor of the University of Muhammadiyah of Malang, after a reorganization of the Working Cabinet on July 27, 2016. The adjustment was likely perceived as a political concession rather than being based on performance considerations; however, there were speculations that Anies did not adequately prioritize the president's Smart Indonesia Card program.

Following his departure from the ministry, Anies officially enrolled in the 2017 Jakarta gubernatorial race, selecting Sandiaga Uno as his vice candidate. Anies advanced to the second round runoff in the initial election on February 15, 2017, after receiving almost 40% of the votes. He trailed behind Basuki Tjahaja Purnama, the acting governor (also known as Ahok), who collected 44% of the votes, but was significantly ahead of Agus, who obtained 16%. Anies became victorious in the runoff election on April 19, 2017, winning almost 58% of the votes, while Ahok trailed behind with 42%. On October 16, 2017, he assumed the position of governor, replacing the interim governor, Djarot Saiful Hidayat.

Although Anies achieved some notable accomplishments during his time as Governor of Jakarta, such as implementing a school meal program in 2019 that benefited 144,000 students in 459 schools, as well as effectively managing the COVID-19 pandemic, he was also involved in several controversies due to his public statements. Anies's actions pertaining to granting building permits on reclaimed land in the northern region of Jakarta and eliminating unauthorized settlements contradicted his campaign pledges made in 2017. In addition, he faced further criticism as a result of an error made by city authorities during the budgeting procedure, leading to exorbitantly inflated pricing, for example, Aibon glue priced at almost 82 billion rupiah (equivalent to $6 million USD). Colosseum Club 1001, a nightclub located in Kuningan, Jakarta, was awarded by the city during his term. Subsequently, this accolade was rescinded upon the discovery of extensive problems in the club involving illicit substances and narcotics.

Andika Perkasa

General Muhammad Andika Perkasa, born Fransiskus Xaverius Emanuel Andika Perkasa on December 21, 1964, is the current 21st Commander of the Indonesian National Armed Forces (Panglima TNI). In November 2021, he was designated by President Joko Widodo of Indonesia as the successor to the retiring ACM Hadi Tjahjanto.

After graduating from the Military Academy in 1987, Andika commenced his professional journey in the Infantry. He was initially appointed to the 2nd Group Para Commandos, which is a part of the Army Special Forces Command. Subsequently, his academic pursuits took him to the United States from 2003 to 2011. During this time, he underwent military training at the National War College and Norwich University. Additionally, he pursued a master's degree at Harvard University and a Ph.D. at George Washington University. After coming back to Indonesia, Andika received a promotion to the position of Colonel and was assigned as the Commander of the Kodam Jaya Regional Training Regiment in 2011. In 2012, he was designated as the Commander of the 023 "Kawal Samudera" Military Area Command (Korem) inside the 1st (I) "Bukit Barisan" Regional Command located in North Sumatera.

In 2013, Andika was elevated to the rank of Brigadier General and assigned as the leader of the Army Public Relations office. Then, he was designated as the Commander of the Presidential Security Force in 2014 and was elevated to the rank of Major General following President Joko Widodo's inauguration. Andika's career significantly advanced at this juncture. In 2016, he was given the position of Commander of the 12th (XII) "Tanjungpura" Regional Command. In early 2018, he was elevated to the rank of Lieutenant General and assigned as the Head of the Indonesian Army Doctrine, Education, and Training Development Command. Perkasa assumed the role of Commander of Kostrad in July 2018. Perkasa was elevated to the rank of four-star general on November 22, 2018 and subsequently assumed the position of Chief of Staff of the Indonesian Army after being appointed and sworn in. Perkasa was among the four candidates recommended by Commander of the National Armed Forces, Hadi Tjahjanto, as a potential replacement for the departing General Mulyono.

Perkasa was chosen as the only candidate by President Joko Widodo of Indonesia on November 5, 2021 to replace the retiring ACM Hadi Tjahjanto in the People's Representative Council. Perkasa was appointed as the Commander of the National Armed Forces by the President of Indonesia on November 17, 2021. During his time as a military chief, Andika gained recognition for implementing unconventional policies, such as allowing the descendants of PKI members, who had been barred since 1966, to join the armed services again. Despite the initial controversy surrounding this move, it could be crucial in garnering the support of the 25 million descendants of the Indonesian Communist Party (PKI) if Andika is nominated for the presidency. While they may not form a unified voting bloc, Andika's background makes him an appealing candidate to advocates of "national reconciliation."

CHAPTER 8

FACTORS THAT WILL INFLUENCE THE 2024 INDONESIAN PRESIDENTIAL ELECTION

Introduction

The 2024 Indonesian general election is set to take place in Indonesia on February 14, 2024. The purpose of this election is to choose the President, Vice President, MPR, and members of local legislative bodies. In order to be eligible as a presidential candidate, one must have the support of a political party or a coalition that holds at least 20% of the seats in the DPR or has received at least 25% of the popular votes in the previous election (specifically, the 2019 election). Political parties must maintain neutrality when they are unable to put forth their own candidate, but they are obligated to nominate their own candidate when they have the ability to do so. The voting mechanism adheres to a two-round approach, when voters select one of the candidate pairs. In order to be declared the winner, a candidate must secure a majority and obtain a minimum of 20% of the votes in more than half of Indonesia's provinces. If there are no candidate pairs that meet this requirement, the election must be redone with a maximum of two participants.

The Role of President Jokowi

In 2022, there were discussions and conjectures about the potential of Jokowi serving a third term. These assumptions were mostly driven by lawmakers expressing their support, asserting that Jokowi needed further time to supervise economic recovery and execute his plan. Although Jokowi had initially aimed to not only solidify the achievements of his first term but also surpass them by initiating more ambitious and visionary endeavors, such as establishing himself as a prominent developer of Indonesia, comparable to Suharto whom he partially emulates, his aspirations were disrupted by the pandemic and the subsequent recession and economic turmoil. His plans encompassed his ambitious $32 billion proposal to transfer the capital city from Jakarta to Kalimantan, 256 infrastructure projects outlined by the Jokowi administration in 2016, and the enhancement of the industrial and technological sectors through the enhancement of skills and human capital via improved education and training, as well as the augmentation of research and innovation capabilities.

Consequently, numerous lawmakers advocated for prolonging Jokowi's tenure in office, either by postponing the 2024 election or modifying the constitution to eliminate the restriction on serving two terms. Notably, investment minister Bahlil Lahadalia, economics minister and chair of the Golkar Party Airlangga Hartarto, National Awakening Party head Muhaimin Iskandar, and minister Luhut Pandjaitan all emphasized this idea. Minister Luhut Pandjaitan specifically mentioned that analysis of "big data" from social media indicated that a majority of Indonesians are in favor of extending the president's term. It is worth noting that the possibility of Jokowi extending his term in presidency is feasible. To do this, a constitutional change would need to be passed through a majority vote in a joint session of the MPR. However, it is important to mention that Jokowi's government now holds over 80% of the seats in the House of Representatives. Although Jokowi's political party has rejected the idea of a constitutional modification that would enable him to serve a third term as president, a pressure group called "Jokpro 2024" advocated for the amendment and claimed that the necessary majority vote may be obtained. However, this move has the potential to undermine political reforms that were carefully developed during the Reformasi era. One of the most significant reforms was the two-term constitutional limit on the presidency, which was put in place to prevent leaders from abusing their power and to avoid a repeat of the Suharto era. Allowing this amendment would set a precedent that could open the door for other constitutional changes that demote democracy.

Nevertheless, Jokowi declined the proposal, viewing it as "an insult" and restated his commitment to adhere to the constitution. Furthermore, the president's key aides refuted any possibility of a third term being part of his program. Jokowi categorically refuted other rumors, disseminated by local media sites, suggesting his likely nomination for the vice presidency. Although Jokowi enjoys a significant level of public support, surveys conducted by Saiful Mujani Research and Consulting (SMRC) and Lembaga Survei Indonesia (LSI) indicate that 70% of respondents are opposed to the notion of a third term for him. However, Jokowi will continue to have a significant impact on the outcome of the 2024 Presidential Elections. Political analysts have observed that Jokowi has the potential to assume the role of a "kingmaker" by leveraging his influence to persuade individuals to back specific candidates. Widodo possesses the capacity to influence a significant number of well-organized votes due to his estimated hundreds of grassroots support organizations that wield substantial influence in attracting votes throughout the country. Importantly, this assistance is anticipated to be extended to candidates whom Jokowi deems will uphold his legacy and the endeavors he has undertaken, including the relocation of the capital city from Jakarta to Kalimantan.

The Crucial Domestic Factors

The Police

An essential factor that will determine the outcome of the election is the role of the Indonesian National Police, referred to as Polri within the country. The country's police force has experienced a significant decline in public trust due to recent well-known scandals. This has further damaged their already notorious reputation for widespread corruption, violence, and favoritism, and has brought their important role in Indonesian society to the forefront of public attention.

In July 2022, a scandal emerged when Nopryansyah Yosua Hutabarat, also known as Brigadier J, a 27-year-old bodyguard and driver for Inspector General Ferdy Sambo, who is a two-star general and the chief of Internal Affairs for the Indonesian National Police, was shot. Upon the discovery of Hutabarat's lifeless body in Sambo's residence, the initial assumption was that he had fallen victim to an unintentional shooting. However, subsequent claims of a pervasive police concealment, the unavailability of crucial CCTV recordings, and speculations of homicide swiftly emerged. The affair, which incited public outrage regarding the police's utilization of force, was then followed by the tragic demise of 135 individuals in a stampede during a football match at Kanjuruhan Stadium on October 1 in the city of Malang, located in East Java. The sad incident occurred when riot police deployed tear gas onto the playing field and into the spectator stands, where women and young children were present, resulting in widespread fear. During the chaotic stampede that followed, onlookers were trampled or asphyxiated by tear gas while attempting to flee the stadium. Despite the football match having already been concluded, several entrances of the stadium were inexplicably sealed.

Both episodes, which indicate a tendency of the police to use excessive force and engage in unjustifiable violence, have caused the Indonesian public to want law enforcement organizations to be held accountable beyond mere administrative penalties. Despite the measures taken, such as establishing a collaborative and impartial team to investigate the incident and prosecuting people involved in the shooting of Brigadier J in the Indonesian court, these efforts have only revealed further evidence of widespread corruption within the police force. A total of 97 officers from various branches of the police force have been implicated in concealing the shooting incident involving Brigadier J, which is considered one of the most severe instances of police corruption in the history of Indonesia. Additionally, the fact-finding team responsible for investigating the stampede accused the police of deleting the CCTV footage at the stadium.

Although the Indonesian police force, known for its corrupt and ruthless practices, has been engaged in a process of self-directed institutional change since the ousting of President Suharto in 1998, significant improvements are still needed. During Suharto's reign, the Indonesian police were notorious for engaging in cronyism and employing aggressive policing methods. Subsequent presidents made attempts to address these issues, albeit with varying degrees of success. One such measure was the establishment of the National Police Commission (Kompolnas), aimed at promoting greater accountability and transparency within the police force. However, during the period of reformasi that occurred after Suharto's downfall in 1998, when the military stepped back, Polri was given more responsibilities and authority, making it the central institution for maintaining internal security.

The persistent misuse of authority by the police has led to a significant decrease in public backing for the Indonesian police. Nevertheless, the Indonesian government has made minimal efforts to address this issue. According to a local polling agency called *Indikator Politik Indonesia*, despite the public's lack of trust, successive governments have shown little interest in monitoring and controlling the increased authority of the police. Consequently, this has created ample opportunities for corruption within the police force. Contrary to expectations, the Polri's political influence greatly increased under the Jokowi administration. Due to Jokowi's limited connections with the military, he increasingly relied on the police for both security and political purposes. This includes using legal means to target government opponents, suppress critics, and take action against individuals who pose a threat to the president's authority. As an illustration, the police have pursued prominent legal cases against individuals who criticize the government, such as Robertus Robet, a human rights activist who performed a satirical song mocking the military at a protest, and Dandhy Laksono, a filmmaker who expresses dissent through his documentaries. In the case involving Muhammad Rizieq Shihab, a Muslim preacher and outspoken critic of Jokowi, there was noticeable police involvement. Rizieq orchestrated the 2016 protests with the objective of ousting former Jakarta governor Basuki "Ahok" Tjahaja Purnama, accusing him of committing blasphemy against Islam. Rizieq was ultimately indicted under the Law on Information and Electronic Transaction, prompting him to voluntarily move to Saudi Arabia.

The dependence that Jokowi has established on the Polri has led to the ongoing bestowal of political favors to the police, resulting in a profound politicization and erosion of the institution's integrity. The recent series of controversies involving the police will inevitably lead to public attention in the 2024 elections being partially focused on the ability of candidates to initiate reforms inside the Polri. Candidates who closely associate themselves with former or current police elites are unlikely to gain popularity among the general public. This is important because Jokowi has appointed police elites to key positions that were previously held by military generals and were considered the army's jurisdiction.

The military (TNI)

In Indonesia, the military has traditionally exerted a substantial influence on politics, with two military leaders, namely, Suharto and Bambang Yudhoyono, having served as presidents of the country. Nevertheless, with the downfall of the authoritarian New Order regime in 1998, there has been a concerted effort to curtail the military's participation in politics and enhance civilian oversight of the government. The TNI is constitutionally obligated to maintain political neutrality and is prohibited from endorsing any political party or candidate. Recently, the military has made efforts to separate itself from politics, and there has been a move toward governance led by civilians.

However, a significant portion of voters still have a preference for presidential and vice presidential candidates who have military experience, as they are seen as authoritative and possessing strong leadership abilities. Due to his accelerated and highly distinguished career, recently retired TNI commander Andika Perkasa may possess a significant edge over other candidates in this regard. During his one-year term as TNI commander, Andika actively pursued strategies to enhance his popularity among both the TNI and the broader public, with the aim of running for the 2024 election. These activities involved the expansion and assumption of hosting responsibilities for the Garuda Shield exercise, which was promoted as the largest-ever collaborative exercise with the United States and played a significant role in improving military relations between the US and Indonesia. Andika's decision to lift the prohibition on enlisting descendants of PKI members in the military not only earned him accolades from human rights organizations but has also raised concerns about his motives in trying to enhance his pro-rights image.

The role of political Islam

Indonesia, with a population of over 230 million, is the largest Muslim-majority country in the world. Muslims make up over 87% of the population. Although Indonesia is officially a secular state, religion and religious identity nevertheless exert influence in Indonesian politics, with numerous political parties aligning themselves with specific religious groups or organizations. However, the Islamic environment has seen substantial changes in recent years. Notably, there has been an increase in conservative Islamic factions and politicians, who have been more outspoken and influential in Indonesian politics. The rise of several Islamic institutions with international connections has led to a growing dispute over religious authority, challenging the dominance of established mainstream religious organizations. The emergence of charismatic preachers (ustadz) with significant social media following is posing a challenge to traditional Islamic clerics (kyai), particularly among individuals aged 40 and below. The endorsements of prominent Indonesian kyais, ustadzs, and other religious leaders are highly valued for their religious influence and their ability to rally supporters to vote for preferred candidates. These endorsements are seen as vital for enhancing the legitimacy of political candidates, especially those running for president. It is widely anticipated that all potential contenders in the 2024 competition will actively seek the support of these diverse Islamic individuals and institutions.

Nahdlatul Ulama

Among the Islamic groups in Indonesia, two stand out as the most notable. The Nahdlatul Ulama (NU), the largest Islamic organization in Indonesia, has greatly profited from its strong association with the Jokowi administration since 2014. The NU played a pivotal role in persuading Jokowi to ban organizations such as the HTI (in 2017) and the FPI (in 2020). According to NU officials, these groups were attempting to supplant the Indonesian government with an Islamic state. As a result, the NU received substantial benefits from the Jokowi administration, evident in the selection of its prominent religious leader Ma'ruf Amin as vice president, the appointment of Yaqut Cholil Qoumas, a former leader of NU's youth paramilitary wing, as minister of religious affairs, and the inclusion of three other members affiliated with the NU as cabinet ministers. The NU was assigned the role of the primary organizer for Religion 20 (R20), a conference that brought together global interfaith religious leaders. The conference was conducted in conjunction with the G20 summit, which was hosted by Indonesia. Given that all senior organizer roles for the conference were filled by leaders and activists from the NU, it conveyed the message that the Jokowi administration has confidence in NU's ability to present Indonesia as a moderate and inclusive Muslim-majority country on the global platform.

Nevertheless, the NU operates in a decentralized manner, granting significant autonomy to its affiliated kyais in the interpretation of Islamic doctrines and the endorsement of political candidates, including those competing for the presidency. The leaders of the group are also fragmented due to personal rivalries and opposing political loyalties. Consequently, several factions within the organization are expected to support different candidates based on their distinct political goals and personal connections. This phenomenon is evident in the preferences of the upper echelon of NU society, who are supporting several presidential contenders. Due to his strong affiliation with Jokowi, Yahya Staquf, the current general chairperson of the NU, would support Ganjar. Currently, the PKB, which is NU's semi-official political party, is endorsing Prabowo. The reason for this is that Muhaimin Iskandar, who is the chairman of the party, belongs to a competing faction within the NU. In order to garner additional support, Prabowo has made visits to prominent NU Islamic boarding schools (pesantren) located in Magelang (Central Java) and Jombang (East Java). With approximately 90 million followers, the NU holds significant influence, particularly in the politically significant provinces of Central and East Java. As a result, all presidential candidates will undoubtedly make efforts to gain the support of grassroots-level NU kyais, who possess considerable abilities to mobilize their extensive follower networks.

Muhammadiyah

Muhammadiyah, the second-largest Islamic organization in Indonesia, is facing challenges in countering the perception that it is being overshadowed by the NU in terms of its national and international standing. To address this, Muhammadiyah is actively promoting its own moderate Islamic ideology. Muhammadiyah has expressed disapproval of NU's strong association with the Jokowi administration, without explicitly addressing the NU by name. Recently, Abdul Mu'ti, the secretary general of the organization, expressed that this kind of interaction gives the impression that the state supports a specific and strict interpretation of Islam. This was a clear allusion to the Jokowi administration's deliberate attempts to gain control over the NU, such as publicly supporting NU's ideology of "Islam Nusantara" as a means to counteract the influence of radical Islamists. Therefore, Muhammadiyah is endeavoring to distinguish its public perception from that of the NU by emphasizing its unwavering dedication to supporting a secular nationalist Indonesian state, while simultaneously promising to maintain political impartiality.

Muhammadiyah is also increasingly worried about the loss of its members, especially the younger ones, to several emerging Islamist movements including the Tarbiyah movement (affiliated with the Muslim Brotherhood), HTI, and numerous Salafi movements. Recent studies indicate a significant reduction of over 50% in the number of individuals identifying themselves as members of Muhammadiyah within the past decade, suggesting a rapid loss of membership. Similar to the NU, adherents of Muhammadiyah are fragmented in their endorsement of political parties participating in the upcoming 2024 parliamentary and presidential elections. The PAN, which is affiliated with Muhammadiyah, is formally part of Jokowi's political alliance. However, it is widely believed that the party has experienced a major decline in support among the Muhammadiyah members. A majority of the organization's members are believed to be backing either the Ummat Party, established by Amien Rais, the former chair of Muhammadiyah and founder of the PAN, or the PKS, which has gained a significant number of new supporters from Muhammadiyah due to its strong performance in the 2019 election. This trend is anticipated to persist in 2024.

Conservative Islamists

Conservative Islamists, a significant faction within the Islamic community, will exert considerable influence in the 2024 Indonesian election. This group encompasses various Islamic organizations that advocate for a stronger alignment between the fundamental principles of Islam and the established regulations of the Indonesian government and society. Prominent conservative Islamist groups and kyais are increasingly reaching a consensus to endorse Anies Baswedan as a candidate for the 2024 presidential election. The PKS, the nationalist-leaning Nasdem, and the Democratic Party are expected to establish a coalition to officially endorse Anies as their candidate. Once Anies's presidential candidature is officially confirmed, his opponents are expecting that he will acquire collective support from these groups, similar to what Prabowo received in 2019.

Nevertheless, Anies and his campaign team have declared their intention to not simply depend on the backing of orthodox Islamists. Instead, they plan to actively pursue endorsement from moderate Islamic organizations such as the NU and Muhammadiyah. Anies had been routinely traveling to Central and East Java to convene meetings with NU kyais in their pesantrens. Several experts have proposed that Anies could contemplate selecting seasoned politicians affiliated with the Nahdlatul Ulama (NU), such as Khofifah Indar Parawansa, the governor of East Java, as his running mate. This strategic move would enhance his prospects in the election, particularly in the regions of Central and East Java where the NU retains significant influence.

The 2024 Indonesian presidential election will see Islamic groups, kyais, and activists playing a crucial role, as all presidential candidates are actively seeking their endorsements. Presidential contenders are motivated to appeal to the NU and Muhammadiyah-affiliated kyais and their followers in the highly populated Central and East Java regions, as the election outcome will be influenced by their votes.

However, due to the theological and political differences between the NU and Muhammadiyah, as well as the fractured state of other conservative Islamic groups in Indonesia, it is unlikely that any one candidate will receive a clear endorsement from a majority of Indonesian Muslims. However, it is probable that Muslim support will be evenly distributed among the several contenders. Furthermore, the decision of Islamic groups and individuals to support specific candidates will not only be driven by ideology but also by the candidates' willingness to meet the demands of each group and its leaders. This includes the possibility of offering political appointments and other forms of favoritism after the candidate's victory.

The possibility of a non-Muslim President?

Given the predominantly Islamic population, the emergence of conservatism will make it exceedingly improbable for a non-Muslim candidate to win the presidency. Although the Indonesian

Constitution and the 2008 law on presidential and vice presidential eligibility do not explicitly require presidential candidates to be Muslims, it is improbable that non-Muslim candidates would be able to secure the support of the significant Muslim majority in Indonesia. This posed a significant challenge for individuals holding fundamentalist or conservative beliefs, as seen by their attempts to depict Jokowi as a leader lacking robust Islamic credentials and intending to enforce policies that would suppress devout Muslims before the 2019 Presidential elections. Although the Islam faction is now divided, it is highly unlikely that any candidate would definitively gain the support of this faction. However, it is clear that a non-Muslim candidate will encounter significant challenges in earning the votes of the growing conservative Muslim component.

The Chinese businessmen bloc

Chinese Indonesians, comprising approximately 4–6% of Indonesia's population of 280 million, possess a disproportionately high concentration of the country's wealth. Despite the anger, prejudice, and violent assaults faced by the group's small elite, the Chinese merchants possess significant political power due to their economic success. This is demonstrated by the endeavors of past presidential contenders, like Prabowo in 2019, to seek the support of the bloc.

The primary concern for the incoming presidential contenders is their capacity to effectively connect with their constituency, particularly about the potential consequences of their presidency on the business interests of Chinese entrepreneurs. With the economic growth of Indonesia, Chinese businesses are increasingly interested in investing in the country. Many Chinese Indonesian businessmen play a key role in facilitating deals between China and Indonesia, often leveraging their positions within Indonesian public and private business associations. The backing of this coalition, whose considerable economic and political influence should not be underestimated, is somewhat contingent on the foreign policy stances of prospective candidates.

Public popularity versus party incumbency

An ongoing topic in the lead-up to the 2024 presidential elections is the conflict between personal popularity and the current party in power. Privately, party leaders have expressed their dissatisfaction with the excessive influence of polling figures, which primarily prioritize popularity, on the selection of their parties' presidential candidates. According to the party elites, a party possesses the constitutional authority to select the candidates for the positions of president and vice president. Many members of the upper class also have the belief that if they become their party's presidential candidate, their party will be able to benefit from their popularity and get more votes in the general elections. The strong desire among party elites to secure their party's nominations for the presidential and vice presidential tickets in 2024 primarily for party chairpersons or senior party members is evident in the Prabowo–Muhaimin ticket from the Gerindra–PKB coalition, as well as in the attitudes of party leaders in the KIB.

If the party elites succeed in excluding the current front-runners in the popular surveys (with the exception of Prabowo, who is currently ahead in most polls) from the 2024 Presidential Election, this might indicate a significant change in the prevailing political climate in Indonesia. Jokowi, initially a regular member of the PDI-P party, defied expectations by emerging as the party's nominee for the presidential election in 2014. Susilo Bambang Yudhoyono (SBY), although not the head of the Democratic Party during the 2004 PE, gained power due to his popularity among the people. Both Susilo Bambang Yudhoyono (SBY) and Joko Widodo (Jokowi) successfully defeated the leaders of prominent political parties, highlighting the significant role of widespread public support in past elections.

Prominent individuals within the party will gain advantages if candidates who are not affiliated with any political party or well-liked regular members such as Anies, Ganjar, and Ridwan Kamil are unable to obtain their party's endorsement. The party leaders seem to be utilizing their veto authority to obtain these tickets for their own benefit. Despite the potential for popular people like Anies and

Ganjar to gain support from political parties, it is probable that they will be compelled to accept the nomination for the vice presidency. This is due to the current situation where a majority of the present party leaders are lagging behind non-party candidates in terms of popularity.

According to a prominent survey, Prabowo's electability remains the highest among party leaders, standing at 38.2% in a poll simulation. In contrast, the percentages for the remaining candidates are considerably lower. Democratic Party (DP) Chairman Agus Harimurti Yudhoyono (AHY) stands at 10%, Megawati at 7.5%, Puan at 5.7%, and Muhaimin at a mere 4.6%. The remaining party leaders obtained significantly lower levels of electability. Curiously, a significant portion of the survey participants, specifically 27%, were unable to provide an answer when presented with simulated candidate names that were restricted to only party chairpersons.

Despite Prabowo's present lead in the polls, the party elites are typically highly confident in their ability to defeat him in the 2024 elections. Prabowo has made two unsuccessful attempts at running for president in 2014 and 2019. His popularity may see fluctuations in the upcoming months; there are already indications that prospective voters have shifted their choice to Anies or Ganjar. According to recent simulated polls that considered candidates outside of political parties or those not affiliated with the political class, Ganjar consistently ranked as the leading contender, while Anies was placed third.

This party elite-driven scenario can occur if all party chairpersons take actions to prevent the nomination of non-elite candidates such as Ganjar or Anies on their party's ticket. Nevertheless, in the event that a party or coalition breaks this informal agreement by selecting Anies or Ganjar as their presidential nominee, the remaining parties would be compelled to seek a well-liked individual, possibly an independent candidate, in order to have a competitive opportunity of winning the presidential election. In the event of this occurrence, the ambitions of party leaders to exert control in the forthcoming PE will once more be thwarted by the influence of mass popularity contests.

The importance of identity politics

Another fundamental concern that has emerged in debates about the 2024 Presidential Elections is the problem of identity politics and the potential consequences that this type of political strategy may have on the voters. The party elites, for instance, had conveyed a wish to transcend the divisive religious polarization that had eroded Indonesia's democracy in the last one to two decades. During the MPR annual meeting on August 16, 2022, Jokowi explicitly called for the eradication of identity politics, the politicization of religion, and societal polarization in the upcoming 2024 General Elections. Specifically, Jokowi urged candidates to maintain the maturity of Indonesian democracy and enhance national unity. Similarly, the Speaker of the DPR, Puan Maharani, urged candidates to promote shared dedication to conducting the democratic process in a secure, peaceful, and harmonious manner, without causing divisions or compromising the unity and integrity of the nation.

Considering the political and social divisions that have emerged after the 2014 presidential election, it is particularly important to engage in discussions on this subject. The Suharto regime employed de-ideological and floating mass politics, which involved reforming the party system, indoctrinating Pancasila, and enacting laws to make Pancasila the sole ideology of the country and its organizations. This approach suppressed ideological debates and disagreements over policy. However, the populist approach adopted by Jokowi and Prabowo in the 2014 Presidential Elections revived ideological conflicts. Prabowo's style of populism was particularly provocative due to his utilization of forceful anti-establishment, anti-foreign, and pro-domestic language when discussing policy matters. The PDI-P's public endorsement of Jokowi, combined with his history of collaborating with non-Muslim running mates, further expanded ideological feelings in a country that is becoming more divided. The discourse on economic matters and the state's role started to encompass religion-based identity politics, with Jokowi being perceived as the leader of a secular nationalist faction, while Prabowo was seen as the representative of a conservative Muslim faction.

This polarization gained further momentum during the 2017 Jakarta regional election. Despite having a Muslim running mate named Djarot Saiful Hidayat, Basuki Tjahaja Purnama (also known as Ahok), who is a Chinese Christian, a double minority, became the target of an Islamist sectarian campaign supporting Anies Baswedan and Sandiaga Uno. This was due to Ahok's straightforward communication style. This issue was exacerbated by a speech made by Ahok on September 27, 2016, in which he acknowledged that certain citizens would not vote for him due to their belief that Verse 51 of Al Maidah from the Quran, as interpreted by Islamic groups opposing his campaign, forbade Muslims from choosing a non-Muslim leader. Ahok's statement provoked a strong negative reaction from society, with many people criticizing him for insulting the Quran. In response to his speech, many Islamic organizations formed a large rally, attended by an estimated 50,000 to 200,000 followers. Although initially peaceful, factions of aggressive protesters incited a riot and engaged in confrontations with law enforcement after dusk. The 2017 Jakarta regional election exacerbated political schisms between Islamists and secular nationalists that had persisted since the 2014 presidential elections. Society became divided into two factions: secular nationalists, consisting of nationalist and moderate Islamists who supported Jokowi and Ahok and Islamic political groups, typically favoring Pabowo and Anies.

The ongoing focus of Indonesian political elites on avoiding divisive speech or campaign techniques is crucial as it has significant implications for democracy. Political polarization has the potential to stimulate political engagement, streamline political decision-making for voters, and fortify political organizations. However, it can also hinder the functioning of democracy. Political polarization can result in democratic regression through two ways. Severe polarization can result in policy deadlocks due to the opposing factions adopting a zero-sum mindset that impairs their ability to collaborate. This has a consequential impact on the execution of policies. Furthermore, intense polarization can provide a rationale for undemocratic actions carried out by one faction against another. As government supporters become more accepting of the illiberal act of restricting the political rights of the opposition, opposition supporters may also endorse non-constitutional methods to oust those currently in power.

Given the absence of clear policy or ideological distinctions among the four main candidates, it is highly likely that Indonesia would once again experience a type of artificially created division, whether it be based on religious identity or some other societal division. For instance, the polarization between advocates and adversaries of Jokowi remains strong, as evidenced by recent opinion polls and online debates on the relocation of the capital city. This could become an issue if supporters from either pro- or anti-Jokowi groups shift their support toward specific candidates.

The Role of External Factors

ASEAN leadership

ASEAN leadership has the ability to impact the 2024 Indonesian presidential elections. Due to Indonesia's significant influence in the area and its status as one of the largest democratic countries and founding members of ASEAN, it is highly probable that ASEAN leadership would closely observe the Indonesian elections. The election of a president who supports ASEAN's political orientation and policy direction is of significant concern. ASEAN aims to achieve deeper economic integration to stay relevant in a rapidly changing global order.

Currently, none of the contenders are advocating for a drastic shift in policy. Despite being considered the de facto opposition candidate, Anies has abstained from using anti-government or excessively patriotic language. Currently, it is probable that all of the contenders would follow the foreign policy vision established by Jokowi. This includes attracting foreign investment within a nationalist economic framework, balancing relationships with China, the

United States, and Japan in terms of geopolitics, and expanding the social safety net.

The fundamental objective of ASEAN, as stated in 2020, is to foster stronger unity among member states and create a community characterized by compassionate societies. This commitment to community-building and regional collaboration is emphasized in the preamble of the ASEAN Charter. Consequently, ASEAN leaders will closely monitor Indonesia's elections to ensure the election of a president who supports their interests, rather than one who would pursue strongly nationalist policies that could disrupt the process of integration.

Aside from the regional ASEAN aspect, the other significant external variables are the influence of major countries in the region, particularly the policies of the US and China toward Indonesia, and how these might impact the presidential elections. This topic will be explored in greater detail in subsequent chapters of the book.

CHAPTER 9

THE 2024 INDONESIAN PRESIDENTIAL ELECTION PLAYBOOK: CANDIDATES, POLITICAL PARTIES, AND STRATEGIES TO WIN THE RACE

Introduction

The 2024 Indonesian presidential election was essentially kicked off when multiple polling agencies began in 2020 to identify potential contenders and their support networks.[1] This paved the way for three prominent political figures to be mentioned as potential 2024 presidential candidates for Indonesia: Prabowo Subianto, the country's defense minister, and two Java governors, Ganjar Pranowo (Central Java) and Anies Baswedan (Jakarta).

In this context, this chapter will examine what might be seen as a blueprint for the ultimate process of selecting the next president of the country. Several factors will impact the course of the

---

[1] See Kurniawan, D. (2020). "Survei Indo Barometer: Mencari Parpol dan Pemimpin 2024". *Indo Barometer*, 23 February.

presidential contest and, perhaps, its conclusion. Consequently, the following will be examined in this chapter:

(a) Key dates involved in the presidential elections;
(b) Key determinants needed for a candidate to win the Pilpres;
(c) Key political parties;
(d) Key candidates;
(e) Kingmakers;
(f) The number of political coalitions;
(g) The quadrant of presidential politics;
(h) The role of predictions;
(i) Campaign and issues;
(j) Number of presidential election rounds.

Key Dates Involved in the Presidential Elections

The following are the key dates in Indonesia's political calendar for the presidential elections:

- October 19 to November 25, 2023: Registration period for all elections in 2024.
- November 28, 2023: Campaign period.
- February 10, 2024: Campaign period ends.
- February 11–13, 2024: Cooling off period (no campaigning allowed).
- February 14, 2024: General Election Voting Day (Presidential and Parliamentary).
- February 14–15, 2024: Counting of votes.
- February 15–March 20, 2024: Verification of vote count and results.
- March 20, 2024: Announcement of first-round results by the KPU.

A second round of voting will be held in the presidential election if no contender receives more than 50% of the vote. Just two candidate pairs would advance to this stage; these would be the top two vote-getters from the previous round. The following are key dates for the second round of the presidential elections:

- June 2–22, 2024: Campaign period.
- July 23–25, 2024: Rest and relaxation (no campaigning permitted).
- July 26, 2024: Election Day.
- October 1, 2024: Parliamentarians' inauguration.
- October 20, 2024: President and Vice President's inauguration.
- Saturday, November 27, 2024: Electing regional heads of state, mayors, and regents.

However, the General Elections Commission declared in mid-September 2023 that it was going to move the presidential and vice presidential candidate registration deadline from late November to mid-October,[2] amounting to a five-week reduction. As a direct result of this statement, political parties had to move quickly to nominate candidates for president and vice president.

Electability/Acceptability Index and Qualities/Conditions Needed for a Candidate to Win the Presidency in Indonesia

Even though there are a lot of things that go into deciding who wins the Indonesian presidential election, there are a few things that must be considered to guarantee not only electability but also victory in the end. These considerations are, to a large extent, specific to Indonesia and its demographics, voting mentality, and historical backdrop. It is implied, but not explicitly stated, that the following are crucial requirements for a presidential candidate in order to be elected as president of the country, especially under the current system of direct presidential election:

(a) Be a Muslim, especially of the moderate persuasion.
(b) Be a Javanese, who constitute more than 50% of the country's population.

---

[2] "KPU plans earlier, shorter registration for presidential candidates". *The Jakarta Post*, September 10, 2023.

(c) Be a male even though Megawati Sukarnoputri, a woman, did become Indonesia's president from July 2001 to October 2004, following the resignation of the then president, Abdurrahman Wahid.
(d) It is helpful to have the support of the security services, especially the military and police.
(e) The candidate must be non-controversial and have a national political appeal. The attractiveness of the candidate would be able to appeal to the wide and changing electorate of the country, especially with the rising importance of the youth and female voters.
(f) The candidate must have an attractive political and economic program as well as a broad-based political party and political coalition support, including a Vice President who can widen the political support of the presidential candidate.
(g) As elections are expensive affairs, the presidential candidate must have the ability to garner financial support from various sources, be it the business community, especially the Chinese, in the country.
(h) The Indonesian constitution also stipulates that the presidential candidate has to be at least 40 years old, be a resident of Indonesia for at least 5 years, and not possess foreign citizenship or a resident permit in a foreign country, either at the time of the election or at any time before.
(i) The role of external political players, especially the great powers, is equally important in influencing and often determining who wins the presidency in Indonesia. This is because the great powers, especially the United States, have been directly influencing and interfering in Indonesia's politics since 1945 due to Indonesia's strategic importance.

Key Political Parties Involved in the Presidential Race

A candidate seeking the presidency in 2024 must have the support of a political party or coalition accounting for 20% of the DPR seats

Table 9.1. Key Political Parties Involved in the 2024 General Elections

Political Party	Party Leader
National Awakening Party (PKB)	Muhaimin Iskandar
Great Indonesia Movement Party (GERINDRA)	Prabowo Subianto
Indonesian Democratic Party of Struggle (PDI-P)	Megawati Sukarnoputri
Party of Functional Groups (GOLKAR)	Airlangga Hartarto
Labour Party (PB)	Said Iqbal
Indonesian People's Wave Party (GELORA)	Anis Matta
Prosperous Justice Party (PKS)	Ahmad Syaikhu
Nusantara Awakening Party (PKN)	I Gede Pasek Suardika
People's Conscience Party (HANURA)	Oesman Sapta Odang
Change Indonesia Guardian Party (GARUDA)	Ahmad Ridha Sabana
National Mandate Party (PAN)	Zulkifli Hassan
Crescent Star Party (PBB)	Yuzril Ihza Mahendra
Democratic Party (DEMOKRAT)	Agus Harimurti Yudhoyono
Indonesian Solidarity Party (PSI)	Giring Ganesha
Indonesian Unity Party (PERINDO)	Hary Tanoesoedibjo
United Development Party (PPP)	Muhammad Mardiono
Ummah Party (UMMAT)	Ridbo Rahmadi

or 25% of the popular votes from the 2019 elections, whichever is greater. A total of 24 national political parties had registered to contest in the 2024 national elections, after the Ministry of Law and Human Rights announced the names of 75 eligible parties in April 2022. After an appeal, the 18th political party, the Ummah Party, was deemed qualified to run in the parliamentary elections, bringing the total number of eligible parties to 18, according to the KPU's December 2022 announcement. There was a rejection of the Just and Prosperous People's Party's application to run in the 2024 national elections. This meant that the following political groups could run for office in the 2024 national legislature and, by extension, would have a strong impact on the 2024 presidential election (Table 9.1).

Key Presidential Candidates

In spite of the abundance of political hopefuls and contenders lined up for Indonesia's 2024 presidential election, three names have stood out since 2020, when polls regarding the field first surfaced. From the beginning, Prabowo Subianto, Ganjar Pranowo, and Anies Baswedan have been the three leading candidates for president. Other names that were initially mentioned as possible candidates included Puan Maharani, Airlangga, Erick Thorir, Agus Yudhoyono, Sandiaga Uno, Riduan Kamil, Khofifah, Mahfud MD, and Risma.

With unsuccessful bids for vice president in 2009, president in 2014, and president in 2019, Prabowo Subianto is no stranger to the Indonesian presidential race. He teamed up with Megawati in 2009 and ran against Sandiaga Uno for vice president in 2009. Prabowo formally accepted Gerindra's nomination of him as their presidential candidate for the 2024 election in August 2022, after the party had announced it in October 2021. Prabowo has always been one of the top contenders for president in political surveys that have included this question.

One of the most prominent politicians to run for president is Prabowo, who has been Indonesia's defense minister since 2019. His parents chose the name Prabowo for him in remembrance of the national hero and martyr who was his father's younger brother and who died defending the Philippines from a Japanese invasion. Gerindra, the political party of the 71-year-old, was just founded in 2008, yet it managed to become the third-largest party in the DPR in 2019. As a member of the Investigating Committee for Preparatory Work for Independence and the first leader of Indonesia's Provisional Supreme Advisory Council, Prabowo comes from a politically significant family. He retired as a Lieutenant-General and was the former commander of the country's Army Special Forces and KOSTRAD. His father, Professor Sumitro Djojohadikusomo, was an economic maestro during Suharto's rule, and his grandfather, Margono, was the founder of Bank Negara Indonesia. Prabowo is the grandson of Margono Djojohadikusomo, who was a member of the Investigating Committee for Preparatory Work for Independence and the first leader of Indonesia's Provisional Supreme Advisory Council. He retired as a Lieutenant-General.

The two-term PDI-P governor of Central Java Ganjar Pranowo is another prominent candidate. The most populous province in the country is Central Java. People look up to him because, like the current president, he comes from a modest family and shares Jokowi's temperament and character traits. He, too, has risen to prominence among Indonesians, particularly the young and on social media, despite his non-political and military roots, much like Jokowi. Voters who identify as female also seem to favor him. Despite taking a hit when he supported the decision to exclude Israel from a World Cup match in Indonesia, he is still at the top of most polls.

Anies Baswedan, who has a strong academic background, is the third front-runner for president. The 53-year-old former Jakarta governor was embroiled in controversy during his ascent to power because he was the front-runner among the hardline Islamists who sought to depose Basuki Tjahaja Purnama, better known as "Ahok," a Christian Chinese national, from Sumatra as he had been convicted of blasphemy against Islam. Anies chose not to separate himself from the extremists who still back him and his presidential campaign, despite his reputation as a moderate Muslim. Additionally, he served as Jokowi's Minister of Education.

Key Vice Presidential Candidates

From the perspective of political discussions and bargaining, each of the three presidential contenders may theoretically be considered as a viable and respectable vice presidential candidate. Though the names of the presidential and vice presidential candidates had not been announced, speculation had already begun about a potential alliance between Ganjar and Prabowo. There were more contenders for vice president who were rather strong in addition to the three mentioned. Included in this group were MD Mahfud, Muhaimin Iskandar, Riduan Kamil, Airlangga Hartarto, Sandiaga Uno, Erick Thohir, Puan Maharani, Tri Rismaharini, Agus Harimurti

Yudhoyono, Basuki Tjahaha Purnama, Andika Perkasa, and Yenny Wahid.

An acting minister of communication and information technology and Jokowi's Coordinating Minister for Political, Legal, and Security Affairs of Indonesia, MD Mahfud was nominated as Ganjar's running partner. It was during his leadership that Indonesia's Constitutional Court was presided over from 2008 to 2013. His family is from Madurese, and he served as President Abdurrahman Wahid's Minister of Law and Human Rights, Minister of Defense, and a member of the People's Representative Council from the PKB in 2004. In 2019, he was widely considered as one of Jokowi's top vice presidential candidates, but senior NU ulama Ma'ruf Amin ultimately won the race.

Muhaimin Iskandar, better known by his nicknames Cak Imin and Gus Imin, had served as both the Deputy Speaker of the DPR and the Chairman of the PKB since 2005. In Bambang Yudhoyono's administration, he was minister of labor and transmigration manpower from 2009 to 2014 and then he served as deputy speaker of the legislative power republic (DPR) from 2018 to 2019. Cak Imin was appointed one of the three deputy speakers of the DPR in 2018, despite his belief that he would have been an asset if chosen as Jokowi's running mate, a position which was instead filled by Ma'ruf Amin.

Having served as Mayor of Bandung from 2013 to 2018, Riduan Kamil is now the Governor of West Java, the most populous province in Indonesia. Although Riduan did not identify with any political party, he received the backing of the PKB and Gerindra in his bid to become Bandung's mayor. Despite remaining independent, Riduan was backed by the PPP in the 2018 mayoral race; they even gave him a running companion. He won the seat again. Riduan officially joined Golkar in January 2023.

Since 2019, Airlangga Hartarto has served as both the chairman of Golkar and the Coordinating Minister for Economic Affairs in Jokowi's cabinet. He follows in his father's footsteps as a lifetime Golkar member and former cabinet minister under Suharto. He became Golkar's treasurer from 2004 until 2009 after being elected to the DPR in 2004. Jokowi appointed him minister of industry in

2016, and he succeeded Setya Novanto as Golkar chairman in December 2017.

The current Minister of Tourism and Creative Economy is Sandiaga Uno, a former businessman turned politician. He had previously served as Jakarta's deputy governor alongside Anies Baswedan, who defeated Basuki Tjahaja Purnama and Djarot Saiful Hidayat to become the city's governor in 2017. After losing to Jokowi and Ma'ruf Amin in the 2019 election, Prabowo and Sandiaga resigned from their positions as Deputy Governor and running mates. Though he became a member of Gerindra in 2015, Sandiaga renounced his membership in 2019 as part of an agreement with coalition partners who were backing the Prabowo–Sandiaga combination. After the Prabowo–Sandiaga team lost, Sandiaga went back to Gerindra, but he left in April 2023.

The current Speaker of the DPR is Puan Maharani, who is a member of the PDI-P, Megawati's daughter, and Sukarno's granddaughter. In that role, she oversaw human development and cultural affairs from 2014 till 2019. After being elected to the legislature in 2009, she oversaw the party's faction until being promoted to the position of minister in 2014. Rumor had it that she and Ganjar, both members of the PDI-P, distanced themselves due to Puan's frequent criticism of Ganjar and her low electability ratings in public opinion polls; the two were reportedly considering running for president together in 2024.

The current Minister of Social Affairs is Tri Rismaharini, who was a member of the PDI-P and the previous mayor of Surabaya.

Current Democratic Party leader Agus Harimurti Yudhoyono is Bambang Yudhoyono's older son. He has a background in the military and resigned as a major in 2016. In 2017, he ran for governor of Jakarta but was defeated by Anies Baswedan and Sandiaga Uno. In March 2020, he was made Democratic Party leader.

One of Indonesia's rare non-Muslim leaders, Basuki Tjahaha Purnama, better known as Ahok, served as Jakarta's governor when Jokowi was elected president. Basuki has served as Regent of East Belitung and a lawmaker in the PDIP. In 2009, he won an election to the DPR; however, in 2012, he stepped down to seek a position as Jakarta's deputy governor. He became governor in 2014 when the Jokowi–Basuki ticket won the election. Charges of blasphemy against Islam were levelled against Basuki before the 2017 Jakarta gubernatorial elections. After losing, he spent two years behind bars.

The former head of the Indonesian military was Andika Perkasa. He was appointed Commander of the Presidential Security Forces in 2014 and to the Panglima TNI in November 2021. He is a highly decorated infantry officer. He resigned from his position as Panglima TNI in December 2022. His marriage to the daughter of Hendropriyono — a former cabinet member and Head of the National Intelligence Agency — also lends credence to his political claims.

There are close ties between the moderate Islamists in Indonesia and Yenny Wahid, the daughter of former President Abdurrahman Wahid and a long-time leader of the NU. Her father established the research center, the Wahid Institute, where she now serves as director.

Political Parties–Candidates Dynamics

Given that only political parties are allowed to nominate candidates for president, one of the main concerns has been how the popularity of a particular candidate relates to the popularity of the party. This has led to situations where a popular candidate — like Anies — may not even be a member of the party. Despite being a member of the PDI-P, Jokowi was once considered more popular and, by extension, electable than Megawati, the party's leader. As a result, Megawati and the PDI-P nominated Jokowi as their candidate due to the urgency of seizing political power. The presidential elections of 2024 have also encountered a comparable predicament.

First, despite reports of backing from three political parties — Nasdem, PKS, and PD — Anies is supposedly an independent and not a member of any party. According to Anies, the outcome of the individual vs party dynamics is still uncertain. The Ganjar issue was just as intriguing, especially since Megawati had originally supported her daughter Puan for the PDI-P candidature. But Megawati and the PDI-P nominated Ganjar as their party's candidate because of Ganjar's growing popularity. Prabowo is an exception to this rule because he is the head of Gerindra and the two parties are in perfect harmony with one another.

The Key Kingmakers in the 2024 Presidential Elections

When compared to other prominent political figures in Indonesia, two so-called "kingmakers" stand head and shoulders above the crowd. President Jokowi is the first and foremost kingmaker. His position as president gives him tremendous influence and power, and he will play a pivotal part in choosing the victor. Secondly, Megawati, the head of the PDI-P and the daughter of Sukarno, the previous president of Indonesia, is another important figure. She will play a significant role as a political mobilizer in addition to being the leader of Indonesia's most influential party with the most DPR seats.

Although Megawati was supposed to support Ganjar, the PDI-P candidate, some had accused Jokowi of "interfering" with the election. Jokowi faced criticism from several quarters, including former vice president Jusuf Kalla, who accused him of attempting to influence the presidential election results by publicly endorsing certain candidates. When their tenure ended, Ibu Mega and SBY did not want to get too involved, whether they liked it or not, so Kalla said that the president should do the same. It is a more democratic choice.

There was an argument put out by Hasto Kristiyanto, Secretary-General of the PDI-P, that President Jokowi was carrying on a long-standing political practice in which the sitting president attempted to influence the outcomes of elections. To maintain policy continuity, Hasto and other Jokowi-supporting political figures have stated that it was customary for an outgoing president to have a preferred successor. Therefore, it was not significant that Jokowi publicly backed and endorsed Ganjar and Prabowo, two presidential contenders. Rumor had it that Jokowi was acquainted with Ganjar and

Prabowo from their time working together, and that he thought they will do their best to ensure that Jokowi's legacy is protected when he steps down from office in October 2024. Prabowo, Erick Thohir, Mahfud MD, and Sandiaga Uno are among the presidential prospects whose potential running mates have been mentioned by Jokowi. Ganjar is one of these candidates. Some have viewed these recommendations as political intervention by the current president, even though they are merely advisory in character (Kalla, for example). Jokowi's opponents accused him of *cawe-cawe*, which means interference in Javanese.[3]

The formation of the United Indonesia Coalition (KIB) — which includes the Golkar Party, the United Development Party (PPP), and the National Mandate Party (PAN), along with the alliance of Gerindra and the National Awakening Party (PKB) — was viewed by many as Jokowi's attempt to shape the 2024 presidential elections to suit his own preferences, and he has since faced accusations of being biased and not impartial. In a similar vein, prominent critics like Kalla accused Jokowi of taking sides in the election when he invited six political party chairs and their leaders to a meeting on May 29, 2023, excluding the leader of the Nasdem party, Surya Paloh. The invited parties included the PDI-P chairwoman Megawati Sukarnoputri, PAN chairman Zulkifli Hasan, PKB chairman Muhaimin Iskandar, PPP representatives Muhamad Mardiono, and Gerindra chairman Prabowo Subianto.[4]

In response, Jokowi defended his actions of meeting with prominent political figures to plot the course of Indonesian politics. He insisted he was acting independently and not utilizing any official channels. He promised to respect the results of the election and work toward a seamless handover of power when he resigns in October 2024. Ensuring elections happen "without polarising [sentiment] or sowing social conflict" was also crucial. "The President also wants assurances that the nation's future leaders would oversee and

---

[3] "Nothing wrong with President Jokowi interfering with politics: PDI-P sec-gen". *The Jakarta Post*, May 11, 2023.
[4] *Ibid.*

continue any strategic policies in the future," Bey Machmudin, Deputy of Jokowi's Presidential Secretariat Protocol and Press Affairs, stated.[5] According to Kalla, "since the press has pointed out that being *cawe-cawe* is about safeguarding democracy and ensuring an honest and fair election, then that is a very good thing."[6] This shift in Kalla's position occurred after Jokowi explained his motivations for engaging in political discussions with important leaders. Having well-run elections is of utmost importance.

Although other prominent figures and leaders in Indonesian politics, such as Surya Paloh and Bambang Yudhoyono, do exist, they lack the political clout and party support necessary to affect the ultimate results of the contest.

The Role of "Javanese Spiritual" Predictions

For many Indonesians, particularly those who identify as Javanese, the wisdom and timing of political and religious leaders' prophecies and projections play a significant role in helping them choose between competing candidates. Mysticism, messianic views, culture, and tradition all have a significant impact on these people, making them crucial in the political choosing process. Notable among these historical personalities are Joyoboyo and Ronggowarsita.

Just as Nostradamus is popular in the West for his prophecies about the future, so is the monarch of Kediri, Jayabaya (Joyoboyo), a seer king in Indonesia who foretold many of the events that would shape contemporary Indonesia some 400 years before Nostradamus. Not only did Joyoboyo foretell that a "white-skinned" race (the Dutch, British, and Spanish) would colonize Indonesia only to be vanquished by "yellow-skinned" men (the Japanese) but he also supposedly foretold that administration of the modern Indonesia would be governed according to 'notonogoro'. One possible explanation related to Joyoboyo's idea of "notonogoro" is that it is connected to the first or

---

[5] "Jokowi's admission of meddling in presidential polls divides public". *The Jakarta Post*, May 31, 2023.
[6] *Ibid.*

Table 9.2. King Joyoboyo's Prophesy of Indonesia's Leaders

Syllable	Leader or President
NO	Sukarno
TO	Suharto
NO	Yudhoyono Mulyono (Jokowi)
GO (Ga)	**Ga**njar Pranowo, Hartarto Airlan**gga**, or **Ga**tot Nurmantyo
RO	Leader after "Go"

last syllable of the names of former presidents of Indonesia. The concept of a Ratu Adil, also known as a Just King, was associated with these so-called "leaders." This idealized figure would rescue the nation from impending doom.

According to Joyoboyo's prophesies, many Javanese have interpreted their fulfilment as follows: No, for Sukarno; To, for Suharto; No, for Yudhoyono and Mulyono; and the nation waits for Go and Ro. Because of their lengthy or complete terms in office, Sukarno, Suharto, Yudhoyono, and Mulyono are all factored into the prediction. Because they were only in office for a limited time, Joyoboyo did not include the three presidents who succeeded Suharto but before Yudhoyono — Habibie, Gus Dur, and Megawati — in his forecast. Now, that the nation is waiting for either Go or Ro, rumors have circulated about three potential candidates: Ganjar Pranowo, Hartarto Airlangga, and even the former Chief of Armed Forces, Gatot Nurmantyo (Table 9.2).

According to Joyoboyo, there are three essential qualities in a leader: *Satrio Panandito*, who is religious and follows God's commands; *Satrio Bhayakara*, who is concerned for the welfare of his people; and *Satrio Raja*, who is a statesman concerned for the well-being of his nation and its citizens. Leaders like these should hail from Java, preferably from the heart or eastern regions, according to Joyoboyo. One of Gerindra's members, Arief Poyuono, hinted that the Javanese majority would not be able to disregard Joyoboyo's prophetic prophecies. According to him, among the current presidential contenders, "like Airlangga, Ganjar also fulfils the qualities to be a president, mainly based on the fact that it should be a Javanese, [and] born in central or eastern Java."[7]

Born in Surakarta in 1802, Raden Ngabehi Ronggowarsita is the second notable national predictor. Known for his work as a court poet and prophet during Sultan Paku Buwani VII's reign, he foretold the rise to power of seven Satrio Peningits (state administrators) from the previous Majapahit Empire in Indonesia. The following are the *satrio peningits*:

1. *Satrio Kinunjoro Murwo Kuncoro*: This is a leader who would be imprisoned (*kinunjoro*) and would eventually free the nation from foreign occupation. This figure came to be associated with Sukarno, the leader of Indonesia's independence who ruled from 1945 to 1967.
2. *Satrio Mukti Wibowo Kesandung Kesampar*: This is the leader who has worldly wealth (*mukti*), authority, and was to be feared (*wibowo*). He would eventually suffer for his mistakes (*kesandung kesampar*). This figure is associated with Suharto who ruled Indonesia from 1967 to 1998.
3. *Satrio Jinumput Sumela Atur*: This figure is associated with B.J. Habibie who served as president in 1998–1999. He is seen as a leader who was appointed (*Jinumput*) on a transitory basis (*Sumela Tata*).
4. *Satrio Lelono Tapa Ngrame*: This is a leader who is well traveled (*lelono*) and with immense religious knowledge (*tapa ngrame*). This is associated with Abdurrahman Wahid or Gus Dur, who led Indonesia from 1999 to 2000, the Fourth President of the Republic of Indonesia.
5. *Satrio Piningit Hamong Tuwuh*: This is associated with Megawati Soekarnoputri, a leader who carried the charisma of her ancestor, namely, Sukarno (*Hamong Tuwuh*).
6. *Satrio Boyong Pambukaning Gapuro*: This is a leader who moved from being a minister or other key positions to a president and

---

[7] Bashkara, P. (2021). "Arief Poyuono Pakai Ramalan Jongko Joyoboyo ungkap pengganti presiden Jokowi di Pilpres 2024, siapa?" TribunBekasi.com, 6 December.

Table 9.3. Characteristics of Indonesian Leaders according to Ronggowarsita

Characteristics of the Leader	Leader
Satrio Kinunjoro Murwo Kuncoro	Sukarno
Satrio Mukti Wibowo Kesandung Kesampar	Suharto
Satrio Jinumput Sumela Atur	Habibie
Satrio Lelono Tapa Ngrame	Abdurrahman Wahid
Satrio Piningit Hamong Tuwuh	Megawati Yudhoyono
Satrio Boyong Pambukaning Gapuro	Jokowi
Satrio Pinandito Sinisihan Wahyu	

the gate opener for Indonesia to achieve prosperity (*Pambukaning Gapuro*). Susilo Bambang Yudhoyono is associated with this type of leadership.

7. *Satrio Pinandito Sinisihan Wahyu*: This leader is seen as a religious figure, ruling on the basis of Allah's guidance (*Sinisihan Wahyu*). Some associate this with Jokowi even though he is also seen as a *Satrio Boyong Pambukaning Gapuro*. Some have seen Jokowi's Vice President, Ma'ruf Amin, as carrying a religious mantle.

The traits that Ronggowarsita mentioned and the Indonesian leader they seem to match are stated in Table 9.3.

Although these are the seven most defining features or *satrio peningits*, it defies easy categorization. It is acceptable to classify Sukarno, Habibie, Suharto, and Gus Dur as part of the first four types of leaders; however, Megawati and Yudhoyono can also be classified as part of the fourth type. This type describes leaders who have gained not only personal but also familial reputation and charisma; Megawati inherited it from her father, Sukarno, and Yudhoyono inherited it from his father-in-law, Sarwo Edhie Wibowo, the general who assisted Suharto in destroying the PKI and Sukarno's followers. Just as Megawati and Yudhoyono can be categorized as *Satrio Piningit Hamong Tuwuh* leaders, Jokowi can be classified as *Satrio Boyong Pambukaning Gapuro*, not *Satrio Pinandito Sinisihan Wahyu*. By resolving critical issues like the Papuan conflict and bringing the rich

Freeport Corporation, which was owned by foreigners, under Indonesian control, Jokowi helped Indonesia become a developed state through infrastructure, earning him the title of "door opener" to a new era. Therefore, the *Satrio Pinandito Sinisihan Wahyu* title would be the eligible for Indonesia's future president.

But Gus Dur, a prominent Indonesian political and religious figure, did foretell that Prabowo would succeed to the presidency in his later years. What if the next president of Indonesia is not Ga from Joyoboyo or Satrio Pinandito Sinisihan Wahyu from Ronggowarsita? That is the big question. Prabowo Subianto or Anies Baswedan would be the other two candidates from the current slate if Ganjar is not already on it. This is not completely out of the question, but it could also indicate that these two contenders may lead Indonesia in a manner similar to Habibie, Gus Dur, or Megawati: for a brief while because they did not receive a clear "mandate" from above.

The Presidential Campaign, November 28, 2023 to February 10, 2024

By November 2023, the presidential and vice-presidential race was set to go with the KPU finalising and confirming the three pairs of candidates along with their election serial numbers. Regardless of the various rumours, there were to be debates involving both the presidential and vice-presidential candidates.

Political party machinery

The efficiency of a party's apparatus is directly proportional to its campaign effectiveness. Golkar, the PDI-P, and Gerindra are just a few of the political parties with deep roots in Jakarta, the provinces, and even the villages. Therefore, a politician's ability to directly reach the archipelago people through the party machinery can greatly impact the amount of support and votes the candidate receives.

Importance of financial resources

Having access to financial resources is closely related to having political might because it is not cheap to run for political office, even in Indonesia. There have been discussions over whether or not to delay the elections owing to financial concerns and, more subtly, the possibility of President Jokowi's term extension. It was the president himself who raised an objection to this. The allocation of Rupiah 25.01 trillion (US$1.7 billion) to finance the election process till the balloting day in February 2024 was announced by Finance Minister Sri Mulyani Indrawati in February 2023. The General Election Commission received Rp 15.4 trillion, the Elections Supervisory Agency received Rp 6.9 trillion, and other ministries received Rp 2.6 trillion.[8]

A person's or a political party's financial situation can determine their success or failure. During his 2004 campaign for vice president alongside Bambang Yudhoyono, Jusuf Kalla said that he spent one to two trillion rupiahs on his campaign. Two to three trillion rupiahs would have been the price tag for the 2024 elections. In addition to the 200,000 to 230,000 Rupiahs needed to pay witnesses at each polling station, candidates also need 500,000 to 750,000 Rupiahs to cover rally expenses (whether by motorbike, foot, or car), purchase campaign swag (flags, banners, etc.), and pay for traditional and online ads. It can end up costing someone anything from 3 to 5 trillion Rupiah.

Moderate orientation

A moderately oriented candidate is vital in Indonesia because the country is predominantly an Islamic majority state with about 90% of its population being Muslims. The way a prospective candidate links themselves to groups that are not perceived as moderate in tone becomes significant in light of the country's current trend

---

[8] "Finance Ministry earmarks Rp25 trillion for election funding". *The Jakarta Post*, February 3, 2023.

toward Islamic conservatism and the existence of numerous extreme Islamist groups. Concerns regarding identity politics, in which a political party or individual advocates for policies based on their religious beliefs rather than secular ones, such as the imposition of Sharia law on the country, must be considered.

Leadership and policies

In the end, voters' perceptions of the candidates will be shaped by what each candidate stands for. Islamists in Indonesia used identity politics to depose the Christian ethnic Chinese governor of Jakarta in 2017, shattering the country's reputation for relatively homogeneous politics. This was also a factor in the 2019 Indonesian presidential elections, when Islamists backed Prabowo over Jokowi.

Number of political coalitions and rounds

There has been a dynamic consolidation of political coalitions since 2022. The PDI-P stood alone, while Golkar, PAN, and PPP joined the United Indonesia Coalition. Later, three political parties supporting Anies — PKS, Nasdem, and the Democrats — united under the Coalition for Change label. Gerindra was initially joined by the PKB in the Great Indonesia Awakening Coalition (KIB). After April 2023, with the backing of Hanura, Perindo, and PPP, the number of political parties joining the PDI-P to endorse Ganjar's candidature climbed to four. Rumor had it that Jokowi and other Indonesian politicians were aiming to form a Grand Coalition with the assistance of lesser parties like Hanura and Perindo. This coalition was to supposedly include the PDI-P, Golkar, Gerindra, PKB, PPP, and PAN.

As a result of several political parties pulling out of a previous coalition, the dynamics of the remaining coalitions shifted. Golkar and the PAN announced their departure from the United Indonesia Coalition on August 13, 2023, in order to become members of Prabowo's Great Awakening Coalition. On September 2, 2023, Anies gained the endorsement of Muhaimin Iskandar, who had previously been a member of Prabowo's alliance; Anies had named Muhaimin as his vice president running mate, all thanks to the efforts of Nasdem head Surya Paloh. The Democrats defected from Anies as a result, and the PKS was dissatisfied as well but uncertain on whether to defect or join Anies. This contributed to the partial collapse of Anies's support. Agus, the party head, had planned to be Anies's running mate for president in 2024.[9]

The Importance of Geopolitics in the 2024 Presidential Elections

Interference in Indonesia's internal affairs by foreign parties, particularly major powers, is not surprising given the country's global significance and strategic importance. Among Indonesia's many noteworthy qualities as a nation are its status as the biggest Muslim state, its relatively moderate Islamic orientation, its vast territory, its abundance of natural resources, and its crucial control over strategic sea lanes of communication like the Makassar, Sunda, Malacca, and Lombok Straits. China and India, two of the biggest states in Asia, are physically close to Indonesia.

Because of these reasons, Indonesia and its politics have long attracted the attention of powerful nations. As part of their Cold War rivalry, the United States and the Soviet Union vied for influence in Indonesia; the former played a pivotal role in the final demise of the Communist Party of Indonesia and the removal of President Sukarno, who was perceived as being antagonistic toward the West. Against Left–Communist forces, particularly those of the Soviet Union, China, and their allies, the Suharto-led New Order sided with the West.

The United States and China, in particular, have been embroiled in a fierce struggle for global sway since the Cold War ended and a democratic Indonesia came into being.[10] Bambang Yudhoyono was

---

[9] See "Indonesia's presidential election: Anies Baswedan picks head of Islamic party as running mate". *The South China Morning Post*, September 2, 2023.

[10] Suryadinata, L. (2023). "Indonesia's potential presidential candidates and two

far more aligned with the West than China, in contrast to Habibie, Abdurrahman Wahid, Megawati, and Jokowi, who were all open to doing business with China. Given this, and the fact that Jokowi's administration leaned more toward China in its political and economic policies beginning in 2014, there was fierce rivalry among the world's superpowers to influence the February 2024 election, with pro-US forces and allies aiming to change Indonesia's focus from China to themselves. The outcome of the presidential elections in February 2024 will have a significant impact on the political trajectory of Indonesia in the years to come, but the influence of external great powers will also be crucial.

The United States has been significantly more proactive in contacting the three major presidential contenders, in contrast to China, which has chosen not to take a stand on the candidates and has avoided endorsing any one of them. Ganjar, out of the three, has had the least amount of international experience and received his education in Indonesia. The other two, Prabowo and Anies, are more accustomed to life outside of their home country because of their American education. The United States has been actively engaging with the candidates through visits to Ganjar in October 2022 and the PKS headquarters in February 2023 by US Ambassador Kim Sung Yong. In November 2022, while Indonesia was hosting the G20 Summit, Anies was invited to speak at the Bloomberg CEO Forum in Bali. The forum covered a range of topics, including Indonesian politics. While in Bali, Anies met with Ambassador Kim as well.

According to Leo Suryadinata, the future president of Indonesia should be cordial with major nations, especially with the U.S.–China competition heating up.[11] While Beijing has not yet taken any steps in this direction, Washington appears to have started reaching out to some of the possible presidential contenders in order to get to know them better. *Republika* reported that Ambassador Kim's visit to the PKS could be "A symbol of support for Anies." Coincidentally,

---

superpowers". *The Fulcrum*. Institute of Southeast Asian Studies, Singapore, 19 April.
[11] *Ibid.*

the PKS formally recommended Anies for presidency a few days after Kim's visit. According to another report, "Washington and Beijing would want a keener sense of each frontrunner, if only to know where the next Indonesian president will stand on the regional and global stage," indicating that the Indonesian presidential elections are not devoid of geopolitical importance, regardless of the real intentions.[12]

---

[12] *Ibid.*

CHAPTER 10

THE POLITICS AND POLITICKING FOR THE PRESIDENCY PRIOR TO D-DAY (FEBRUARY 14, 2024)

Introduction

There were a lot of events that changed the mood and intensified the competition for the presidency long before the political parties settled on their candidates and the Indonesian people chose R1, representing the President and R2, the Vice-President. What follows is a list of these changes.

Ganjar Pranowo Selected as PDI-P's Presidential Candidate

Megawati finally announced Ganjar Pranowo as the PDI-P presidential candidate on April 21, 2023, after a long period of internal politics and debate.[1] It was widely believed before the announcement that Megawati intended to nominate her daughter, Puan Maharani, the speaker of parliament, as the presidential candidate. However, ongoing electability polls revealed that she was performing poorly,

---

[1] Afifa, L. (2023). "PDIP appoints Ganjar as presidential candidate, Ganjar: Hopefully I am able". Tempo.Co., 21 April.

consistently falling below 10% compared to powerful contenders like Prabowo and Ganjar. Also, at first, it was thought that President Jokowi would back Megawati's pick of Ganjar as the PDI-P candidate, but that did not happen.

Arrest of Ministers for Corruption prior to the Presidential Elections

An intriguing turn of events occurred just before the presidential elections: Several ministers in Jokowi's government were either arrested or interrogated on corruption charges. Both the Nasdem and Golkar ministries were involved in this. Since 2019, Nasdem has been an integral part of Jokowi's alliance. But Nasdem leader Surya Paloh had sided with Anies Baswedan for president since June 2022, and he has forged a coalition with the Democratic Party and the PKS to back Anies. Given that Ganjar had been nominated by Jokowi's party, the PDI-P, and the president had been making clear his tight relationships with Prabowo, the question remained as to whether Surya's participation in endorsing Anies would be tolerated or penalized.

Johnny Plate, a senior Nasdem cabinet minister, was arrested in May 2023 for corruption related to the "4G Base Transceiver Station (BTS) construction project all across Indonesian regions," which resulted in a loss of 8.32 trillion rupiahs. Plate served as both the Secretary General of Nasdem and the Minister of Communications and Informatics. Surya Paloh, leader of the Nasdem, said that "the high-value corruption case upset him" and expressed concern that it could impact "the electability of the party in the 2024 election, as well as the party's presidential candidate Anies Baswedan."[2] According to Mahfud MD, the Coordinating Minister for Politics and Security, the public should not be concerned that the

---

[2] Arkyasa, M. (2023). "Minister Johnny G. Plate accused of corruption, NasDem defends". *Indonesia Business Post*, 19 May.

prosecution was politically motivated but rather centered around Plate's legal infraction.[3]

Two Nasdem ministers were suspected of wrongdoing and resigned in October 2023, following Plate's alleged misconduct. Claiming to have been involved in fraudulent projects using private vendors and taking bribes tied to job promotions at the ministry, Syahrul Yasin Limpo, Indonesia's agricultural minister, formerly from Gokar, switched party to Nasdem, was alleged to be involved in corruption by using private vendors and taking bribes tied to job promotions at his ministry. The KPK searched Syahrul's home while he was away and found 1.9 million US dollars worth of cash, guns, and foreign and local currency. According to the media, Mahfud, the Coordinating Minister for Political, Legal and Security Affairs, stated that Syahrul was officially designated as a suspect.[4]

While Johnny Plate was on trial, another minister from Jokowi's cabinet was accused. The government's internet infrastructure project in the country's most distant regions was allegedly hindered by Johnny's involvement in a dark conspiracy and his acceptance of payments. There are multiple packages with large budgets for the commercial entities that are required to create the 4G base transceiver stations (BTS) and other infrastructure that covers about 7,900 communities in the furthest regions. The consortiums FiberHome, Telkominfra, and Multi Trans Data would each receive Rp 2.9 trillion, Lintasarta, Huawei, and SEI would each receive Rp 1.58 trillion, and IBS and ZTE would each receive Rp 3.5 trillion. Up until March 2022, 4G BTS coverage was limited to 958 locations, even though the project's goal was to deliver cellular services in 4,200 sites by the end of 2021. Jussie Jhonny was allegedly corrupt and cost the state Rp 8 trillion ($533.7 million).

Anang Achmad Latif, a former chief executive officer of the Information and Telecommunication Accessibility Agency (BAKTI) within the Ministry of Communication, and Yohan Suryanto,

---

[3] *Ibid.*
[4] Karmini, N. (2023). "Indonesia's agriculture minister resigns amid a corruption investigation". 5 October.

a consultant from the University of Indonesia, allegedly received Rp 5 billion and Rp 453 million, respectively. Irwan Hermawan, commissioner of Solitech Media Sinergy, Galumbang Menak Simanjuntak, chief executive officer of Mora Telematika Indonesia, Mukti Ali, account director of Huawei Tech Investment, Windi Purnama, director of Multimedia Berdikari Sejahtera, and Muhammad Yusriki Muliawan, director of Basis Utama Prima, were alleged to be involved in corrupt practices. The initiative allegedly brought in about US$5 million for Yusriki, while Irwan took home Rp 119 billion.[5]

Regarding this matter, Irwan Hermawan, who is the co-defendant, informed the Jakarta Anti-Corruption Court that he had sent Rp 27 billion to Dito Ariotedjo, the Minister of Youth Affairs and Sports from Golkar. Dito has been asked to appear as a witness by the anti-corruption court.[6] Similarly, Airlangga Hartarto, leader of the Golkar party and the country's Coordinating Minister for the Economy, was questioned by the Attorney-General's Office in connection with a cooking oil shortage and an alleged corruption case involving three palm oil companies.[7]

Celebrating Sukarno's Anniversary in June 2023

The politics of promoting the PDI-P on a national level and Jokowi's public image were both intriguing aspects of what has become an annual event honoring Indonesia's independence hero. Jokowi was publicly humiliated by Megawati's verbal attacks and criticisms, which likely influenced him to support Prabowo over Ganjar for president. The PDI-P's stated goal in hosting the event was to showcase Sukarno as their "political mascot" and rally supporters for a national campaign. The main concern was whether or not it would

---

[5] *Ibid.*

[6] Ali, I. (2023). "Co-defendant in major graft trial implicates sports minister Dito". 27 September.

[7] "Airlangga Hartarto questioned as witness in alleged corruption case involving 3 palm oil companies". *Indonesia Business Post,* July 25, 2023; "AGO investigators examine Airlangga Hartarto on cooking oil scarcity policy". Tempo.Co., July 25, 2023.

be successful. The June celebrations, known as the Bung Karno Month, have grown into a significant event that highlights the political might of the PDI-P. However, the 2023 celebration marked a new high point in the Jokowi–Megawati clash, and thus it was unclear if it was a positive or negative development.

Andika Perkasa's Link with the PDI-P and Ganjar Pranowo

General Andika Perkasa, the former head of the Indonesian military, was ensnared by Ganjar Pranowo and added to his "success team," which was an intriguing occurrence. As part of June 2023's "Remembering Sukarno Month," Andika paid a public visit to the grave of Indonesia's first president, Sukarno, in Blitar, East Java, East Java, and then went to the Gelora Kung Karno Stadium in Jakarta for the penultimate "Remember Sukarno" event, openly demonstrating his closeness to the PDI-P. Members of the PDI-P faction in parliament, Andreas Pareira and Djarot Saiful Hidayat, were among the prominent PDI-P leaders who accompanied him on his visit to the burial site in Blitar. Because Andika and his family had been making the journey to Blitar for a long time, he supported the practice. Andika met with PDI-P leaders Ganjar Pranowo and Megawati at the Sukarno celebrations.

To coordinate Ganjar's expected victory in the presidential election scheduled for February 2024, the PDI-P and its electoral partners from the PPP, Hanura, and Perindo announced on September 4, 2023 that Arsjad Rasjid would be head of the Ganjar Winning Team (TPN) and Andika Perkasa would be vice head of the same. Now, Arsjad serves as the Indonesian Chamber of Industry and Commerce's General Chairman.[8]

---

[8] Firmansyah, T. (2023). "PDIP akan Gandeng Mantan Panglima TNI Andika untuk Jadi Tim Sukses Ganjar". *Republika*, 4 July.

The American Ambassador Openly Gets Involved in Indonesian Domestic Politics

Indonesia has taken a minor turn toward China since Jokowi took office in 2014. This is mostly attributable to the growing economic relations between the two countries and, more specifically, to China's involvement in Indonesia's infrastructure initiative. However, with the upcoming presidential elections in Indonesia rapidly approaching, US Ambassador Kim Sung Yong paid a visit to Ganjar Pranowo in Semarang, not long after Nasdem announced Anies as its preferred candidate. At the Bloomberg CEO Forum, where he met Ambassador Kim and spoke about his time as Jakarta governor, Anies was also invited to share his thoughts.

The Jakarta headquarters of the Prosperous Justice Party (PKS) was also visited by Ambassador Kim in this regard. In spite of the PKS's long-standing animosity against the United States, particularly in relation to its Middle Eastern policies, the US ambassador met with PKS officials to supposedly discuss democracy and human rights in Indonesia. Subsequently, the PKS formally supported Anies for president.

Jokowi and Megawati's Deteriorating Relationship

Much has been said about the icy relationship between Jokowi and Megawati over the years, and rightfully so, given their insurmountable disagreements over their respective approaches to the 2014 presidential elections. When Jokowi performed better than Megawati in multiple polls and surveys as the PDI-P presidential candidate in 2014, Megawati felt pressured to nominate Jokowi, and the rift between them began to widen. Despite Jokowi's status as the highest political official in the country and his victories in the 2014 and 2019 presidential elections, Megawati has repeatedly referred to him as a "party worker" (*petugas partai*) since Jokowi's ascension to the office. Although they have not spoken about their disagreements in public, there is a belief that they exist over several matters.[9]

Despite Megawati's PDI-P having declared Ganjar as its favored candidate since April 2023, the president's subtle and occasionally obvious support for Prabowo as the country's future president is supposedly the main point of contention between Megawati and Jokowi.[10] Jokowi has been the target of political attacks from high-ranking PDI-P leaders like Secretary-General Hasto Kristynanto. Jokowi's huge food estate project was deemed an economic bust and even an "environmental crime" due to the extensive cutting down of trees that it entailed, according to Hasto. Although Hasto may have had Prabowo in his sights, the president appointed him to handle the project. However, there have been claims that monies meant for the project ended up in the pockets of different political factions, particularly those backing Prabowo. Although Prabowo was perhaps Hasto's last objective, the project was actually launched in 2020 by Jokowi as part of Indonesia's food security policy, and Hasto fired a bullet in his direction. Hasto also probably would not have been so outspoken about the program if Megawati had not given him the go-ahead. Global food shortages, particularly of rice, the country's major staple, have been argued by Jokowi as the reason the food security plan was necessary.[11]

The daughter of Megawati, Puan Maharani, attempted to defuse the issue in response to Hasto's accusation of environmental criminality by suggesting that "maybe it is going too far to say that." Jokowi defended the food estate program by saying that "Every region, every state, is now facing a food crisis. Wheat is a problem in every country. Food prices are also rising drastically, for example, sugar and rice." As a result, "Food Estate is necessary as a stock,

---

[9] "Analysis: Tension between Megawati and Jokowi about to get worse". *The Jakarta Post*, August 28, 2023.
[10] *Ibid.*
[11] "Jokowi to proceed with food estate program despite criticism". Tempo Co., August 19, 2023.

whether it's strategic stock or, when [the domestic supply] is abundant, for export."

Megawati has also directed her criticism at Jokowi by saying that the KPK, the Corruption Eradication Commission, should be abolished as it was ineffective, indirectly criticizing the president for his ineffective policies at stemming corruption in the country. Another constant irritant in the Megawati–Jokowi relations is the issue of being loyal to the PDI-P, with Megawati and even Puan stating that Jokowi was a PDI-P member and, hence, expected to be loyal to the party. While this is true and the PDI-P did endorse Jokowi as its party candidate, the president does not hold any formal leadership position in the party. Still, Jokowi is not powerless as he commands the loyalty of millions of non-partisan supporters who would vote for the candidate the president suggests. Hence, Jokowi has a lot of power, not just as the incumbent president but also due to the intense support he has among his supporters, referred to as "relawans" or even "Jokowers." Partly due to Jokowi's "unwillingness" to openly endorse Ganjar, there was growing pressure within the PDI-P to crackdown and discipline party members who were showing disloyalty to the party, especially with regard to the presidential elections. One clear case relates to Budiman Sudjatmiko, a PDI-P veteran, who was told to quit or face party sanctions, due to his open support for Prabowo in the presidential race, something Budiman refused to do. How Megawati deals with internal dissent, including Jokowi and even Gibran's unwillingness to openly back Ganjar, would play a part in the ongoing Jokowi–Megawati tensions.

A new source of tension between Megawati and Jokowi before the presidential elections was over Golkar and the PAN joining the coalition supporting Prabowo in August 2023, something believed to have been undertaken with Jokowi's blessing, even encouragement. While Jokowi did not publicly indicate his preference for a presidential candidate and many would expect him to "toe" the PDI-P line of endorsing Ganjar, there also seemed to be a belief that Jokowi was leaning toward favoring Prabowo, the candidate whom he defeated in the 2014 and 2019 presidential races. Whatever the reasons may be for this, one clear important factor is the belief that

Prabowo and not Ganjar was more likely to safeguard and continue Jokowi's legacy and programs, including Jokowi's "peace policies" in Papua, the nation's infrastructure projects, the move to set up a new national capital in East Kalimantan, and Jokowi's neutral foreign policy internationally with regard to the great powers but somewhat aligned to China when it comes to economic ties.

Since August, an additional sweetener had been added to Prabowo's political fortunes with the possibility of Gibran Rakabuming Raka, Jokowi's eldest son and current Mayor of Solo, being touted as Prabowo's running mate, should the Constitutional Court agree to lower the minimal age of presidential and vice presidential candidates from 40 to 35.[12] This was eventually confirmed by the Constitutional Court, announcing that any citizen below the age of 40 who has been elected and held regional offices could seek the office of president and vice president. Jokowi's critics were concerned not only that it showed a highly popular president backing Prabowo but also because of the fact that the Constitutional Court's chief justice was the president's brother-in-law and uncle of Gibran. With strong support from Golkar, Prabowo eventually named Gibran as his running mate. The point being, if a PDI-P member, Gibran was thinking of supporting Prabowo, then Jokowi's younger son's decision, Kaesang, to join and lead the PSI, a party opposed to the PDI-P, would also rile the PDI-P. This would not only signal the move of Jokowi's family members away from the PDI-P but could also threaten the PDI-P's standing in certain constituencies where Gibran or Kaesang decided to contest, especially against a PDI-P member.[13]

Although it seemed that Gibran's alliance with Prabowo might have bolstered Prabowo's presidential campaign, there was an immediate reaction to the decision by the Indonesian Constitutional

---

[12] Widianto, S. and Teresia, A. (2023). "Indonesia court clears path for Jokowi's son to run for vice presidency". *Reuters*, 16 October.

[13] "Jokowi takes a huge chance with son's political elevation". *East Asia Forum*, October 23, 2023; "Jokowi's relations with PDIP hit a new low". *The Star*, September 26, 2023.

Court, which was led by Jokowi's brother-in-law. The result was the removal of Anwar Usman, the head of the court, for ethical violations following the court's decision to allow his nephew and Jokowi's son to be eligible as a vice presidential candidate. The Honorary Council allowed Usman to remain a member of the court but barred him from being involved in any adjudication in the court over election disputes in 2024. However, the decision by the Constitutional Court to allow Gibran to become Prabowo's running mate in the 2024 presidential elections cemented the escalating distance between Jokowi and Megawati, and especially between Jokowi and the PDI-P.[14]

Jokowi's tilt toward Prabowo was also seen to be evident from a number of statements that he made as president. During his speech at the Musyawarah Rakyat on May 14, 2023, Jokowi stated that his supporters should refrain from rushing to pick a candidate that was endorsed by him and that he would tell them quietly in the future despite the PDI-P having endorsed Ganjar in April 2023. Jokowi also stated on various occasions that the next president of the country must be firm, courageous, hear the voice of the people, and not be influenced by elites, clearly showing his preference for Prabowo and not Ganjar. Though denied by the PDI-P, this dig was seen as a criticism of Ganjar as he was believed to have agreed for Megawati to choose the vice presidential candidate and the composition of the cabinet should Ganjar win the presidential election. Jokowi's lack of enthusiasm for Ganjar was partly attributed to the fact that he was not involved in the party's decision to nominate Ganjar as its candidate.

Jokowi's decision to support or not support a particular candidate was significant primarily because of his high public approval rating. According to a poll by LSI and SMRC, Jokowi's approval rating reached 82%, which is unusual for a president who is approaching the end of his 10-year term.[15] In this respect, Prabowo's ranking

---

[14] Syam, F. (2023). "Court panel removes Indonesia's chief justice for ethical breach that benefited president's son". *ABC News*, 7 November.

[15] Muhtadi, B. (2023). "Battle of Indonesia's kingmakers: A rift between Jokowi and Megawati?" *The Fulcrum*. Institute of Southeast Asian Studies, Singapore, 31 May.

had risen partly because people believed Jokowi supported him, while Ganjar's ranking had fallen because Jokowi distanced himself from him, particularly after Ganjar's opposition to the Israeli soccer team's participation in the FIFA U-20 World Cup that was planned to take place in Indonesia. Jokowi could have also veered toward Prabowo as Prabowo, once president, could be likely to provide him political protection once Jokowi stepped down in October 2024.

Generally speaking, the Jokowi–Megawati feud was precipitated by a number of circumstances, such as their long-standing animosity dating back to 2014, Jokowi's rejection of Puan as the PDI-P presidential candidate, Megawati's open denigration of Jokowi's role within the party, Jokowi's vision for Indonesia's future, which differed significantly from Megawati's, Jokowi's tacit and overt endorsement of Prabowo as the most qualified leader of the country, and lastly Jokowi's actions as president to sanction his son's alliance with Prabowo, thereby severing ties to the PDI-P and permitting the use of state resources and apparatus to back Prabowo and Gibran's presidential campaign.

The big puzzle and mystery about the Jokowi–Megawati clash is that this was not supposed to happen as Jokowi is a very Javanese person, believing in the "right way of doing things," in the traditional Javanese world of *Kejawean*, which among others things does not condone or encourage one to be disrespectful or disloyal, especially since it was the PDI-P that was behind Jokowi's rise as a politician in Indonesia, from being a mayor and governor to being president for two terms. Why then did this happen? First, it could be due to the power of incumbency where Jokowi believed that he was much more powerful than Megawati and that he was likely to triumph in any contest with Megawati, including in public support. Second, there was the "mutual assured deterrence" in the Jokowi–PDI-P relationship wherein if anyone dislodged the other openly, both would suffer, and hence there were limits to what the PDI-P could do to Jokowi and vice versa. Third, the PDI-P and Megawati were somewhat weakened as they were out of touch with modern-day Indonesian politics, especially in dealing with the youth and in a technologically driven world. Fourth, it was the support Jokowi had from the security services, especially the TNI, Police, and public service, that gave him the confidence to take on Megawati and the PDI-P, in particular the support of senior generals like Wiranto, Bambang Yudhoyono, Agum Gumelar, and Luhut Panjaitan. This eventually made the difference and allowed Jokowi to move confidently toward Prabowo as he also had the support of the bureaucracy, Golkar, Gerindra, and the Democrats, three powerful political parties. Finally, he also had the economic support of most businessmen, especially the "9 Nagas," the leading Chinese businessmen who controlled Indonesia's economy. In short, power was asymmetrically in Jokowi's hands and he could take on Megawati and the PDI-P and show his support to Prabowo and Gibran. As Jokowi was without a party of his own and not a party leader, the next best thing was to find an arrangement that would mutually benefit him and his benefactor, in this case, the cementing of the Jokowi–Prabowo relationship, especially since early 2023.

Jokowi's Relations with Ganjar and Prabowo

As president and a highly respected political leader in Indonesia, Jokowi plays an important role in influencing the direction of Indonesian politics, including possibly the choice of the country's next president. In this regard, while Ganjar may be popular in Central Java and Prabowo in West Java and parts of Sumatra, the role of Jokowi in indicating his choice of candidates, including the news that he was attempting to broker a possible alliance between the two competing presidential candidates, will have important consequences on the outcome of the presidential elections. This was partly the consequence of Jokowi's March 9, 2023 invitation to both Prabowo and Ganjar to join him on a rice field visit in Central Java, where there is alleged to have been some discussion of the two candidates joining forces. Following this, surveys indicated that the joint Ganjar–Prabowo alliance would be hard to beat in the presidential elections. Various sources, including those close to Jokowi indicated that this was something the president was inclined to support. According to Budi Arie Setiadi, the head of ProJo, one of the key groups of Jokowi's supporters, the president was working toward bridging the political divide between the two presidential frontrunners. Speaking to Kompas, Budi said Jokowi had long considered pairing Prabowo and Ganjar as this was "ideal" for the 2024 presidential election. According to Budi, "Whether it is Prabowo-Ganjar or Ganjar-Prabowo, [the President] wants these two figures to [join forces]."[16]

During a PDI-P national meeting on October 1, 2023, its leader, Megawati, strongly denied rumors of a Prabowo–Ganjar alliance in the presidential elections. According to Megawati, the joint Prabowo–Ganjar scenario was highly improbable. She urged that media reports claiming Prabowo would run for president with Ganjar as his running mate be disregarded, saying, "I, as the chairwoman, have no knowledge of such an arrangement, so we should refrain from giving it credence." The PDI-P national congress that concluded on October 1, 2023 simply recommended "that the chairwoman announce Ganjar's running mate at an appropriate moment". Megawati responded by saying that people should not attempt to partner "a man and woman who are not compatible with each other" even though there were "parties that continue to try to unite them".[17]

The Political Importance of Generation X and the Millennials in the Presidential Election

In the 2024 presidential and general elections in Indonesia, the millennial generation was bound to take the lead, according to data given by the Indonesian General Election Commission. There were a total of 204,807,222 voters: 203,056,748 located within the country

---

[16] Utama, V. R. (2023). "Jokowi, Ganjar, and Prabowo: A look at Indonesia's pre-election landscape". *The Diplomat*, 24 March.

[17] Paat, Y. (2023). "Megawati dismisses speculations of Prabowo-Ganjar pairing for 2024 election". *Jakarta Globe*, 1 October. Hashem, H. (2024). *BNN Network*, 3 October 2024. See https://bnn.network/politics/political-unrest-in-indonesia-megawati-dismisses-rumours-of-prabowo-ganjar-alliance-for-2024-elections/.

and 1,750,474 overseas. With 102,218,503 male voters and 102,588,719 female voters, the gender gap was barely noticeable. But the politically crucial demographic was the age bracket or generational divide among voters. Within this, there were 68,822,389 millennials (33.60%), 57,486,482 Gen Xers (28.07%), 46,800,161 Gen Zers (22.85%), 28,127,340 baby boomers (13.73%), and 3,570,850 pre-baby boomers (1.74%). The age group of 40 and over had the largest turnout (98,48,775 people, or 48.07 percent), followed by the 17–30 age group (63,953,031 people, or 31.23 percent), and finally the 31–40 age group (42,398,719 people, or 20.70 percent).[18]

In the 2024 presidential elections in Indonesia, does the majority of voters being under the age of 40 have any bearing on the outcome? "If young Indonesians were to go to the ballot box today, they would choose either Central Java Governor, Ganjar Pranowo or outgoing Jakarta Governor Anies Baswedan as their president," stated a 2022 article in the *Straits Times*. In addition to being honest, non-corrupt, populist, straightforward, strong, and having integrity, millennial and Gen Z voters were seeking a leader with a capacity to create a difference, lead during crises, and develop innovative policies, according to a CSIS Survey. A leader's priorities should also include a healthy environment, jobs, democracy, the elimination of corruption, improved civil freedoms, and robust law enforcement. It was thought that Anies and Ganjar were both better at using social media. "Prabowo will face a tough situation if he were to run in 2024."[19] This was based on the argument that Prabowo was "seen as an old elite and does not represent the spirit of the young people now." The importance of regeneration was emphasized, with Anies and Ganjar being viewed as the new elites who could bring new ideas, vision, and progress to Indonesia. It was clear that something had changed when the majority of Indonesian voters preferred

---

[18] Millennial Generation Voters Dominate the 2024 Election, a Total of 33.6 Percent". *Voice of Indonesia*. https://voi.id/en/news/290967, July 2, 2023.

[19] Arshad, A. (2022). "Indonesia's young voters set to pick change over 'old elite' Prabowo: Survey". *The Straits Times*, 12 October.

Prabowo over Ganjar and Anies, as most electability surveys had put Prabowo far ahead of them.

The growing influence of young voters, however, prompted political parties to focus on this demographic specifically and craft policies that appeal to them. As an example, Djarot Saiful Hidayat, a prominent member of the PDI-P, said that "from the start, the PDI-P has been paying special attention [to voters] from Generation Z by turning the PDI-P into a digital-based party."[20] Similarly, Sandiaga Uno, who was the leader of the campaign team for the PPP after joining from Gerindra, said that the PPP's strategy to get 11 million votes in the 2024 parliamentary elections would center on appealing to Generation Z and millennials.[21] As PD chairman Agus Harimurti put it, "youth is strength." Meanwhile, Democratic Party campaign chief Kamhar Lakumani declared that the party's attention would be directed at addressing the issues faced by millennials and Generation Z.[22] In a similar vein, Golkar enlisted the help of Riduan Kamil, the former governor of West Java, who was highly regarded by both young people and social media users, to co-chair the party's election committee.[23]

As a direct result of the younger voters' growing importance, there has been a shift on platforms that affect them. Since millennials are information savvy, Djarot reasoned that his party should encourage its members to start their own podcasts. Consequently, the significance of the October 2022 CSIS study, aimed at prospective voters aged 17–39, cannot be overstated: It found that social media was the primary source of knowledge for 59% of respondents about current events.

---

[20] Suhenda, D. (2023). "Indonesia's political parties draw up strategies to entice Millennials, Gen Z". *The Jakarta Post*, 10 July.
[21] *Ibid.*
[22] *Ibid.*
[23] Suhenda, D. and Loasana, N. A. (2023). "Gen, millennials comprise majority of 2024 voters in Indonesia". *The Jakarta Post*, 6 July.

Changing Political Coalitions since April 2023

There were already political coalitions in place when Ganjar Pranowo was named the PDI-P presidential candidate in August 2022. Golkar had formed the United Indonesia Coalition with the PAN and PPP, Gerindra and the PKB had formed the Great Indonesia Awakening Coalition to back Prabowo, and Anies Baswedan's candidature had been backed by the Change Coalition for Unity, which consisted of Nasdem, the Democrats, and the PKS.

By April 2023, the early twofold coalitions were beginning to disintegrate. To rally around Anies, the PKB severed ties with the Great Indonesia Awakening Coalition in August 2023 and joined the Change Coalition for Unity. The PPP had already broken away from the UIC to align with Ganjar's PDI-P, Hanura, and Perindo. Then in August 2023, Prabowo received the endorsements of Golkar and the PAN. The Democrats defected from the Change Coalition for Unity coalition to the Great Indonesia Awakening Coalition, led by Prabowo, partly out of frustrations and disagreements. The most powerful coalition now in existence is the one that backs Prabowo. It consists of Gerindra, Golkar, the PAN, PKB, Democrats, and two non-parliamentary parties, the PBB and Gelora.

The following were the constituent parts of the three coalitions just before the commencement of the presidential and vice presidential candidate registration[24]:

Coalition Supporting Prabowo Subianto:
Gerindra with 78 seats in the DPR (13.57%)
Golkar with 85 seats in the DPR (14.78%)
PAN with 44 seats in the DPR (7.65)
Democrats with 54 seats in the DPR (9.39%)
Non-parliamentary parties of PBB, Gelora, and Garuda
Total: 261 seats in parliament (45.39%)

---

[24] Hutajulu, M. (2023). "8 Hari Sebelum Pendaftaran Capres-Cawapres, Ini Peta Koalisi Terkini". *Detik News*, 11 October.

Coalition Supporting Anies Baswedan:
Nasdem with 59 seats in the DPR (10.26%)
PKS with 50 seats in the DPR (8.76%)
PKB with 58 seats in the DPR (10.09%)
Non-parliamentary party of Ummat
Total: 167 seats (29.05%)

Coalition Supporting Ganjar Pranowo:
PDI-P with 128 seats in the DPR (22.26%)
PPP with 19 seats in the DPR (3.30%)
Non-parliamentary parties of Perindo and Hanura
Total: 147 seats (25.56%)

Who Will Be the Running Mates of Prabowo, Ganjar, and Anies?

With Prabowo, Ganjar, and Anies as the front-runners for president, choosing a running mate was a major (and perhaps growing) concern. Prabowo laid out many requirements for his vice president early on: that he should be a patriot who believed deeply in Indonesia, its foundational principles (Pancasila and the Constitution), and the national anthem, Bhinneka Tunggal Eka (Unity in Diversity). Additionally, the candidate should have a stellar reputation for honesty and have a high electability rating according to national polls.

The PDI-P nominated Ganjar, who sought a running mate who believed in the same things he did. On the other hand, Megawati and the PDI-P are widely believed to have significantly influenced Ganjar's choice of running partner.

Anies, who had the backing of Nasdem, the Democrats, and the PKS from the beginning, said that his running mate should be capable of helping them win by being highly electable and relatively unshakable, as well as stable for the coalition, capable of running the government efficiently, and willing to work toward unity as a peaceful pair. But by mid-July 2023, Anies had thrown in the "0" criterion, which was seen to be very significant. This is where a vice presidential or RI2 candidate's spotless record is crucial. The future coalition could be held captive by the vice president's legal issues, according to Anies, who claimed he was afraid such an occurrence. At one point, Anies was considering Ahmad Heryawan, the deputy chairman of the PKS Shura Council, and Agus Harimurti Yudhoyono, the general chairman of the Democrat Party, as possible running mates. Heryawan and Yudhoyono are both friends of Nasdem and have supported Anies's presidential campaign.

Nevertheless, Anies declared Muhaimin Iskandar, the PKB Chairman (Gus Imin), to be his running companion on September 2, 2023. The prevalent belief that presidential contenders would seek out a vice president with NU ties was validated by this. The Democrats' criticism of Anies and Surya Paloh, the one responsible for arranging the "marriage," had immediate and severe consequences for the coalition behind Anies.

The official registration of candidates was to take place between October 19 and 25, 2023, which was also "D-Day" for the announcement of Prabowo and Ganjar's running mates. Earlier, a number of names were being considered for Prabowo and Ganjar, such as Erick Thorir, MD Mahfud, Khofifah, Airlangga Hartarto, Sandiaga Uno, and Riduan Kamil. Another unexpected contender was Gibran, the eldest son of Jokowi. He was not eligible to be considered until October 16, 2023, when the Constitutional Court reduced the age requirement for candidates from 40 to 35. This opened the door for him to potentially run as a running mate for either Prabowo or Ganjar.

Nevertheless, Ganjar's running mate was declared by PDI-P Chairperson Megawati at a meeting held on October 18. Mahfud MD, who served as Jokowi's Coordinating Minister for Political, Legal, and Security Affairs, was selected for this role. Megawati praised Mahfud as an accomplished thinker who had worked in the legislative, executive, and judicial departments. Among Mahfud's many accomplishments, he served as Minister of Defense and Law under President Abdurrahman Wahid, presided over the

Constitutional Court, has strong ties to Northwestern University (NU), attended Northwestern University's boarding school, and was active with the university's Youth Wing and Wahid Institute. Additionally, he had maintained a prominent public image while handling other massive corruption cases, including the Samba case, which involved the death of a police officer, and internet gambling.[25]

As previously stated, Prabowo eventually chose Gibran as his running mate. This indicates that Jokowi's influence was apparent in all three of the contending coalitions: Ganjar, who served as governor of Central Java for two terms, Mahfud, who was Jokowi's Coordinating Minister for Politics, Law and Security, Prabowo, who was Jokowi's defense minister, Gibran, the president's son, Anies, who was Jokowi's education minister, and Cak Imin, who was Jukowi's Deputy Speaker of the People's Representative Council until he decided to run with Anies.

Importance of Political Islam including Hardline Islamic Movements and Leaders

Hardline Islamic leaders and movements played a significant role leading up to the 2019 presidential elections. This was most clearly seen in the ouster of Ahok, a Christian Jakarta governor of Chinese descent, and the triumph of Anies Baswedan, who had the support of the "212 Group," an organization headed by the fiery Islamist leader Habib Rizieq. Despite losing to Jokowi in the 2019 presidential elections, hardline Islamist leaders and groups rallied around Prabowo. Many years later, Habib Rizieq escaped to Saudi Arabia, only to be arrested and put under house arrest upon his return. Even though the hardline movement has died down a bit, there are still groups like these, and it will be important to see how these groups support the three individuals running for office.

---

[25] Lai, Y. (2023). "Breaking: MD Mahfud tapped as Ganjar's running mate". *The Jakarta Post*, 18 October.

Concerning this matter, the question of "identity politics" and the possibility that Habib Rizieq and other Islamist hardline groups would support Anies in the 2024 presidential elections were brought to the forefront when Anies and his prospective running mate, Cak Imin, attended Rizieq's wedding in September. Although Habib Rizieq's support for Anies is not new, the historical animosity between the NU and Habib Rizieq and his groups and the potential escalation of differences if Anies were to receive Habib Rizieq's endorsement in the next presidential elections were intriguing. According to a commentator, "Anies was in a position of a dilemma; does it mean that he will distant his image from the right-wing Islamic groups that have been him all this time in order to gain the sympathy of NU?"[26]

Indonesia and the Israel–Hamas War, October–November 2023

Several political groups were able to use the October 7, 2023 Hamas attack on Israel as a political wedge issue. Despite its current lack of diplomatic ties with Israel, Indonesia has a long history of supporting Palestinian organizations in the West Bank and Gaza. During the Israel–Hamas War, which started in early October 2023, all presidential candidates criticized Israel and its backers in the West, particularly the United States, and supported Hamas.

The Rise of Anti-Jokowi Sentiments

Megawati and Jokowi's feud had been simmering for a while, but it really took off in 2023 when Jokowi was reluctant to support the PDI-P and Ganjar Pranowo, Megawati's nominee for the 2024 Indonesian presidential election. Many took Jokowi's repeated statements about the necessity for an independent strong leader and his

---

[26] "Anies-Cak Imin hadiri pernikahan putri Rizieq Shihab, 'politik identitas' muncul lagi?" *BBC News Indonesia*, September 29, 2023.

decision to let his son Gibran join Prabowo's ticket as proof that he had broken with the PDI-P and Megawati.

With the entry of his sons, Kaesang and Gibran, into political positions and his support for his nephew Bobby Nasution, mayor of Medan, many commentators publicly accused Jokowi of forming a political dynasty. In addition to becoming the head of the Constitutional Court until his removal on November 7, 2023, but able to continue to serve as a member until 2028, Kaesang quickly rose to the post of PSI leader. Jokowi's brother-in-law was also a member of the court. According to many observers, Jokowi's close relatives would not be in these positions now if he had not meddled and influenced on their behalf.

Some see these claims and the anti-Jokowi attitude as a catalyst for the resurgence of nepotism and a decline in Indonesia's democratic ideals. Professor Ikrar Bhaki, who had previously been appointed as an ambassador by Jokowi, was among those who criticized the president, calling him a "big Suharto" for abusing his power by placing his relatives in high-ranking political positions (the only time Suharto did this was when he appointed his daughter Tutut to a ministerial post).

Is Jokowi Building a Political Dynasty?

The PDI-P was an integral part of Jokowi's political career, which included stints as Solo's mayor, Jakarta's governor, and Indonesia's president for two terms. But even as one approached the 2024 presidential elections, there were indications that Jokowi was beginning to distance himself from the PDI-P and maybe even preparing to challenge the PDI-P by forming his own political dynasty or support base.

Tensions between Jokowi and the PDI-P began to rise in the middle of 2022, and they had their roots in the widespread suspicion that Jokowi was establishing a political dynasty through the cultivation of personal support. The widespread assumption that Jokowi did not back the PDI-P's nomination of Ganjar Pranowo for president was a major factor in igniting this schism. The conviction that

Jokowi would persistently defend his legacy — the infrastructure he had built, his policies toward Papua, the new capital he was planning to construct in Kalimantan, and his foreign policy — was another important factor.

Being the daughter of Indonesia's first president and a former president herself, Megawati has had strong opinions on Jokowi and other members of the PDI-P. "Mr. Jokowi, I am making you a presidential candidate, but you are a party officer who must carry out party obligations," Megawati publicly announced in July 2014, a few months before the presidential elections.[27] While Megawati's stance remained unchanged, Jokowi shifted his focus to building his own identity and base of support while portraying himself as a new generation of political elite, distinct from the previous crop of elites descended from Indonesia's political and military families. This further established the fact that Jokowi was not a pawn of Megawati or the PDI-P. "Without PDI-P, Mr Jokowi is just a poor thing," Megawati claimed in January 2023, at an event to commemorate the 50th anniversary of the PDI-P, which Jokowi attended.[28] This was not surprising.

In 2022, Megawati's disillusionment with Jokowi became apparent when he showed support for Ganjar, not Puan Maharani, Megawati's daughter, as the presidential candidate of the PDI-P. As Ganjar soared to the top of the popularity charts, Puan Maharani's chances of winning diminished. The Indonesian president started to hint that he preferred Prabowo over Ganjar and that Prabowo would be a worthy successor due to his political experience, strength, and ability to make decisions in the national interest [rather than simply being a "party worker"]. Tensions between Jokowi and the PDI-P escalated once Ganjar was named the PDI-P's presidential candidate.

Another indication of the growing divide between Jokowi and the PDI-P was Ganjar's nomination as the party's presidential candidate. While Jokowi was in Bogor in April 2023, the PDI-P announced Ganjar's decision. But it was revealed just one day before the Muslim

---

[27] Siregar, K. (2023). "Analysis: Tensions brewing between Indonesia's ruling PDI-P and Jokowi, but both sides to play nice for now". *CAN*, 28 October.
[28] *Ibid.*

holy month of Eid, and Jokowi had already traveled to Solo to partake in the festivities. It appears that Jokowi was just told of the decision at the eleventh hour since he had to return to Jakarta and Bogor because of the PDI-P's statement.

Megawati also announced Mahfud as Ganjar's running mate on October 18, 2023, but Jokowi was overseas at the time, so he missed the announcement. The PDI-P could have waited for Jokowi to return to Indonesia if they needed his participation; the registration period ended on October 25 after all, and he was to return on October 21. But this fell through, further demonstrating how far apart Jokowi and the PDI-P, and Megawati in particular, really were. Afterward, the nomination of Jokowi's son Gibran, a PDI-P member, as Prabowo's presidential running mate caused a deep split between Jokowi and the party. On October 22, while Jokowi was in Jakarta and registration was closing, Prabowo opposed Megawati and the PDI-P by announcing Gibran as his running mate.

Accusations that Jokowi is seeking to establish a political dynasty have emerged as a significant consequence of the disagreement between him and Megawati. His political legacy and his family will be protected from any form of retaliation once Jokowi steps down as president in October 2024. Having completed all of Indonesia's national strategic projects is a significant component of Jokowi's legacy.

In 2021, when Gibran became mayor of Solo at the age of 34, a political rookie, the beginnings of a Jokowi dynasty were already visible. Bobby Nasution, Jokowi's 32-year-old son-in-law, was elected mayor of Sumatra's capital city Medan in 2021. Upon joining the Indonesian Solidarity Party (PSI) in 2023, Kaesang Pangarep, the youngest son of Jokowi, became its leader. The Onward Indonesia Coalition, of which Prabowo is a member, included the PSI. In order to allow Gibran to be named as Prabowo's running mate, the Constitutional Court — headed by Anwar Usman, Jokowi's brother-in-law — lowered the minimum age limit for presidential and vice presidential candidates.

Even though Jokowi was falsely accused of engaging in "*cawe cawe*," or meddling in national politics, the president dismissed these accusations. In June, during the PDI-P national meeting, Jokowi stated that he wanted to make sure that the transition to power was seamless due to which he had a moral obligation to interfere in the next elections. "I have already expressed that it is my moral role as president during the transitional time in 2024 so that the national leadership may run well without any ripples that could damage the nation." In reference to interfering, Jokowi said on June 6, 2023, "I will not remain silent if there are tremors."

Given the growing opposition and disobedience from Jokowi and his relatives, the crucial question was what Megawati and PDI-P would do. Because they relied on each other's political capital and support base, both sides were likely caught in a "catch-22" situation, a state of "mutual hostage," where they were unable to openly engage in hostilities. Being the largest political party in parliament, the PDI-P is essential to the Jokowi government's stability and, more specifically, to the funding of Jokowi's important initiatives until October 2024. Even though there is friction, Jokowi's reputation and the political future of his family and children will suffer if he is unable to enact many important measures. Similarly, the PDI-P needs to tread carefully because Jokowi is still the most well-liked leader in the nation, with widespread support from both inside and outside political parties. So, the PDI-P needs to tread carefully unless it wants to face criticism. Therefore, both sides must keep their relations amicable until they are able to afford to separate from the other, which is likely to happen after February 2024 or after Jokowi's resignation in October 2024, even though relations have been deteriorating since mid-2022 over a number of issues, the most important of which is the choice of presidential candidate.

The Indonesian Election Commission Approves Three Presidential Candidates and Their Running Mates

The three presidential candidates and their running partners for the February 2024 election were approved by the Indonesian Election Commission on November 13, 2023, following much public hype about the candidates. Despite the contentious 5–4 decision by the Constitutional Court, which permitted Jokowi's son Gibran Rakabuming Raka to run for vice president at the age of 36, all three candidates met the legal requirements, according to the KPU. There was an exemption for Gibran, who is the current mayor of Solo and a regional delegate, because the court was presided over by Jokowi's brother-in-law. Ganjar and Mahfud are supported by the PDI-P and friends, while Prabowo and Gibran are endorsed by the Advanced Indonesia Coalition. Anies and Muhaimin Iskandar are endorsed by the Coalition of Change for Unity.

The announcement that would motivate voters to elect their selected candidates for the 2024 presidential and vice presidential elections was made on November 14, 2023, following a draw by the KPU for the candidates' serial numbers. First place went to Anies and Muhaiman, second place went to Prabowo and Gibran, and third place went to Ganjar and Mahfud.

The Presidential and Vice Presidential Election Campaign, November 28, 2023 to February 10, 2024

On November 28, 2023, the presidential campaign was underway after the KPU confirmed the candidates for president and vice president on November 13, 2023 and announced the three contesting pairs' serial numbers. The vice presidential and presidential debates were supposed to be a big deal during the campaign. Despite rumors to the contrary, the KPU announced on December 3, 2023 that the vice presidential and presidential debates would indeed take place, albeit in a revised format.

There would be a shared platform between the presidential and vice presidential candidates in the 2024 race, with the former receiving more time for debates. Although the Prabowo and Ganjar groups were early adopters of the new format, all of the contestants eventually came around. Law, human rights, governance, anti-corruption, democracy, defense, security, geopolitics, international relations, economics, social welfare, investment, trade, financing, infrastructure, energy, natural resources, environment, public services, disinformation, education, health, and employment were among the themes and topics that the KPU has listed for the debates. The dates of the discussions were 12 and December 22, 2023, 7 and January 21, 2024, and February 4, 2024.[29]

The significance of carrying on Jokowi's legacy, in terms of infrastructure building, the construction of the new capital in Kalimantan, policies toward Papua, and foreign and defense policy, was among the main points brought up in this context. The presidential contenders' first set of debates focused on the rule of law, the democratic process, and government bureaucracy. During the first discussion, Prabowo was strongly criticized for allegedly being engaged in the kidnapping of activists in 1997 and 1998, an accusation that he denied. The new capital in Kalimantan, the economy, and infrastructure were topics covered in the second discussion between the vice presidents.

A One- or Two-Round Presidential Contest?

In early 2020, when the topic of presidential elections began to circulate and several candidates were named as potential applicants, a related question arose regarding Jokowi's term extension and, more specifically, the possibility that the vice president- and president-elect could each win their respective races in the first round without a runoff. There would be no need for a rerun if a presidential contender received more than 50% of the total votes and 20% of the votes in 20 provinces in the first round, according to the election legislation (Election legislation 416).

With Prabowo–Gibran comfortably ahead of the pack by a margin close to 50%, many have argued that whether or not a two-round fight would be necessary in this context. These debates have intensified in the six months leading up to the February 14, 2024 election. A two-round battle was necessary, according to those who argued for

---

[29] "Indonesia's 2024 presidential election: New debate format and data security concerns". *BNN*, December 3, 2024.

it, because democracy and popular choice are paramount.[30] In the spirit of democracy, they claimed, there ought to be a two-round battle, as the statutes allowed for one and there was a budget of IDR 76.6 trillion for it. Those who advocated for a two-round race tended to be supporters of Anies–Muhaimin and Ganjar–Mahfud. It was also believed by this group of opinion makers that the Prabowo–Gibran team was afraid of a two-round contest because, in that scenario, if Prabowo–Gibran finished first in the first round without receiving more than 50% of the votes, the supporters of Ganjar–Mahfud and Anies–Muhaimin would likely band together to defeat Prabowo–Gibran in the second round.

Supporters of Prabowo–Gibran and others who wanted a one-round race said the nation would be better off with a one-round fight because it would promote "budget efficiency" and avoid possible political tensions and hostilities. Proponents of this view, including social media influencer Kiky Saputri, contended that "it would not only be the budget that would increase but also the debates and hostility" if the presidential elections were conducted in two rounds.[31] A one-round presidential election would save the country about IDR 30 trillion, according to Jokowi's Investment Minister Bahlil Lahadalia. Zulkifli Hasan, the country's trade minister, said that the country's political atmosphere would benefit from a one-round presidential election. In a similar vein, prominent members of the Nahdatul Ulama, like Saifullah Yusuf, contended that holding the presidential election in a single round would save money and allow Muslims to "carry out our worship devoutly" during the fasting month, rather than being overly preoccupied with campaigns and other forms of chaos.[32]

---

[30] Muryani, T. (2024). "Challenging the grand narrative of 'one round' of the 2024 presidential election". Kompas, 5 February; "Pilpres 2024, Satu atau Dua Putaran?" Indonesiabaik.id, see https://indonesiabaik-id.translate.goog/infografis/pilpres-2024-satu-atau-dua-putaran?_x_tr_sl=id&_x_tr_tl=en&_x_tr_hl=.

[31] "Mengapa penyebaran narasi 'satu putaran' Pilpres 2024 dituding bermotif 'politis'?" BBC Indonesia, February 6, 2024. See https://www.bbc.com/indonesia/articles/c3gkn2ye0j5o.

[32] Ibid.

CHAPTER 11

THE RESULTS OF INDONESIA'S 2024 PRESIDENTIAL AND VICE PRESIDENTIAL ELECTIONS

Introduction

On February 14, 2024, Indonesia organized the largest single-day elections in modern history. According to Reuters, "The world's biggest single-day election saw nearly 259,000 candidates and 18 parties contest 20,600 posts across the archipelago of 17,000 islands." The U.S. State Department said the vote was "a testament to the durability and strength of the Indonesian people's commitment to the democratic process."[1] Similarly, *The Sydney Morning Herald* observed that the presidential elections, in conjunction with the legislative elections, were "the biggest single-day election on Earth."[2] The presidential elections, to elect a president and vice president, the fifth such elections to be held since the fall of Suharto in 1998, were held together with the legislative elections to elect members of the House of Representatives, the Upper House or Senate, and local legislative

---

[1] See Teresia, A. and Widianto, S. (2024). "Indonesia's Prabowo claims victory after presidential election rout". *Reuters*, 15 February.
[2] Hope, Z. and Rompies, K. (2024). "'Gentler' strongman Prabowo looks to have scored first-round knockout". *The Sydney Morning Herald*, 15 February.

provincial and municipal councils, throughout Indonesia. According to the KPU, for the national elections, for the 580 seats in the DPR, there were 9,917 candidates, and for the DPD's 152 seats, there were 668 candidates. At the regional level, for the 2372 seats in the Provincial People's Representative Council or DPRD, there were 32,880 candidates and for the 17,510 Municipal People's Representative Councils seats, there were 214,915 candidates.[3]

Pre-Official Results through the Quick-Count System

Following the close of the voting on February 14, very early, using the Quick-Count system, the Prabowo–Gibran team, in line with earlier surveys, led the race, signaling that it would win in the first round without the need for a runoff.[4] While Real Counts were also taking place, as were done by the KPU, the Quick-Count system quickly established that Prabowo and Gibran would be Indonesia's next president and vice president, respectively, with competitors unable to defeat the Prabowo–Gibran team as they were trailing badly.

From the moment the Quick-Count results started coming in, the standing of the candidates hardly changed, in line with predictions made by earlier surveys prior to the February 14, 2024 elections, with Prabowo–Gibran leading way ahead of Anies–Muhaimin and Ganjar–Mahfud. Hence, even a news site critical of the Prabowo–Gibran team, such as the *AP News*, stated on February 15, 2024, that "According to unofficial tallies conducted by Indonesian polling

---

[3] See Lingga, R. A. (2023, 3 November). Ninditya, F. (ed.). "KPU tetapkan 9.917 DCT anggota DPR RI di Pemilu 2024". *Antara News*; "Daftar Caleg DPRD Provinsi di Seluruh Indonesia". goodkind.id; Nurrahman, A. and Zagoto, N. (eds.) (2023, May 20). "Sebanyak 10.341 Orang Daftar Bakal Caleg DPR 2024". validnews.id.

[4] The Quick-Count system is a calculation method using a representative sample with a small margin of error expected. When it was first implemented nationally in Indonesia in 2004, one of the goals was to prevent voter fraud in tiered counting from counting centers at the village, sub-district, district, provincial, and national levels. See Harbowo, N. and Basyari, I. (2024). "Exit poll, quick count, and official count what's the difference?" *Kompas*, 14 February.

Table 11.1. Quick-Count Results of Presidential Elections with More Than 90% of Votes Counted

	Anies–Muhaimin (%)	Prabowo–Gibran (%)	Ganjar–Mahfud (%)	Votes Collected (%)
Indonesian Election Commission	24.55	56.11	19.34	41.01
Indikator	25.32	58	16.68	97.63
CSIS	24.8	58.4	16.7	95.9
LSI Denny JA	25.21	58.16	16.64	97.0

Source: Quick-Count Results from Independent Pollsters.

agencies, Subianto had 57% to 59% of votes, with more than 80% of the vote counted in polling places that were sampled. The Quick Counts are based on actual votes at a sample of polling stations across Indonesia. The laborious official count may not be finished for up to a month, but Quick Counts have provided an accurate picture of the results of all four presidential elections held in Indonesia since it began direct voting in 2004."[5] On February 18, 2024, one of the key survey portals, Lingakaran Survei Indonesia Denny JA, announced that it had tabulated 100% of the votes and that Prabowo–Gibran received 58.47%, Anies–Muhaimin received 24.98%, and Ganjar–Mahfud received 16.55% of the total votes (Table 11.1).[6]

The results of the Quick Count were also being confirmed with the then ongoing Real Count with the Prabowo–Gibran team leading by garnering between 56% and 58% of the total votes. On March 4, 2024, the total Real Count votes amounted to some 78% and the Prabowo–Gibran team was still leading with 58.83% (Table 11.2).[7]

---

[5] Karmini, N. and Tarigan, E. (2024). "Former Indonesian general linked to human rights abuses claims victory in presidential election". *AP News*, 15 February. See https://apnews.com/article/indonesia-presidential-election-voting-dd732ad-b2d0f3b674fc92aee4f547c6a.

[6] See "Quick Count LSI Denny JA 100%, Prabowo Menang 58.47%". *CNBC Indonesia*, February 18, 2024.

[7] See "Real Count KPU: Suara Masuk 78,08^%, Prabowo-Gibran Masih Unggul". *CNBC Indonesia*, March 4, 2024.

Table 11.2. Real Count by the KPU Following 41.0% of Votes Being Counted

Candidates	Party	Votes	%
Prabowo Subianto–Gibran Rakabuming	Gerinda & Independent	12,476,925	56.11
Anies Baswedan–Muhaimin Iskandar	Independent and PKB	5,459,425	24.55
Ganjar Pranowo–MD Mahfud	PDI-P & Independent	4,300,835	19.34

Source: Author.

Table 11.3. Quick-Count Results by Provinces

Provinces	Prabowo–Gibran (%)	Anies–Muhaimin (%)	Ganjar–Mahfud (%)
Sumatra	57.18	31.87	10.95
Banten	55.92	34.26	9.82
DKI Jakarta	43.29	41.42	17.31
West Java	57.91	32.02	10.06
Central Java/DIY	52.07	13.0	34.93
East Java	65.03	17.40	17.57
Bali NTB NTT	60.20	13.29	26.51
Kalimantan	64.97	23.84	11.19
Sulawesi	62.65	28.57	8.84
Maluku Papua	56.25	21.27	22.48

Source: LSI Denny JA. https://www.cnnindonesia.com/nasional/20240217122141-617-1063909/hasil-akhir-quick-count-pilpres-versi-lsi-denny-ja-seluruh-indonesia.

As of March 4, 2024, the results of the Quick Count, confirmed by the Real Count, showed that only three political parties had crossed the 10 million votes, namely, the PDI-P, Golkar, and Gerindra, receiving a total percent of 16.39, 15.05, and 13.3, respectively. The other political parties in the race garnered the following figures: PKB, 11.54%; Nasdem, 9.42%; PKS, 7.5%; Democrats, 7.41%; PAN, 6.95%; PPP, 4.01%; PSI, 3.13%; and the rest getting less than 2% of the votes.[8]

---

[8] See Setiawti, S. (2004). "Real Count KPU: hanya 3 partai tembus 10 juta surara". *CNBC Indonesia*, 4 March.

Table 11.4. Final Results of the Presidential and Vice Presidential Election

Candidate	Total Votes	% of Total Votes
Prabowo–Gibran	96,214,691	58.6
Anies–Muhaimin	40,971,906	24.9
Ganjar–Mahfud	27,040,878	16.5

Source: Author.

The Prabowo–Gibran team was also leading in the majority of the provinces in the country, where they were only required to capture 20 out of the 38 provinces in order to win. For instance, one set of figures, as released by LSI Denny, showed the following results in the provinces (Table 11.3).

The Official Presidential and Vice Presidential Results

On March 20, 2024, just before midnight and in the presence of the Coordinating Minister for Politics, Law and Security, Hadi Tjahjanto, Minister of Internal Affairs, Tito Karnavian, and the Head of National Intelligence, Budi Gunawan, the KP Chairman, Hasyim Asy'ari, as was scheduled, announced the official results of the presidential and vice presidential elections, confirming the results from the Quick Count that started on the night of February 14, 2024. The delay in the announcement of the final results was partly due to the recounting that took place in two Papuan provinces. This would mean that once all the legal issues associated with the presidential elections are resolved, Prabowo and Gibran would be sworn in on October 20, 2024 in the parliament. The KPU final tally of the presidential and vice presidential elections was as follows (Table 11.4).

The results of the 2024 presidential and vice presidential elections were significant on a number of counts. First, the Quick-Count system very accurately predicted the final results, signaling the trustworthiness and credibility of the Quick-Count system in Indonesia. Second, the Prabowo–Gibran win in the first round was a whopping endorsement from the public with 58.59% of the votes versus the total votes given to Anies–Muhaimin and Ganjar–Mahfud at only

41.42%. Third, the Prabowo–Gibran team won in all of Indonesia's provinces except two. The defeat was only in the Aceh and West Sumatra provinces, with Prabowo–Gibran even winning by a razor margin in Jakarta where Anies was formerly governor (Table 11.5).

Furthermore, this victory stands out as the most exceptional achievement by a presidential contender at the regional level since the implementation of direct presidential elections in 2004. The analysis and editorial published by *The Jakarta Post* on March 21, 2024, titled "Mixed Results," effectively encapsulated a significant part of the implications of the Prabowo–Gibran triumph:

> But only on Wednesday could we finally see the scale and magnitude of those wins, and in the case of the presidential election, finally gauge to what extent Prabowo has upended some established practices in post-New Order electoral politics. The quick count correctly predicted that Prabowo would get 58 percent of the votes, and the official result announced by the General Election Commission (KPU) on Wednesday confirmed that. The KPU's final tally can give us details on how sweeping the victory was.
>
> Based on the KPU's final tally, Prabowo is the only candidate in the reform era presidential elections who could pull off a win in three battleground provinces; West, Central and East Java in the first round of election. (Fellow Army general Susilo Bambang Yudhoyono achieved the feat in 2004 but only in the second round). Not even President Joko "Jokowi" Widodo, arguably the most popular politician in the past two decades, could win West Java in the presidential election. In fact, Jokowi lost twice in 2014 and 2019 to none other than Prabowo himself.
>
> Prabowo could even score a win in Jakarta, the home turf of its former governor and opposition presidential candidate Anies Baswedan. In Jakarta, Prabowo gained 2.6 million votes, leading with a slim margin of about 40,000 votes. A slim margin indeed, but impressive nevertheless. As for Anies, never before in a reform era presidential election has

Table 11.5. The Indonesian 2024 Presidential and Vice-Presidential Election Votes by Provinces

Provinces	Anies-Muhaimin Votes	%	Prabowo-Gibran Votes	%	Ganjar-Mahfud Votes	%	Total Votes Total
Aceh	2,369,534	73.56	787,024	24.43	64,677	2.01	3,221,235
North Sumatra	2,339,620	29.25	4,660,408	58.26	999,528	12.49	7,999,556
West Sumatra	1,744,02	56.53	1,217,314	39.45	124,044	4.02	3,085,400
Riau	1,400,093	37.96	1,931,113	52.35	357,298	9.69	3,688,504
Jambi	532,605	24.15	1,438,952	65.23	234,251	10.62	2,205,808
South Sumatra	997,299	18.98	3,649,651	69.47	606,681	11.55	5,253,631
Bengkulu	229,681	18.10	893,499	70.42	145,570	11.47	1,268,750
Lampung	791,892	15.49	3,554,310	69.55	764,486	14.96	5,110,688
Bangka Belitung Islands	204,348	23.08	529,883	59.85	151,109	17.07	885,340
Riau Islands	370,671	32.15	641,388	55.64	140,733	12.21	1,152,792
Banten	2,451,383	34.02	4,035,052	55.99	720,275	9.99	7,206,710
Jakarta	2,653,762	41.67	2,692,011	41.67	1,115,138	17.26	6,460,911
West Java	9,099,674	31.68	16,805,854	58.50	2,820,995	9.82	28,726,523
Central Java	2,866,373	12.58	12,096,454	53.08	7,827,335	34.35	22,790,162
Yogyakarta	496,280	19.80	1,269,265	50.63	741,220	29.57	2,506,765
East Java	4,492,652	17.52	16,716,603	65.19	4,434,805	17.29	25,644,060
West Kalimantan	718,641	22.34	1,964,183	61.05	534,450	16.61	3,217,274

(Continued)

Table 11.5. (Continued)

Provinces	Anies-Muhaimin		Prabowo-Gibran		Ganjar-Mahfud		Total Votes
	Votes	%	Votes	%	Votes	%	Total
Central Kalimantan	256,811	16.98	1,097,070	72.53	158,788	10.50	1,512,669
South Kalimantan	849,948	35.16	1,407,684	58.23	159,950	6.61	2,417,582
East Kalimantan	448,046	20.09	1,542,346	69.15	240,143	10.77	2,230,535
North Kalimantan	72,065	17.67	284,209	69.71	51,451	12.62	407,725
Bali	99,233	3.70	1,454,640	54.26	1,127,134	42.04	2,681,007
West Nusa Tenggara	850,539	26.20	2,154,843	66.37	241,106	7.43	3,246,488
East Nusa Tenggara	153,446	5.27	1,798,753	61.80	958,505	32.93	2,910,968
North Sulawesi	119,103	7.30	1,229,069	75.31	283,796	17.39	1,631,968
Gorontalo	227,354	29.39	504,662	65.24	41,508	5.37	773,524
Central Sulawesi	386,743	21.50	1,251,313	69.57	160,594	8.93	1,798,650
Southeast Sulawesi	361,585	23.09	1,113,344	71.11	90,727	5.79	1,565,656
West Sulawesi	223,153	27.23	533,757	65.14	62,514	7.63	819,424
South Sulawesi	2,003,081	37.94	3,010,726	57.02	265,948	5.04	5,279,755
Maluku	228,557	21.16	665,371	61.59	186,395	17.25	1,080,323
North Maluku	200,459	26.85	454,943	60.93	91,293	12.23	746,695
Papua	67,592	10.81	378,908	60.62	178,534	28.56	625,034

West Papua	37,459	11.32	172,965	52.26	120,565	36.43	330,989
Southwest Papua	48,405	13.53	209,403	58.54	99,899	27.93	357,707
Central Papua	128,577	11.66	638,616	57.94	335,089	30.40	1,102,282
Highland Papua	284,184	21.89	838,382	64.56	175,956	13.55	1,306,740
South Papua	41,906	13.31	162,852	51.74	110,003	34.95	314,761
Overseas Voters	125,110	18.64	427,871	63.73	118,385	17.63	671,366
Total	**40,971,906**	**24.95**	**96,214,691**	**58.59**	**27,040,878**	**16.47**	**164,227,475**

Source: Compiled by author with inputs from Hasil Hitung Suara Pemilu President & Wakil Presiden RI 2024", https://pemilu2024.kpu.go.id/; "The 2024 Indonesian General Elections", *Wikipedia*; "Indonesia announces official election result in 33 provinces", *Sinar Daily*, 18 March 2024, https://www.sinardaily.my/article/216403/focus/world/indonesia-announces-official-election-result-in-33-provinces.

a runner-up only scored a meager win in two provinces, Aceh and West Sumatra. In 2019, even when President Jokowi was at the height of his political power and was on track to win a second term, Prabowo could snatch victories from the jaws of defeat in 12 provinces.

PDI-P presidential candidate Ganjar Pranowo suffered an even worse fate than Anies. Not only was he crushed by Prabowo on his home turf in Central Java, where he served as governor for two terms, he even lost Bali, the province that has perennially been the stronghold of the PDI-P. In Central Java, Ganjar, who was once touted by Jokowi himself to be his successor, could only gain 7.8 million votes, while Prabowo garnered more than 12 million. In Bali, Prabowo came out top, beating Ganjar by a margin of more than 300,000 votes.[9]

Although the Prabowo–Gibran duo achieved success in the presidential elections, Prabowo's party, despite performing admirably overall, had to share the spotlight with other well-established parties. The PDI-P achieved a hat trick by obtaining the largest number of parliamentary seats for the third time, solidifying its position as the most influential political party. It won 16.72% of the total votes. Golkar closely followed with 15.29%, while Gerindra and PKB had 13.22% and 10.62%, respectively, of the votes (see to Table 11.6).

As per Article 6A (3) of Indonesia's constitution, the winner in the presidential elections must meet three specific conditions: They must obtain a minimum of 50% of the total votes, win in at least 20 out of the 38 provinces, and receive at least 20% of the votes in all provinces. The Prabowo–Gibran alliance met these requirements, resulting in their decisive victory in the 2024 presidential elections. Although the Prabowo–Gibran coalition emerged victorious in all provinces, it faced a close contest in Jakarta and was unsuccessful in Aceh and West Sumatra. The Anies–Muhaimin alliance garnered 2.3 million votes in Aceh, whereas Prabowo–Gibran received 787,000 votes and

---

[9] "Editorial: Mixed Results", *The Jakarta Post*, March 21, 2024.

Ganjar–Mahfud obtained little over 64,000 votes. The Anies–Muhaimin ticket garnered over 1.7 million votes in West Sumatra, while Prabowo–Gibran obtained around 1.2 million votes and Ganjar–Mahfud secured about 124,000 votes. Curiously, the Ganjar–Muhaimin duo failed to secure victory in any of the provinces in Indonesia.

Eight political parties successfully surpassed the parliamentary threshold by receiving more than 4% of the votes. These parties are the Indonesian Democratic Party of Struggle (PDI-P) with 16.72% of the votes, the Golkar Party with 15.29%, the Great Indonesia Movement Party (Gerindra) with 13.22%, the National Awakening Party (PKB) with 10.62%, the National Democratic Party (Nasdem) with 9.66%, the Prosperous Justice Party (PKS) with 8.42%, the Democratic Party with 7.43%, and the National Mandate Party (PAN) with 7.24%. On the other hand, several parties failed to meet the threshold and are considered non-parliamentary political parties. These include the United Development Party (PPP) with 3.87% of the votes, the Indonesian Solidarity Party (PSI) with 2.81%, the United Indonesia Party (Perindo) with 1.29%, the Gelora Party with 0.84%, the People's Conscience Party (Hanura) with 0.72%, the Labour Party with 0.64%, the Ummat Party with 0.42%, the Crescent Star Party (PBB) with 0.32%, the Garuda Party with 0.27%, and the Nusantara Awakening Party (PKN) with 0.22% (Table 11.6).

The parliamentary representation of different political parties is crucial as it will indicate the level of support that the Prabowo–Gibran team will have in parliament after October 2024. It will also determine how the new leaders will need to collaborate with other political parties in order to secure a majority in parliament. Therefore, although Prabowo succeeded in winning the presidency, he could not rely on his popularity to help his political party achieve victory in the legislative elections. It is crucial for Prabowo to form political alliances in order to secure a majority in parliament and pass laws that align with his policies. This will require him to negotiate and make compromises with other political parties, such as the Nasdem and PKB, who supported Anies alongside the PDI-P and PKS. These parties may either be unwilling to support Prabowo or demand favorable terms in exchange for their support in parliament.

Table 11.6. Votes for Political Parties in the 2024 Indonesian Legislative Elections

Party	Votes	% of Votes	Parliamentary Seats
PDI-P	25,387,279	16.72	110
Golkar	23,208,654	15.29	102
Gerindra	20,071,708	13.22	86
PKB	16,115,655	10.62	68
Nasdem	14,660,516	9.66	69
PKS	12,781,353	8.42	53
DP	11,283,160	7.43	44
PAN	10,984,003	7.24	48
PPP	5,878,777	3.87	0
PSI	4,260,169	2.81	0
Perindo	1,955,154	1.29	0
Gelora	1,281,991	0.84	0
Hanura	1,094,588	0.72	0
Labour Party	972,910	0.64	0
Ummah Party	642,545	0.42	0
PBB	484,486	0.32	0
Garuda Party	406,883	0.27	0
PKN	326,800	0.22	0
Total	**151,796,631**	**100**	**580**

Source: Compiled by author with inputs from *Statista*, see https://www.statista.com/statistics/1450989/indonesia-national-legislative-election-result-2024/; "2024 Indonesian general election", *Wikipedia*; "Results of the national legislative election in Indonesia in March 2024, by political party".

Despite Prabowo's favorable outcome in the presidential campaign, the Gerindra Party did not experience the same success. According to the official KPU total, the party secured third place in the parliamentary election, receiving slightly over 13% of the votes. Prabowo's political party in the presidential election did not benefit from the coattail effect, which could make it difficult for him to form an effective government. He will have to form a broad coalition in the House with limited political resources. Prabowo can take comfort in the fact that the current president, who has already provided significant support during the election, will continue to assist him in the upcoming weeks and months. Prabowo could, however, face a potential legal challenge at the Constitutional Court and an investigation at the House about electoral violations. *The Jakarta Post* editorial states the following:

> Prabowo's good luck in the presidential race, however, did not rub off on the Gerindra Party, as the final KPU tally put the party in third position in the legislative election with a little over 13 percent of the votes. For the first time, the political party of the winner in the presidential election failed to capitalize on the so-called coat-tail effect, a situation that could complicate Prabowo's efforts for an effective government as he has to cobble together a grand coalition at the House with only meager political capital. The good news for Prabowo is that he still has an outgoing President who not only has helped him tremendously in the election but will continue to lend a hand in the coming weeks and months. As Prabowo deals with possible legal challenge at the Constitutional Court and an inquiry at the House on election irregularities, that is one thing that he can definitely count on.[10]

Why Did Prabowo–Gibran Win Big in the 2024 Presidential Elections?

Prabowo's remarkable victory in the presidential contest, without the necessity for a runoff, can be attributed to several causes. This is the first time such an outcome has occurred since the introduction of direct presidential elections in 2004. In the end, Prabowo–Gibran's political rivals were too feeble and unable to overcome their dominance that had developed in the six months leading up to the February election day. The Anies–Muhaimin and Ganjar–Mahfud teams, despite their personal appeals and charms, failed to

---

[10] *Ibid.*

deliver on their promise to collaborate in order to overcome the challenge posed by Prabowo–Gibran. Prabowo's success can be attributed to several factors. These include his personality and family lineage, the support of Gerindra and other parties in the coalition, the backing of the TNI, particularly respected senior generals, Prabowo's appealing programs, especially for lower-income groups, the weak opponents he and Gibran faced, the failure of Megawati and the PDI-P, possible external support for Prabowo's opponents, the broad-based support of the NU, the role of President Jokowi in supporting the Prabowo–Gibran team, the importance of the youth vote, the influence of the silent majority, and the fear factor that prompted Indonesians to support Prabowo after overseas results largely endorsed Anies. Political analysts and commentators generally agree on the factors and reasons behind the one-round victory of the Prabowo–Gibran team. However, there is a tendency to have an outsider's perspective or be influenced by a rational, Western mindset. Additionally, there are uniquely Indonesian factors that defy a simple explanation.

Prabowo, the man with a long personal and familial history

Prabowo Subianto is an exceptional figure and statesman in Indonesia. He hails from a distinctive lineage in which four consecutive generations of his family have held or currently hold positions of national leadership. The fourth generation includes Prabowo's nephew, Aryo Djojohadikusumo, who is a parliamentarian, as well as other members who occupy significant roles within Gerindra. His grandfather, Raden Mas Margono Djojohadikusumo, belonged to a noble family and was the founder and inaugural president of Bank Negara Indonesia.[11] He was born into a noble Javanese family in Banyumas, Central Java, which actively resisted the Dutch during

---

[11] See Purdey, J. (2016). "Narratives to power: the case of the Djojohadikusumo family dynasty over four generations". *South East Asia Research*, 24(3), 369–385.

the Java War. Subsequently, he received his education at Dutch schools and pursued a career as a civil servant. Amidst the Japanese Occupation, he served on the Investigating Committee for Preparatory Work for Independence.

After the proclamation of independence in August 1945, Margono was named Chairman of the Supreme Advisory Council in September, but he stepped down two months later. Subsequently, he established Bank Negara Indonesia and assumed the role of its inaugural president. In 1948, he was temporarily held by the Dutch authorities before being selected as a member of Indonesia's delegation to the Dutch–Indonesian Round Table Conference. However, he was later substituted by his son, Sumitro Djojohadikusumo. After achieving independence, Margono was selected to serve as a member of the Provisional People's Representative Council, representing the Great Indonesia Party or PARINDRA (*Partai Indonesia Raya*). Due to his son Sumitro's participation in the separatist Revolutionary Government of the Republic of Indonesia in 1958, Margono was compelled to leave the country and could only come back in 1966 after Sukarno's downfall. Margono passed away in 1978.

If Prabowo's grandfather played a significant role in the historical events of the 1940s and 1950s, then his father, Sumitro, also had a notable and distinguished reputation. Throughout his career, he established himself as a prominent economist in Indonesia, occupying many high-ranking positions in the government, including Minister of Industry and Trade, Minister of Finance, and Minister of Research, during the administrations of President Sukarno and Suharto. After completing his education and spending time in the Netherlands, he came back to his home country at the conclusion of World War II. He was then appointed to the Indonesian mission in the US, primarily with the purpose of raising funds and gaining international backing for Indonesia's fight against the Dutch. He participated in the Dutch–Indonesian Roundtable Conference and, after Indonesia gained independence, he became a member of the Natsir government representing the Socialist Party. In the 1950s, he held positions in the ministries of Wilopo and Burhanuddin Harahap. As a result of disagreements in policies with Sukarno,

Sumitro backed the Revolutionary Government of the Republic of Indonesia. After its loss, Sumitro escaped abroad but later came back when Sukarno was overthrown in 1965. He served as the Minister of Trade and subsequently as the Minister of Research during Suharto's tenure. Prabowo, the son of Sumitro, eventually married Titiek, the daughter of Suharto. Sumitro maintained significant influence in Indonesia until his demise in 2001.

Prabowo, like his grandfather and father, also made a significant impact on Indonesian history, but his influence was accompanied by some controversy. Sumitro, Prabowo's father, chose not to give him the family name Djojohadikusomo. Instead, he named him after his deceased brother, Lieutenant Soebianto Djojohadikusumo, who was a member of the Military Police. According to Prabowo, "In 1946, his uncle, Soebianto was assigned to IV, under the command of Major Daan Mogot, with the responsibility of accepting the surrender of the Japanese and disarming them in Lengkong, near Tangerang. Lieutenant Soebianto was killed with another officer named Daan Mogot, Lieutenant Soetopo, and thirty other Indonesian military cadets, including Prabowo's other uncle, military cadet Sujono, by the Japanese during that incident."[12]

Prabowo gained prominence after he joined the Indonesian Military Academy in 1970, completed his studies in 1974, and married Suharto's daughter in 1983. Prabowo, a member of the prestigious special forces unit, Kopassus, participated in several crucial military missions in East Timor and Papua. Eventually, he rose to the position of Commander of both Kopassus and Kostrad, the Strategic Reserve Command, which was previously led by Suharto, his father-in-law. After Suharto was ousted in May 1998, Prabowo was discharged from the military in August 1998, partially due to his admission of involvement in the abduction of political activists who opposed Suharto.

After being released from the military, Prabowo traveled to Jordan to engage in several commercial endeavors, working with his

---

[12] See "Peristiwa Lengkong, Gugurnya Mayor Daan Mogot". Kompas Com., November 10, 20; "*Kematian Daan Mogot dan Sejarah Pertempuran Lengkong*". tirto. id, January 25, 2019; and "Peristiwa Lengkong, Semangat Pemuda yang Tak Pernah Mati". Kompas Com., August 15, 2016.

brother Hasyim. In 2004, he began his involvement in national politics. Curiously, this has also been a customary practice, as both his grandfather and father had to depart Indonesia before coming back to their homeland. In 2004, he made an attempt to secure the leadership of Golkar, but was unsuccessful. In February 2008, Prabowo created the Gerindra Party with the help of long-standing family friends who were connected to Sumitro's network in the 1950s and early 1960s. These friends had strong ties to the Socialist Party and Masjumi. Gerindra is short for Partai Gerakan Indonesia Raya, which translates to the Great Indonesia Movement. Curiously, his grandfather, Margono, was affiliated with the Great Indonesia Party, indicating a connection to his family's history. Gerindra has positioned itself as a nationalist, right-wing, populist party in the country.

Gerindra took part in the 2008 general elections and secured 26 seats. In 2009, Prabowo served as a vice presidential candidate alongside Megawati, who ran for the presidency. Prabowo contested the presidential elections in 2014 and 2019, but was defeated by Jokowi on both occasions, despite Gerindra's significant rise as a prominent political party since 2014. In January 2023, Prabowo declared his candidature for the presidency in 2024. He then formed a ticket with Gibran as his vice presidential running mate and ultimately emerged victorious in the election. This outcome serves as a clear indication that persistence yields success in the realm of politics.

Prabowo and his political party

Gerindra was established by Prabowo's dedicated supporters on February 8, 2008. Since then, the political party has had significant growth, becoming the third-largest party in parliament in 2019.[13]

---

[13] In the 2019 general elections, Gerindra won 78 seats compared to Golkar's 85, but garnered 12.57% of the vote share compared to Golkar's 12.31%. See Putri, Z. (2019, May 21). "KPU Tetapkan Hasil Pileg 2019: PDIP Juara, Disusul Gerindra-Golkar". *Detik.com*; Syaiful, A. (2019, April 19). "Parpol Lolos ke Senayan Versi Quick Count Pileg 2019". liputan6.com.

Table 11.7. Presidential (and Vice Presidential) Elections Involving Gerindra

Year	Presidential Candidate	Vice Presidential Candidate	No. of Votes	% of Vote Share	Outcome
2009	Megawati	Prabowo	32,548,105	26.79	Lost to Bambang Yudhoyono
2014	Prabowo	Hatta Rajasa	62,576,444	46.85	Lost to Jokowi
2019	Prabowo	Sandiaga Uno	68,650,239	44.50	Lost to Jokowi

Source: Author.

Table 11.8. Legislative Elections and Gerindra's Vote Share

Year	Total Votes	Share of Votes	No. of Seats in Parliament
2008	4,642,795	4.46	26
2014	14,760,371	11.81	47
2019	17,594	12.57	78

Source: Author.

Additionally, it has consistently nominated candidates for the positions of president and vice president since 2009.

Tables 11.7 and 11.8 unequivocally illustrate the increasing political prowess and impact of Gerindra in Indonesian politics, including in presidential and legislative elections, from 2008/2009 to 2019.

Gerindra has become a significant political party due to its well-organized and influential political infrastructure, supported by ample funding and charismatic leaders. Within just 16 years of its establishment, Gerindra successfully positioned its leader, Prabowo, as the president of the country.

Prabowo and his political coalition

During the final countdown, a total of eight political parties were involved in the Prabowo–Gibran presidential campaign. The political parties that were featured on the list include Gerindra, Golkar, the Democratic Party, National Mandate Party, Crescent Star Party, Garuda Party, Indonesia's People's Wave Party, and Indonesian Solidarity Party. The PKB, a significant political party in the parliament, initially backed Prabowo's candidature for the presidency starting from August 2022. However, in September 2023, the party withdrew its support and instead aligned itself with Anies, with its leader Muhaimin Iskandar becoming Anies's running partner.

After the 2019 legislative elections, the coalition consisting of Gerindra, Golkar, Democrats, and PAN, which supported Prabowo–Gibran, had control of over 45.39% of the parliamentary seats. In comparison, the coalition supporting Anies–Muhaimin, which included Nasdem, PKB, and PKS, had 29.0% of the seats, while the coalition endorsing Ganjar–Mahfud, comprising PDI-P and PPP, had 25.56%. The Crescent Star Party, Garuda Party, Indonesia's People's Wave Party, and Indonesian Solidarity Party, which backed Prabowo–Gibran, did not have any representation in parliament, similar to the Ummah Party, which endorsed Anies and Muhaimin.

The significance of these parliamentary parties should not be underestimated, as many of them, including Gerindra, Golkar, the Democratic Party, and PAN, have deep roots among the Indonesian electorate. This factor played a crucial role in the Prabowo–Gibran team's triumph in nearly every province of Indonesia, with the exception of Jakarta and Aceh.

Prabowo and the TNI

The role and significance of the TNI in Indonesian politics have always been unquestioned, both prior to and following the downfall of the New Order in May 1998. Despite Prabowo's contentious military background, which led to his removal from the TNI due to his alleged involvement in the abduction of political activists following the downfall of the New Order regime, the support he received from the TNI, particularly from senior and esteemed military figures, was a notable factor in the 2024 presidential race in Indonesia. This support significantly contributed to Prabowo's resounding victory in a single round of voting.

Although a few retired military and police generals showed their support for the Anies–Muhaimin and Ganjar–Mahfud candidatures, with notable figures such as Andika Perkasa, the former

Commander-in-Chief of the Armed Forces, serving as the deputy of the Ganjar–Mahfud success team, and Gatot Nurmantyo, another former Commander of the Armed Forces, endorsing Anies and Muhaimin, it was truly remarkable to see a significant number of senior retired military personnel officially endorsing Prabowo. The list of senior generals supporting Prabowo included General Wiranto, Admiral Widodo AS, General Agum Gumelar, General E.E Mangindaan, General Agustadi Sasongko Purnomo, Admiral Muhammad Jurianto, Air Marshall Ida Bagus Putu Dunia, General Sutanto, General Sutarman, Marshall Imam Sufaat, General Sjafrie Syamsudin, Admiral Achmad Sucipto, General Gautama Wiranegara, Admiral Arie Soedewo, and General Musa Bangun. In addition, he was also supported by senior retired police generals, such as Yovianes Mahar, Ari Dono Sukmanto, Condro Kirono, Adnas, Boy Rafli, Moekhlas Sidik, and Muhammad Iriawan.

Although the military and security institutions claimed to be neutral in the elections, it is undeniable that the public and voters were greatly influenced by the visible support of these senior former anchors of national security for Prabowo and Gibran. This was particularly significant considering that many of them had previously been critical of Prabowo. Former two-term president Bambang Yudhoyono, who is also a former general, actively supported both Prabowo and Gibran. This significantly favored Prabowo and Gibran in the presidential contest, increasing their chances of winning.

President Jokowi's deliberate decision to surround himself with loyal generals in important posts played a critical role in securing Prabowo's win.[14] In the recent months leading up to the presidential elections, Jokowi managed to appoint military generals who were loyal to him, such as Agus Subiyanto as the Chief of the Armed Forces. Jokowi has known Agus since 2009, when Agus served as the Commander of the Surakarta Military District while Jokowi was the Mayor of Solo. Another significant military figure, who held a

---

[14] Haripin, M. and Priamarizki, A. (2023). "Jokowi consolidates influence over TNI as elections looms". *New Mandala*, 4 December.

comparable job, was Hadi Tjahjanto, the former Chief of Armed Forces. Prior to this role, he served as the Commander of the Adi Soemarno Air Base in Solo during Jokowi's tenure as Mayor of Solo. In addition to Agus and Hadi, Jokowi also had other influential generals in his tight circle, such as Mohammad Hasan, Novi Helmy Prasetyo, Tri Budi Utomo, Widi Prasetijono, and the recently appointed Chief of Police, Listyo Sigit Prabowo. This situation clearly demonstrated a strong influence, as the generals were observed to have a close relationship with Jokowi. While remaining impartial, they actively supported their defense minister, Prabowo, in his successful bid for the presidency.

The TNI's shift in attitude toward Prabowo was most clearly demonstrated by the endorsement he received from Wiranto, who had been his longstanding opponent. During a campaign address in Langowan, Minahasa, Sulawesi, on February 5, 2024, Wiranto presented several compelling justifications for his endorsement of Prabowo and highlighted Prabowo's exceptional qualifications for the presidency of Indonesia. Wiranto stated the following:

> I remember how Mr. Prabowo once said that he would dedicate his life to serving this country. He has been blessed by God and has received a mandate from this country. He has completed his life for himself; now, for the rest of his life, he wants to serve and dedicate to this country. God has given him much wealth and this nation has given him much respect. Now all that remains is that he dedicates his life to this beloved country.
>
> A president should also know the nation's challenges. Prabowo is also someone who truly understands domestic and foreign affairs – a trait that is pivotal for a leader's policymaking. Prabowo is also our defense minister. As he would often accompany President Jokowi, that is why he knows domestic and foreign affairs.
>
> Another important trait for a leader to have is that he must be someone who is able and is certain to continue building this country and the various programmes that had

been launched by President Jokowi to make Indonesia great. This is something Prabowo has committed to do.

He also must love to dance. [This is because he is] a person who understands our culture and the youth. Dancing is an important part of our culture for a long time, all-over Indonesia. This country will be dominated by young people in the future. Why? Because they are smarter and more educated, and there are opportunities to learn more. Mr. Prabowo knows that in the future young people will take over the national leadership.

[I also have experience of working with five presidents: Soeharto, Habibie, Gus Dur, Megawati, and Jokowi]. I have experience of knowing how a president works. And what makes a good president. And that person who is fit to be this country's next president is Prabowo.[15]

Therefore, Wiranto's public endorsement of Prabowo over the other two presidential candidates, Ganjar and Anies, suggested that senior generals in the TNI, like Wiranto, Bambang Yudhoyono, Agum Gumelar, and Luhut Panjaitan, believed that Prabowo possessed the necessary abilities and dedication to be the most suitable president for the country. Additionally, the reasoning assumed that Prabowo's advancing age and limited remaining lifespan may restrict his ability to serve as president for an extended period of time. However, it was deemed valuable to support and endorse him, and this significantly contributed to Prabowo's victory in the presidential elections.

Prabowo and His Programs

The Prabowo–Gibran team unveiled 17 priority programs that were successful in benefiting all Indonesians, regardless of their age or gender. Many of these programs were also a continuation of

---

[15] See "Prabowo to dedicate his life to serve the country, Wiranto says". *The Jakarta Globe*, 7 February.

initiatives and policies started by President Jokowi in 2014. These programs encompassed the following:

- Attain autonomy in the production of food, energy, and water.
- Enhancement of the state's revenue system.
- Reforms pertaining to politics, law, and bureaucracy.
- Combating and eliminating corruption.
- Poverty eradication.
- Drug prevention and elimination.
- Guarantee universal access to healthcare for all Indonesians by expanding the coverage of BPJS Health and ensuring the provision of medication to the population.
- Enhancing education, advancing research and technology, and promoting digitalization.
- Enhancing domestic defense and security capabilities while fostering favorable foreign relations.
- Enhancing gender parity and safeguarding the rights of women, children, and individuals with disabilities.
- Prioritize the conservation of the environment.
- Facilitate direct distribution of fertilizers, seeds, and pesticides to farmers.
- Guarantee the development of cost-effective, high-quality housing with proper sanitation facilities for both rural and urban populations, as well as individuals who are in need.
- The goal is to promote economic equality and enhance the growth of Micro, Small, and Medium Enterprises (MSMEs) by implementing business loan programs and supporting the development of the Indonesian Capital City (IKN) and other independent creative cities.
- Pursue the development of downstream industries and industrialization that rely on natural resources, particularly maritime resources, in order to create a wide range of employment possibilities and achieve economic fairness.
- Promote and safeguard interreligious harmony, the right to practice one's religion freely, and the establishment and upkeep of religious sites.

- Preserving arts and culture, enhancing the creative economy, and promoting athletic accomplishments.[16]

In addition to this, a fundamental element of the Prabowo–Gibran program package was to sustain President Jokowi's social welfare initiatives. This would be achieved by improving them through the implementation of "social welfare cards," "Healthy Children Card," and business credit schemes for different sectors across the nation. By implementing "food estates" managed by the Ministry of Defense and offering financial support to millennial businesses, it was thought that one could enhance food production. This would contribute to the efforts to eliminate poverty and enhance human development in the country. One notable scheme launched by the Prabowo–Gibran team is the provision of complimentary lunch and milk for school students, with a particular focus on rural communities and eventually the entire country.[17] This initiative aims to improve the nutritional intake, particularly protein, of Indonesian children attending school. This welfare provision gained significant popularity, which may be attributed to Prabowo's initiative as a Vice President candidate in 2009. He initiated a campaign known as the "white revolution" with the aim of increasing milk consumption among youngsters.

Prabowo and His Weak Political Opponents

The Prabowo–Gibran team's success in winning without a runoff was largely due to the lackluster performance of their opponents. The Anies–Muhaimin and Ganjar–Mahfud combinations were much worse in terms of overall strength and attractiveness compared to the power and appeal of the Prabowo–Gibran duo, regardless of how one evaluates them. Prabowo stood out as a prominent

---

[16] See "17 Priority Programes: Prabowo-Gibran 2024, Bersama Indonesia Maju". https://prabowogibran2.id/17-program-prioritas/.

[17] Belinda, Y. (2024). "Prabowo team says poor regions will get free meals first". *The Jakarta Post*, 20 February 2024.

presence when contrasted with Anies and Ganjar individually. Prabowo's strong family background, extensive political and military experience spanning over 30–40 years, and well-executed campaign, supported by Jokowi, guaranteed his win, making Anies and Ganjar seem less impressive in comparison. The overwhelming majority of scales were tilted in favor of Prabowo–Gibran, which greatly contributed to their victory in 36 out of the 38 provinces in Indonesia. The appeal of the personalities and programs of Anies–Muhaimin and Ganjar–Mahfud was inferior to that of Prabowo–Gibran's. Furthermore, Anies–Muhaimin and Ganjar–Mahfud were unable to effectively and publicly critique and emphasize the weaknesses of the Prabowo–Gibran duo, despite their attempts. This ultimately resulted in a near-landslide victory for Prabowo and Gibran.

The Failure of the PDI-P and Megawati in Relation to Prabowo

Undoubtedly, a significant determinant of the Prabowo–Gibran victory was the substantial shortcomings of Megawati and the PDI-P, the dominant political party in parliament throughout the 2019–2024 term. Megawati's main downfall was her failure to collaborate effectively with Jokowi, as well as her persistent public humiliation of the president. Additionally, the PDI-P's refusal to support Jokowi and their criticism of his government's programs, although being a crucial part of the Jokowi administration, further contributed to Megawati's difficulties. Ultimately, Megawati and the PDI-P displayed a great deal of arrogance, greatly offending Indonesians, particularly those from Java, when they witnessed Megawati, a former president and the daughter of the country's founding president, showing disrespect toward President Jokowi, who was widely regarded as a successful leader for all Indonesians. This had a significant impact on the PDI-P and its candidate, Ganjar, causing a surge in support for Prabowo–Gibran. They were perceived as unjustly targeted by Megawati and the PDI-P, which further boosted their popularity. Essentially, Megawati and the PDI-P were unsuccessful in terms of culture and society compared to Jokowi and his endorsed candidates, Prabowo and Gibran.

Prabowo and the open and covert external support

An often overlooked although potentially significant issue is the influence of external assistance, both direct and indirect, in support of Prabowo and Gibran. Prabowo, a prominent figure, served as the defense minister under Jokowi from 2019 until 2024. During this time, he successfully portrayed himself as a capable and accountable leader of Indonesia on the global stage. On the other hand, concerns were raised about Anies, who enjoyed the backing of extremist Islamists. Their anger was evident in 2016 when the Chinese Christian Governor of Jakarta, due to the disruptive actions of the Islamists, not only lost the gubernatorial elections but also ended up being incarcerated. The prospect of an Anies administration evoked a sense of apprehension over its implications for the non-Muslim world. Moreover, the PDI-P's strong support for China, as well as the endorsement of Prabowo–Gibran by Jokowi, could have raised concerns, particularly in the Western countries. After almost a decade of a highly pro-China approach, the endorsement of Prabowo–Gibran with Jokowi's approval offered the potential for a more equitable foreign policy in the future, which was partially shaped by Jokowi during his visit to the United States in 2023.

Initially, there were concerns that the United States, through its intelligence agencies like the CIA, might want to financially support a "color revolution" by using US front organizations such as the National Endowment for Democracy and International Republican Institute.[18] The goal would be to defeat a Jokowi–Megawati presidential candidate who was likely to continue the previous pro-China domestic economic and foreign policy. The credibility of these accusations was such that high-ranking military, police, and intelligence

---

[18] See Klarenberg, K. (2023). "Leaked: CIA front preparing colour revolution in Indonesia". Mintpressnews.com, 6 September.

officials allegedly convened with American intelligence operatives in Jakarta to caution them about the potential repercussions of engaging in this form of meddling.[19]

Prabowo and the Broad-Based NU Support

Although all the candidates in the presidential race asserted that they had the backing of the country's largest Muslim organization, Nahdatul Ulama (NU), such as Muhaimin who is the Chairman of the NU-affiliated PKB and Mahfud who claimed to have ties to the NU, ultimately NU's support predominantly went to the Prabowo–Gibran team. This was evident in their victory in Java as a whole, particularly in central and east Java, which are NU's stronghold regions. Surveys published in November 2023 have already shown that a majority of NU members are likely to endorse Prabowo–Gibran in the presidential elections.[20] Poltracking's poll results, released in November 2023, revealed that Prabowo and Gibran earned significant support from Muhamadiyah. However, the support from the NU amounted to 42.4%, while Anies–Muhaimin received 23.7% and Ganjar–Mahfud obtained 30.4%. According to a Poltracking survey conducted in early February 2024, barely one week before the polling, the Prabowo–Gibran team received 60.9% of support from NU (Nahdlatul Ulama) in East Java, which is considered the main base of NU support. In comparison, Anies–Muhaimin received 15.3% of support, while Ganjar–Mahfud received 16.3%. The study revealed a significant surge in support for Prabowo–Gibran, increasing from the previous percentage of 41.7% in January 2024. There was a minor increase in support for Anies–Muhaimin, rising to 14.6%, while there was a substantial decline in support for Ganjar–Mahfud, dropping to 37.5%.[21] According to exit

---

[19] Author's interview with senior police, military, and intelligence officers in Jakarta, October 2023 and February 2024.
[20] Wiryono, S. and Rastika, I. (2023). "Survei Poltracking:Suara NU dan Muhammadiyah Dikuasai Prabowo-Gibran", 10 November.
[21] "Poltracking: Pemilih dekat dengan NU di Jatim condong Prabowo-Gibran". February 7, 2024.

surveys conducted by Indikator Politik after the 14 February election, it was shown that 59% of NU supporters voted for the Prabowo–Gibran team. This played a crucial role in their victory in the single-round election, defeating the Anies–Muhaimin and Ganjar–Mahfud teams.[22]

A significant factor behind this was the explicit and implicit endorsement by influential NU leaders toward the Prabowo–Gibran alliance. This is due to the fact that in the NU both the institutional and cultural aspects hold equal significance, particularly when influential leaders express their endorsement for a specific candidate using the phrase "sami'na wa atho'na all-powering," which translates to "we hear and we follow/obey." Notably, prominent leaders of the Nahdlatul Ulama (NU), such as Yahya Cholil Staquf, often known as Gus Yahya, who serves as the Chairman of the PBNU, have publicly advocated for the NU to endorse President Jokowi's initiatives, including the establishment of a new capital city in Kalimantan. Gus Salam clearly instructed people to provide support for the Prabowo–Gibran squad. Similarly, Rais 'Aam Miftachul Akhyar of PBNU, explicitly advocated for endorsing the candidate with "No. 2", namely, Prabowo-Gibran, by showing his two fingers to NU members. The individuals in question are Prabowo and Gibran, both of whom are referred to as "2." Kyai Miftachul explicitly said that Anies and Muhaimin had a strong association with radical Islamists, while Ganjar and Mahfud were merely affiliated with political parties.[23] Consequently, Prabowo and Gibran were the sole converts to Islam and were, therefore, deemed worthy of NU's endorsement. It is widely thought that leaders of the Nahdlatul Ulama (NU) organization, including Gus Yahya, showed their support for Prabowo and Gibran on multiple occasions, particularly during important NU meetings in late 2023. While some NU

---

[22] "Indikator Politik: Prabowo-Gibran unggul telak pengaruh suara kalangan NU". February 21, 2024; Prasetyo, "Indikator Politik sebut suara NU berperan menangkan Prabowo-Gibran". February 21, 2012.

[23] Wahyono, E. (2024). "Gerilya Sesepuh NU Menangankan Prabowo-Gibran". news.detik.com, 10 January.

leaders, including Yenny Wahid, daughter of Gus Dur, and Mohamad Syafii Alilha, head of the PBNU, supported Ganjar and Mahfud and Nihayatul Walfiroh, NU leader from Yogyakarta, and Nasirul Mahasin from Pondok Pesantren Al-Tahfidzal Quran Narukan supported Anies and Muhaimin, a majority of NU's key leaders, such as Habib Muhammad Lutfi, Machfudhoh, Ali Mashyukur, Nusron Wahid, Muhamad Irfan Yusuf Hasyim, Arifah Choiri Fauzi, Abdul Ghofur, and Juri Ardiantoro, supported Prabowo and Gibran. This strong support largely contributed to their victory in a single round.[24]

Equally intriguing were the opinions of the general population, particularly those affiliated with the NU, about Anies and Ganjar, which resulted in NU's endorsement shifting toward Prabowo. During the author's conversation with Kyai Mohammad Hassan, a prominent NU leader, he expressed his dissatisfaction with Ganjar as the Governor of Central Java for two terms. According to Kyai Mohammad Hassan, Ganjar did very little to support the NU as an organization. Based on Kyai Hassan's perspective, Ganjar showed minimal enthusiasm and regard for the NU, the affiliated pesantrens, and the constituents, suggesting his lack of will to establish proximity with Islamic organizations. This can also be attributed to the fact that Ganjar's family, particularly his in-laws, held significant positions within the Muhammadiyah.

In regard to Anies, he maintained a certain level of separation from the NU, instead aligning himself more closely with Himpunan Mahasiswa Indonesia and displaying a preference for Arabic-Islamic organizations. The confrontation between the NU and Anies during the "Ahok Incident" in 2016 and the NU's disapproval of the 212 Movement that backed Anies and ultimately resulted in his win as Jakarta Governor were previous matters that caused most NU members to distance themselves from both Anies and Muhaimin in the presidential elections.

---

[24] *Ibid.*

Backlash and Backfire from Negative and Black Campaigns against Prabowo and Gibran

The Prabowo–Gibran team faced significant hostile and defamatory attacks, targeting their character, abilities, past experiences, and their association with President Jokowi. These advertisements were criticized for alleging interference on behalf of Prabowo. Prabowo was depicted unfavorably in numerous accounts, both from within and outside of Indonesia. *The Guardian's* story highlighted that according to critics, Prabowo's campaign received unjust advantages from the president's funding and support. Jokowi was alleged to have utilized his influence and state resources to bolster Prabowo, who had made a commitment to uphold his own policies. *The Guardian* also stated that a video titled "Dirty Vote," directed by the renowned Indonesian investigative journalist Dandy Laksono, had gained widespread attention since its release on Sunday, three days before polling day, in a bid to undermine Prabowo and Gibran. The documentary alleges that Jokowi utilized state staff and funding to support Prabowo's campaign. It went viral and has been viewed by millions of people. The aforementioned research noted that Prabowo, a former commander of special forces, is a contentious individual who is persistently accused of committing human rights violations. He was discharged from the military due to accusations of his involvement in the abduction and brutal treatment of pro-democracy activists in 1997 and 1998. Additionally, he is also accused of violating human rights in Papua and East Timor.[25]

Several Western journalists constantly criticized Prabowo, while remaining silent about the Israeli military's genocidal actions in Gaza from October 2023. An instance of this may be seen in *The Economist*, which published a report on January 11, 2024 with the headline, "The preferred candidate in Indonesia's presidential election has a scandalous history." Furthermore, *The Sydney Morning Herald*, a prominent Australian newspaper known for its

---

[25] Ratcliffe, R. (2024). "Indonesia election: President criticized over alleged interference on behalf of Prabowo". *The Guardian*, 13 February 2024.

longstanding opposition toward Indonesia, published an article on February 15 titled "'Gentler' strongman Prabowo looks to have scored first-round knockout":

> Former Indonesian general Prabowo Subianto, a two-time runner-up with a murky past as a military strongman, is poised for an outright first-round victory in his bid to lead the world's third-largest democracy ... Prabowo's past contains allegations of human rights abuses in Timor-Leste and of fomenting deadly anti-Chinese riots in 1998, charges he has long denied. But he was dismissed by the military following the fall of dictator Suharto in 1998 for his role in the abduction of democracy activists, 12 of whom remain missing. He says he has no knowledge of where they are or what happened to them. Successive US administrations nonetheless barred him from entry, until Joko brought him into his tent in 2019.[26]

Similarly, *Tempo*, a prominent weekly publication in Indonesia led by Goenawan Mohammad, launched criticism against both Jokowi and Prabowo, aligning with *The Guardian*'s stance. According to a report published prior to the February 14, 2024 elections, *Tempo* stated that "civil groups and academic figures have already voiced their concerns regarding Jokowi's misuse of authority in anticipation of the upcoming presidential election."[27] The premiere of the "Dirty Vote" film on Sunday, just before polling day, further contributed to the prevailing apprehension. Airlangga Hartarto, the Coordinating Minister for Economic Affairs, strongly criticized the *Tempo* report, particularly its mention of the "Dirty Vote," as a deliberate attempt to discredit Prabowo and Gibran Rakabuming Raka. Trade Minister Zulkifli Hasan also condemned the report, specifi-

---

[26] Hope, Z. and Rompies, K. (2024) "'Gentler' strongman Prabowo looks to have scored first-round knockout". *The Sydney Morning Herald*, 15 February.
[27] Fauziah, N. N. (2024). VP Maruf Amin says criticisms in dirty vote must be welcomed". Tempo.Co., 12 February.

cally the "Dirty Vote" aspect, as a covert effort to undermine both Prabowo and the president.[28]

The Jakarta Post, a newspaper in Indonesia known for its longstanding opposition to Prabowo, reported that a documentary alleging President Joko "Jokowi" Widodo's use of state resources to influence the presidential election in favor of his defense minister quickly gained popularity, accumulating millions of views in just one day. The English language daily, affiliated with the Center of Strategic and International Studies, reported that Jokowi faced allegations from NGOs and legal experts of manipulating eligibility requirements to appoint his eldest son as Prabowo's running mate. Additionally, it claimed that he increased welfare handouts prior to the election to indirectly support the frontrunner, who campaigned on maintaining the president's policies.[29]

Despite the widespread demand for a fair campaign and the opposition's insistence on a clean campaign, various publications, both domestic and international, attempted to discredit Prabowo and his running mate Gibran. They alleged that Prabowo benefited from President Jokowi's support, portrayed him as a dangerous individual due to his past, and argued that someone with such a background should not be selected to lead Indonesia. The presence of a predominantly liberal media during the Jokowi administration, along with the availability of technologies that facilitated the expression of opinions, significantly influenced the political landscape. Opponents of Jokowi and Prabowo aimed to prevent the Prabowo–Gibran team from winning, but their efforts backfired. The anti-Prabowo–Gibran and anti-Jokowi campaign actually ended up benefiting the Prabowo–Gibran team, leading to their victory in a single round. The Prabowo–Gibran team effectively refuted the claims made against them, dismissing them as false and malicious,

---

[28] *Ibid.*

[29] "'Dirty Vote' documentary claims Jokowi improperly backed election frontrunner". *The Jakarta Post*, 12 February 2024.

which greatly contributed to their victory and weakened the negative efforts targeting them.[30]

Prabowo and the Youth Vote

The 2024 presidential and legislative elections were significantly influenced by the substantial participation of Generation Z and Millennials, who accounted for around 56.5% of the total votes cast.[31] Based on one investigation, several reasons contributed to the resounding triumph of Prabowo and Gibran. The argument made is that the high voter turnout, particularly among the youth, ethnic Javanese, and Nahdatul Ulama, was the main factor contributing to this triumph. The argument asserts that Generation Z (Gen Z) voters exercised their voting rights, constituting approximately 23% in our sample, which is somewhat higher than the national average of 22%.[32] Contrary to popular belief, younger voters did not show enthusiasm for boycotting the voting process. The younger the voter, the higher the likelihood that they would vote for Prabowo.[33]

Although the accuracy of the data and facts has not been confirmed, one significant factor contributing to the electoral victory of the Prabowo–Gibran team was the utilization of advanced techniques, such as political micro-targeting. Artificial Intelligence was employed to precisely target voters by utilizing extensive data analysis. This enabled the customization of local campaign efforts to cater specifically to the unique demands and attributes of the youth. Political micro-targeting was employed in the 2019 Indonesian

---

[30] Baharudin, H. (2024). "Documentary on Indonesian elections 'slanderous', says Prabowo campaign team". *The Straits Times*, 12 February.
[31] See Rachman, J. (2024). "From K-pop to 'Top Gun,' Indonesia's presidential hopefuls battle it out with TikTok gimmicks". CNBC Com, 10 February. See https://www.cnbc.com/2024/02/05/indonesias-presidential-hopefuls-on-tiktok-to-woo-gen-zs-millennials.html.
[32] "Indikator Politik: Prabowo-Gibran unggul jauh di Pilpres 2024 kerana suara dari pemilih muda Jawa and NU". Kompas.Com, February 22, 2024.
[33] *Ibid.*

presidential elections, particularly by the Jokowi team.[34] However, it is believed that the technique and strategy were significantly improved in the 2024 presidential elections to favor the Prabowo–Gibran team over the other two competing teams. Analysts definitively determined, after the 2016 Jakarta gubernatorial and 2019 presidential elections, that Indonesian politics had entered the post-truth age in a significant and irreversible manner. This statement implies that appeals to emotion and personal belief have a greater impact on shaping public opinion than objective facts. Some suggest that political micro-targeting can improve political involvement and facilitate more efficient communication between political parties or movements and potential voters and supporters.[35] The Prabowo–Gibran duo is highly skilled in this tactic, which significantly appealed to young people and ultimately played a significant role in their triumph.[36]

Prabowo and the Silent Majority

Another significant aspect contributing to the resounding success of the Prabowo–Gibran alliance was the influence of the so-called "silent majority." This term refers to the diverse parts of society that were not included in numerous surveys or individuals who chose to keep their preferences undisclosed. However, on voting day, they decided to lend their support to the Prabowo–Gibran team. Their preference for the Prabowo–Gibran team was primarily driven by their admiration for the team's leadership and programs, as well as their enduring support and respect for Jokowi, who was perceived to be endorsing the Prabowo–Gibran team. It was widely assumed that

---

[34] See Masaaki, O. and Akihiro, K. "Politics of new tools in post-truth Indonesia: Big data, AI and micro-targeting". In *The Jokowi-Prabowo Election 2.0*. Singapore: Institute of Southeast Asian Studies, pp. 67–89.

[35] *Ibid.*

[36] Witzleb, N. and Paterson, M. (2021). "Micro-targeting in political campaigns: Political promise and democratic risk". In U. Kohl and J. Eisler (eds.), *Data Driven Personalisation in Markets, Politics and Law*. Cambridge University Press, 2021.

the silent majority was likewise dissatisfied, for various reasons, with the performance of Anies–Muhaimin and Ganjar–Mahfud.

Prasetya's theory suggests that during the rapid count, it became clear that the Prabowo–Gibran duo emerged as the winners of the presidential contest. Prasetya attributes this victory to the "silent majority," which refers to people who have remained quiet but have offered evidence of their support through their votes. These individuals are those who opt to remain silent in public discussions but have the potential to wield significant influence.[37] Dr. Verdy Firmantoro, a lecturer at Brawijaya University, describes the silent majority as grassroots individuals who may not have significant impact in public debates but actively participate in voting and express their wishes at polling stations. That appears to be the reason for the increase in number of votes for candidate pair 02. According to Dr. Verdy, the "silent majority" rely on social assistance and experience some kind of prosperity at lower socio-economic levels. The influential social circles have the power to sway the public's vote, which is why the vote for 02 holds significant importance.

Verdy believes that the general population is not motivated by public discussions and gaining recognition in sophisticated discussions about democracy. Instead, they prioritize their daily existence. In general, both Javanese people and Indonesians as a whole do not appreciate public criticism or humiliation of leaders like Prabowo. Instead, such actions tend to elicit sympathy for him. People view it as a younger individual hurting an elder for political gain. Furthermore, Prabowo is respected and admired for his persistence in entering the presidential competition four times and his determination to overcome challenges. The Constitutional Court's decision on the voting age of a president or vice president is considered an "elite issue" that is not relevant to the general public. Prabowo's election campaign techniques, including portraying him as a

---

[37] Prasetya Online, "Silent majority phenomenon wins the presidential candidate in quick count, this is FISIP UB academician's thoughts". February 16, 2024, see https://prasetya.ub.ac.id/en/fenomena-silent-majority-menangkan-paslon-di-quick-count-ini-kata-akademisi-fisip-ub/.

charismatic and engaging character and implementing approaches and programs that directly impacted the lives of the youth, ultimately proved to be effective in influencing votes. These opinions revealed that the "silent majority" significantly contributed to Prabowo's victory, a factor that was rather underestimated.[38]

Prabowo's Support and the Javanese Spiritual World and Endorsement

Throughout the author's three research expeditions to Indonesia, specifically in November 2023, January 2024, and after the 14th of February 2024 elections, which took place from February 24–29, 2024, individuals interviewed in Yogyakarta, Solo, and Klaten, all cities located in Central Java, consistently emphasized the significant influence of the "spiritual realm" being "in harmony" with Prabowo and Gibran. The Chinese refer to this as the "Mandate of Heaven." To individuals who are not familiar with Javanese culture, this may seem peculiar. However, the Javanese perspective is shaped by their historical background, socio-cultural structure, and their pursuit of balance and unity with the universe. This is the world that past presidents, including Sukarno, Suharto, Abdurrahman Wahid, Megawati, and Bambang Yudhoyono, and the current president, Joko Widodo, are believed to have been strongly influenced by. They try to show their connection and loyalty to this world to gain support from Javanese voters. It is also believed that their authority comes from a higher power, referred to as the "Supreme Being." This decree is known as "Wahyu" and it bears a striking resemblance to the historical Chinese concept of the Mandate of Heaven in politics.

Repeatedly, the opinions conveyed were that the Prabowo–Gibran duo were considered the favored candidates, and that compared to other teams, they were deemed the most suitable for both the individuals expressing these views and for Indonesia as a whole.

---

[38] *Ibid.*

It is anticipated that the leadership of Prabowo–Gibran will have a significant impact on guiding Indonesia's progress in the coming years and beyond. The writings and acceptance of the ideas proposed by Joyoboyo and Ronggowarsita among the Javanese people hold great significance, relevance, and enduring influence. Although it may be challenging for those unfamiliar with Javanese culture, particularly non-Javanese individuals, to comprehend these factors, it is crucial to consider the cultural aspects of power and leadership when analyzing the overwhelming victory of the Prabowo–Gibran team in February 2024. This victory was further bolstered by the strong endorsement of leaders such as Jokowi and Wiranto, who are staunch believers in the Javanese spiritual realm.[39] It is important to acknowledge the influence of these cultural dimensions, especially since the Javanese constitute the majority of voters in Indonesia.

Prabowo and the Support of Jokowi, and the President's Support Base

The primary and most influential factor contributing to the victory of the Prabowo–Gibran team was the widely acknowledged and visible support from Jokowi. This was demonstrated by Jokowi's decision to have his eldest son as Prabowo's running mate and endorsing his younger son, Kaesang, to lead the PSI, a political party that advocates for the welfare of young Indonesians. Jokowi expressed his belief that it was appropriate for Prabowo to assume leadership of the country. He acknowledged Prabowo's excellent leadership qualities and stated that Prabowo was the most suitable candidate to continue the national initiatives implemented over the past decade. Prabowo officially agreed to this proposition. Given Prabowo's impressive track record, high approval rating, and the endorsement of key national volunteers who previously supported him, it was not

---

[39] Purwadi. (2006). *Jongko Joyoboyo: Jongko Jangkah Jangkaning Jaman*. Yogyakarta: Gelombang Pasang; Purwadi. (2003). *Sosiologi Mistik R. Ng. Ronggowarsito: Membaca Sasmita Jaman Edan*. Yogyakarta, Persada; Sri Wintala Achmad. (2014). *Satria Peningit: Menyingkap Tabir Falsafah Kepimpinan Ratu Adil*. Yogyakarta, Koreksi Aksara.

a matter of whether Prabowo–Gibran would win but rather by what margin they would win in the first round.

To summarize, the elements contributing to the Prabowo–Gibran triumph can be listed as follows:

- The significance of the Indonesian National Armed Forces (TNI) and prominent senior generals, like Wiranto, Agum Gumelar, and Susilo Bambang Yudhoyono, endorsing Prabowo this time around is noteworthy.
- The significance of President Jokowi's support for the Prabowo-Gibran alliance as he is himself an accomplished leader, who enjoys popular and mass backing.
- Megawati's flaws are primarily attributed to her perceived arrogance, lack of respect toward the nation's president, and detachment from contemporary reality.
- Gerindra as a popular political party surpassed the PDI-P in terms of grassroots support, aided by other parties in the KIM coalition.
- Anies and Ganjar were perceived to have a weaker position compared to Prabowo. The public was concerned about entrusting the country's destiny to them.
- There was external support for Prabowo, specifically aimed at undermining Anies, who received backing from radical Islamists. Additionally, this support aimed to distance Prabowo from Megawati's pro-China policies and position.
- Prabowo, known for his resilience and charisma, commanded respect as a powerful leader. Despite efforts to discredit him, the anti-Prabowo narrative was unsuccessful in weakening his influence.
- The significance of Jokowi's volunteers (Projo), along with Prabowo's volunteers, including the Mawar Group, lies in the effective alliance of Golkar, PAN, Gerindra, Garuda, PSI, and PBB. This coalition enjoys robust grassroots support.
- The support provided by the NU, both structurally and culturally, is crucial, particularly in central and eastern Java. The value of the pro-NU leaders, like as Khofifah, cannot be overstated.

- An efficient media and non-media campaign, together with strategic tactics, was implemented to secure a victory for Prabowo, who was widely recognized as a seasoned, renowned, and prominent leader.
- "Geng Solo," operating covertly, weakened Ganjar's influence in central Java, particularly in Semarang, Solo Raya, and Yogyakarta.
- Ganjar and Anies employed ineffective communication methods and engaged in nasty campaigning, which ultimately had severe consequences.
- Voters' weariness in the post-COVID-19 era and their desire for stability and progress as pledged by Prabowo were important factors.
- The PDI-P's emphasis on legislative elections rather than presidential elections significantly contributed to Ganjar's defeat.
- The effective coordination and cohesive teamwork between Prabowo and Gibran were significant.
- The significance of the youth vote and Prabowo's transformation through "gemoy," a charming and affectionate persona, as well as his public dancing, were important factors.
- The silent majority played an important part.
- The significance of the "spiritual realm" in supporting Prabowo and Gibran was immense.
- Ganjar and Anies failed to recognize that Jokowi's policies, such as those aimed at fostering economic growth, political stability, and international and cultural respect, including the establishment of a new capital, were widely popular. The Prabowo–Gibran team took advantage of these policies and gained significant public support, which is not surprising.

Megawati emerged as a significant adversary, particularly as she led the opposition against a popular and populist president. With Anies having little relevance among the majority, particularly the impoverished and less educated rural population, voters were left with no option but to strongly support the Prabowo–Gibran team. This team had the endorsement of the current President, a former president, Bambang Yudhoyono, as well as crucial support of state institutions such as the military, police, and key economic ministries led by Jokowi's associates. Ultimately, the presidential elections resulted in an asymmetrical race, with the Prabowo–Gibran alliance emerging as the surprising winner. This victory established a powerful president supported by a robust coalition. The collective votes of Anies–Muhaimin and Ganjar–Mahfud were insufficient to rival the substantial public backing gained by the Prabowo–Gibran duo.

Summarizing the Prabowo–Gibran One-Round Victory

The Prabowo–Gibran one-round victory can be attributed to several elements, primarily four major ones. The Indonesian presidential election occurred on February 14, 2024. After voting ended, Quick Counts were undertaken, which revealed that Prabowo Subianto, the Defense Minister of Indonesia, was leading with almost 60% of the votes. This was significantly higher than what the pre-election opinion surveys had predicted. Anies Baswedan, the former governor of Jakarta, secured second place in the election with a vote share of 24.04%. Ganjar Pranowo, the former governor of Central Java, came in third with 16.64% of the votes. Prabowo's vote total was above the 50% level needed to secure victory in a single round, thereby preventing the need for a potential second round of voting with the candidate in the second place. On the night of February 14, Prabowo confidently declared his win, citing his significant lead and vote count over his two opponents. This claim was supported by all pollsters, even those who were biased toward Anies and Ganjar. Nevertheless, his rivals chose not to accept their loss, stating that they would wait for the final vote tallies, which was to be disclosed by the General Election Commission (KPU) on or before March 20.

The four crucial causes were Prabowo's political transformation, the selective memory of a youthful voting base, significant errors made by his political adversaries, and the pivotal position of Jokowi as the unrivaled kingmaker.

Prabowo's Political Transformation

Prabowo's success may largely be credited to his strategic transformation in order to appeal to the younger demographic and get their support. In the 2014 and 2019 elections, Prabowo presented himself as a strict and resolute military figure, which sharply contrasted with the relaxed and relatable image of his opponent at the time, Joko Widodo. Aware that the bulk of voters in the 2024 elections were from younger demographics, Prabowo chose to present himself in a more gentle and meticulously controlled manner. The campaign team strategically portrayed Prabowo, a former Special Forces Commander and Lieutenant-General, as an endearing grandfather by utilizing artificial intelligence (AI) to create a digital character that presented him as youthful and innocent on several social media platforms. Prabowo's campaign events featured films of him gyrating his hips and gesticulating with his arms, which gained popularity on TikTok. Additionally, videos of him affectionately cuddling his cat while making a love heart symbol with his hand were shared on Instagram. As a result, the term "gemoy," which refers to being attractive or lovely, became strongly linked to Prabowo on social media. Supporters even went to the extent of producing clothing goods with charming cartoon representations of him. This effort, to some extent, significantly altered public opinions of Prabowo by distancing him from his controversial history, thereby garnering extensive backing from a growing Indonesian population that is adept at using social media.

A significant portion of Prabowo's campaign also focused on enhancing the image of Prabowo as an approachable and relatable grandfather figure. This was achieved through several means, including the use of social media platforms to showcase this representation. Additionally, Prabowo's dances at the conclusion of campaign rallies further reinforced this image. In a survey conducted by Indikator in mid-January 2024, it was shown that 63% of the participants were familiar with Prabowo's gemoy nickname. In contrast, a mere 17.5% of individuals were familiar with the term "desak Anies," which refers to the dialogue initiative pursued by presidential candidate Anies Baswedan in order to engage with younger people. Prabowo's attempts to manipulate the narrative were significantly more effective than those of his rivals. In fact, the study revealed that 72% of respondents below the age of 21 expressed their support for Prabowo. This achievement was partly attributed to his substantial financial resources, which enabled him to outspend his competitors in advertising. According to Facebook's data on political commercials, between November 2, 2023 and January 30, 2024, the five most prominent Facebook accounts purchasing political ads in Indonesia collectively spent Rp 4 billion (US$254,000). Out of the total ad purchases, 65% were made by Prabowo campaign accounts or individuals affiliated with his coalition, such as Agus Harimurthi Yudhoyono. By comparison, 35% of the funding originated from Ganjar Pranowo's campaign, while Anies's campaign had minimal advertising expenditure on Facebook. Consequently, the outcome of the presidential campaign was clearly not determined by strategies for attacking opponents or solid policy proposals but rather by the ability to dominate the narratives that were accessible or attractive to the younger voting base. Both Anies and Ganjar attempted to leverage social media in their campaigns, but neither achieved the same level of success as Prabowo. Anies, for instance, aimed to add a personal element to his social media presence by creating an Instagram account only dedicated to his cats, named "Pawswedan family." On the other hand, Ganjar chose to present himself as a humble and relatable individual by traveling across the country to engage with voters.[40]

Political Amnesia of a Young Voter Base

An anticipated challenge for the Prabowo–Gibran ticket was Prabowo's controversial background. Prabowo, who was mentored

---

[40] Ratcliffe, R. and Mulyanto, R. (2024, January 9). "From military leader to 'harmless grandpa': The rebranding of Indonesia's Prabowo". *The Guardian.* https://www.theguardian.com/world/2024/jan/09/indonesia-election-prabowo-subianto-rebranding-kidnapping-accusations.

by Suharto, quickly climbed the military hierarchy, and became Indonesia's youngest general at 47 years old after marrying Suharto's daughter. Prabowo was perceived as a strong supporter of Suharto's government. While serving in Kopassus, Indonesia's special forces, Prabowo was accused of planning and executing the abduction and disappearance of 22 activists who were critical of Suharto between 1997 and 1998. To this day, 13 of these activists have not been found. Prabowo was dismissed from the military in August 1998 due to his involvement in the abduction and alleged violations of human rights; however, he was never subjected to legal proceedings.

Given that over 50% of Indonesia's eligible voters are under the age of 40, it can be inferred that they were either not yet born or too young to fully comprehend the claims of human rights abuses against Prabowo. Consequently, the attacks launched by Anies–Muhaimin and Ganjar–Mahfud against Prabowo had minimal influence. Prabowo's human rights record has primarily been the subject of discussion among his opponents, activists, scholars, and individuals with a university education. A study conducted by the Indonesian Population and Civil Registration Office in 2022 revealed that only 6.41% of Indonesia's 280 million population possess a university degree, while 35% of the people, equivalent to 95 million people, have not completed elementary school. Moreover, Indonesians have developed a growing skepticism toward the reliability of accusations of human rights abuses against Prabowo. This skepticism is partly due to a significant portion of the population not having experienced the controversial period firsthand. Additionally, Prabowo has been able to evade punishment due to the unwillingness and repeated inability of past governments to hold him accountable. Several generals who previously court-martialed and dismissed Prabowo have now joined his campaign team, including Wiranto and Agum Gumelar, who are widely respected and influential military leaders in Indonesia. This lends credibility to the belief held by many Indonesians that the accusations against Prabowo were driven by political motives. The demographic shift toward a younger voting population and the increasing perception of Prabowo's alleged human rights abuses as lacking credibility were significant factors that reduced the impact of Prabowo's controversial history on the election outcome.

The expungement of the previous accusations of human rights violations against Prabowo was a recurring motif throughout and following the election. On February 28, 2024, Jokowi awarded Prabowo the honorary rank of a four-star general based on the suggestion of General Agus Subiyanto, the Armed Forces Chief.[41] This decision was made despite Prabowo having been discharged from the military 26 years prior. Political analysts have determined that the purpose of the move was mainly to invalidate Prabowo's participation in previous human rights abuses, thereby providing legitimacy before he becomes president. This observation was further substantiated by two lines of criticism: firstly, that the conferment was redundant considering Prabowo's automatic assumption of the position of TNI Supreme Commander if elected president and, secondly, that the honorary general rank was exclusively bestowed upon active soldiers and officers, as stipulated in Indonesia's Law No.34/2004, despite the fact that non-active soldiers had also received this rank.[42] To a certain degree, this supports the argument that the honorary general award was used to enhance Prabowo's reputation and downplay the negative aspects of his past. It also helped to reinforce his image as a leader, as the same honorary title was given to Susilo Bambang Yudhoyono, the sixth president of Indonesia.

Prabowo's win can also be ascribed to his campaign team's strategic use of criticisms from other candidates to his advantage. Recognizing the Indonesian aversion to politicians engaging in personal attacks, Prabowo's campaign staff strategically reframed criticisms and attacks against him as evidence of rudeness and

---

[41] Armandhanu, D. and Haizan, R. Y. A. (2024, February 28). *Prabowo awarded four-star general rank by Jokowi, who fends off talk of a political transaction*. CNA. https://www.channelnewsasia.com/asia/indonesia-jokowi-prabowo-military-general-four-star-rank-free-lunch-politics-4156271.

[42] Rayda, N. (2024, February 16). *A controversial former general is set to become Indonesia's new president. How did Prabowo Subianto pull it off?* CNA. https://www.channelnewsasia.com/asia/indonesia-presidential-election-prabowo-subianto-4127931.

impropriety. This approach aimed to elicit sympathy, comfort, and support for Prabowo. During their election campaign, both Anies and Ganjar criticized Prabowo by scrutinizing his human rights track record, expressing concerns about his suitability for the presidency due to his frequent emotional outbursts, and alleging irregularities in various military procurement projects that occurred during his tenure as Jokowi's defense minister.

Missteps by Prabowo's Opponents

Prabowo gained support by promising to maintain Jokowi's initiatives if elected president. Similarly, Ganjar was also expected to continue most, if not all, of Jokowi's programs. Ganjar's electoral campaign, however, was noticeably less triumphant compared to Prabowo's, primarily due to substantial errors made throughout the process. Although Ganjar had been consistently leading in surveys throughout 2022 and 2023, his popularity declined as he became embroiled in a controversy related to anti-Semitism. This controversy arose due to his opposition to Israel's involvement in the FIFA Under-20 World Cup, which was scheduled to take place in Bali. The competition scheduled for May 2023 was subsequently relocated from Indonesia. Observers argued that Ganjar was only adhering to his party's position on the matter. However, the scandal led to FIFA revoking Indonesia's hosting rights, which was met with disapproval from regular Indonesians, especially younger voters in the football-enthusiastic nation.[43]

Ganjar's backing also diminished as a result of his association with the party chairwoman and former president, Megawati Sukarnoputri. There were rumors that Megawati would have the sole authority to select Ganjar's cabinet members. This raised concerns among non-PDI-P members of Jokowi's coalition, as they

---

[43] Yuniar, R. W. (2023a, March 30). *Indonesians angry, sad as Fifa pulls U20 World Cup over its Israel stance.* South China Morning Post. https://www.scmp.com/week-asia/politics/article/3215447/indonesias-jokowi-sad-football-fans-angry-fifa-pulls-u20-world-cup-over-israels-participation.

feared losing their representation in decision-making. Ganjar dismissed the allegations, but shortly thereafter, officials from coalition parties, Golkar and the National Mandate Party, were observed having a meeting with Prabowo.[44] Ganjar's lack of success in the election can be attributed, at least in part, to his inability to establish a distinct and independent identity separate from being a candidate of the PDI-P and being associated with Megawati. In contrast, Prabowo's well-established image as a strong and authoritative figure, although somewhat subdued, effectively conveyed his independence and capability to be a forceful and resolute leader in his own capacity.

Jokowi, the Kingmaker

Prabowo's achievement can also be largely credited to his depiction as "Jokowi's ally," with his campaign focused on upholding the policies of his predecessor. Prabowo consistently expressed his intention to uphold Jokowi's political and economic initiatives if he were to become president in February. This includes the continuation of the development of a new capital called Nusantara in Kalimantan, with an estimated cost of US$32 billion, as well as the restructuring of the domestic mining sector. Prabowo selected Jokowi's son, Gibran Rakabuming Raka, as his vice-presidential candidate, resulting in a substantial increase in his popularity among voters. Gibran's inclusion in Prabowo's campaign boosted Prabowo's popularity, giving him a significant lead over Anies and Ganjar.

Although Jokowi did not explicitly declare his endorsement of the Prabowo–Gibran ticket, the Indonesian media had extensively speculated about his support for the duo. This speculation intensified after Jokowi was observed meeting Prabowo and the Golkar Chair, Coordinating Minister for Economic Affairs Airlangga

---

[44] Sood, A. (2023, July 23). *Indonesia's Prabowo casts himself as 'Jokowi's man' in third bid for presidency*. South China Morning Post. https://www.scmp.com/week-asia/politics/article/3228519/indonesias-prabowo-subianto-sheds-strongman-image-he-guns-top-job-being-jokowis-man.

Hartarto, individually in January 2024. These meetings took place despite previous announcements that Jokowi would concentrate on governing in preparation for the elections. The Indonesian media had a significant role in presenting Prabowo's policies and political stance as an extension of Jokowi's. They also supported the notion that Prabowo will continue the programs that contributed to Jokowi's popularity during his presidency.[45] The selection of Gibran as Prabowo's vice presidential candidate was interpreted as Jokowi's official backing of Prabowo, leading to support from networks like Projo, a prominent group of volunteers who played a crucial role in Jokowi's election victories in 2014 and 2019.[46]

The perception of Prabowo as Jokowi's successor is supported by their close working relationship. After losing to Jokowi in the 2014 and 2019 presidential elections, Prabowo accused the government of electoral fraud in the latter, leading to violent riots in Jakarta. However, the two politicians eventually reconciled and Prabowo was appointed as the defense minister in Jokowi's cabinet. Prabowo strategically enhanced his political image by emphasizing his cooperative and amiable nature, while also highlighting his close association with Jokowi. He positioned himself as a valuable member of Jokowi's administration and portrayed himself as Jokowi's ally. This was evident through the widespread display of Jokowi–Prabowo portraits on Indonesian streets in the six to eight months leading up to the February 2024 elections. The strong collaboration between the two individuals, along with Prabowo's commitment to uphold Jokowi's policies, created the perception that Prabowo was closely aligned with Jokowi. As a result, Jokowi's image was prominently featured on unofficial campaign posters supporting the Prabowo–Gibran ticket. Jokowi's endorsement of the Prabowo–Gibran team in the struggle

---

[45] Wulan, M. K., Martiar, N. A. D., and Salam, H. (2024, January 7). *Sinyal Jokowi Dukung Prabowo Kian Kasat Mata*. kompas.id. https://www.kompas.id/baca/polhuk/2024/01/06/sinyal-jokowi-dukung-prabowo-kian-kuat.

[46] Ismail, S. (2024, February 13). *Indonesia Elections 2024: How the "Jokowi effect" has influenced the electoral landscape*. CNA. https://www.channelnewsasia.com/asia/indonesia-elections-joko-widodo-jokowi-effect-kingmaker-influence-4118726.

against the Anies–Muhaimin and Ganjar–Mahfud teams was reinforced by the emergence of his second son, Kaesang, as the leader of the PSI with his support for the Prabowo–Gibran team.

Prabowo's election success was largely influenced by the latter factor, namely, perception of a close collaboration between Prabowo and Jokowi. The Indonesian electorate, as demonstrated by Jokowi's consistently high approval ratings and personal popularity, was satisfied with how the country had been governed under Jokowi's leadership. A majority of voters were willing to support a candidate who was seen as Jokowi's successor and who would promise to carry on his policies. These portrayals were partly influenced by Prabowo's strong public commitment to follow Jokowi's path. Prabowo had pledged to continue Jokowi's policies, such as building Nusantara, a new capital city in Kalimantan. He also promised to provide free meals and milk to schoolchildren from preschool to senior high, as well as to pregnant women. Additionally, he aimed to eliminate extreme poverty within two years.

The connection between Jokowi and the Prabowo–Gibran ticket has been evident. Prabowo and Gibran also gained advantages from Jokowi's policy decisions throughout the campaign season. During the 75-day campaign period, Jokowi allocated 6.8 trillion rupiah (US$434 million) to assist farmers impacted by the El Nino weather phenomenon, despite Indonesia already being in the rainy season. Additionally, he implemented an 8% salary increase for all civil servants, resulting in a rise in his own approval ratings. This, in turn, indirectly benefited Prabowo and Gibran by leveraging Jokowi's popularity. Prabowo and Gibran have pledged to uphold Jokowi's social assistance initiatives and infrastructure projects, which were crucial factors in Jokowi's strong public support throughout his ten-year presidency. Prior to the February elections, the state had expanded its allocation of social aid. This action was widely thought to be a covert effort to bolster support for Prabowo.

These efforts worsened the challenges faced by Anies and Ganjar in controlling the narrative. Attacks on Prabowo failed for the same reason that attacks on Jokowi consistently failed. As long as the policies they supported and implemented remained popular, and the challengers struggled to present clear and convincing alternative visions, a majority of voters found these developments acceptable. Prabowo's electoral success can be largely attributed to Jokowi. This is because people perceived a connection between Prabowo and Jokowi. Despite controversies during the election, such as the Constitutional Court ruling on Jokowi's son's eligibility as a vice presidential candidate and the politicization of social assistance, Jokowi remained popular. Additionally, Jokowi continued to implement popular policies. A significant amount of Prabowo's platform and campaign was intentionally evocative of Jokowi's own campaign. This was seen in their rally where both Prabowo and Gibran wore identical blue plaid shirts, following the revelation of the Quick-Count vote.[47] Although the Prabowo–Gibran team's color is blue, Jokowi opted for checkered jerseys for his presidential campaigns in 2014 and 2019. As a result, some volunteer organizations that previously backed Jokowi and played a crucial role in his election wins now embraced Prabowo. Prabowo's electoral triumph was largely due to the shift of votes from Jokowi to Prabowo, which played a crucial role in Prabowo–Gibran's one-round victory in the election on February 14.[48]

The Final Clincher — The Javanese Way and Thinking of Supporting and Selecting a Leader

Indonesia, being a civilizational state, has had most of its historical empires centered in Java, with the exception of Srivijaya which was based in Sumatra. Consequently, Javanese political concepts, particularly those pertaining to leadership (*kepemimpinan*), play a crucial role in elucidating the reasons behind the election of a specific

---

[47] Guild, J. J. (2024, February 7). *IP24012 | How Prabowo Subianto Is Closing In on the Indonesian Presidency—RSIS*. https://www.rsis.edu.sg/rsis-publication/idss/ip24012-how-prabowo-subianto-is-closing-in-on-the-indonesian-presidency/.

[48] *Highlights: Indonesia elections 2024 results – Prabowo Subianto claims presidential victory based on early counts*. (2024, February 14). CNA. https://www.channelnewsasia.com/asia/indonesia-elections-2024-live-results-anies-baswedan-prabowo-subianto-ganjar-pranowo-4119676.

leader, even in present times. According to Javanese beliefs, in order for someone to become the national leader, such as the president (or sultan in the past), they must have the *wahyu*, which is considered to be God's mandate. Often, this position is held by a male rather than a female. However, Megawati became president by chance after Abdurrahman Wahid was impeached. As the Vice President, she assumed the presidency after Wahid lost his position. Furthermore, the leaders who have successfully attained the presidency have demonstrated in diverse ways that they possess a divine mandate. This is evident through the weapons they wield, such as the legendary or historically significant *keris*, as well as their ability to fulfill past predictions, whether through their names or the qualities they are supposed to exhibit.

Overall, there was a widespread agreement that, despite allegations of electoral fraud and manipulation, the Prabowo–Gibran duo had decisively emerged as the winners of the 2024 presidential election in a single round. According to Survei and Polling Indonesia, there were four reasons why Prabowo and Gibran triumphed over the other two candidates in October 2023: the role and support provided by President Jokowi, referred to as the "Jokowi Effect"; the blunders made by Prabowo's opponents such as Ganjar opposing the Under-20 FIFA World Cup in Indonesia and questions about Ganjar's independence and being a proxy of Megawati; programs championed by Prabowo, including the "food estate," which were actually Jokowi's programs that were popular but were criticized by both Ganjar and Anies, with even the PDI-P, Jokowi's political party, criticizing it; and the blunder made by the Hanura chief that for someone to be a president, he must have a wife, directly criticizing Prabowo who is divorced but still close to his former wife, Titiek, Suharto's daughter.[49] These four variables persisted and had a significant impact on Prabowo's triumph in the elections, as well as on Ganjar and Anies.

During the author's field trip to observe the outcome of the presidential elections in February 2024, it was generally concluded

---

[49] See "Empat factor Prabowo kalahkan Ganjar dan Anies, ini alasnya". *AntaraYogya*, October 13, 2023.

that the superior candidate and team, namely, Prabowo and Gibran, emerged victorious in the political competition. Those who were defeated are now making various excuses to justify their loss and attributing Prabowo and Gibran's victory to irregularities, unfairness, and the advantage of Jokowi's support. A prominent Islamic scholar, Kyai Mohammad Hassan, from a renowned Islamic boarding school, Pondok Pesantren Ar-Risalah, in Mlangi, Yogyakarta, central Java, eloquently conveyed this sentiment.

According to Kyai Hassan, the grounds for the success of the Prabowo–Gibran team were obviously apparent. Initially, the general populace expressed their anger and dissatisfaction toward democracy campaigners, as they perceived them to be neglecting or failing to promote the welfare of the common population. In his perspective, the democracy advocates primarily consisted of individuals from different privileged groups and affluent Indonesians, whose interests and worries did not coincide with those of a majority of citizens who were facing financial difficulties. After the downfall of Suharto's New Order, although democracy advocates had a strong presence on various platforms such as the Internet and media, their concerns and expressed issues did not align with the economic objectives of the general populace. These average Indonesians believed that Suharto and, more recently, Jokowi were the best leaders for promoting their welfare. However, these activists who advocate for democracy have been preoccupied with criticizing Jokowi's governance, despite the fact that their main concerns align with the basic issues that Jokowi and his cabinet are addressing. Essentially, the democracy activists' concerns did not resonate with them, and these individuals, frequently without expressing their support, endorsed Jokowi and his selection of the future president, specifically, Prabowo. While democracy may have seemed appealing in theory, the primary concern for the common citizens was the fulfilment of their basic necessities. This was the main focus for Prabowo and his team, rather than the Ganjar–Mahfud and Anies–Muhaimin teams.[50]

---

[50] Author's interview with Kyai Mohammad Hassan at Pondok Pesantren Ar-Risalah, in Mlangi, Yogyakarta, central Java, February 29, 2024.

Furthermore, Kyai Hassan argued one should not overlook the significance of the "silent majority," as elucidated by Dr. Verdy Firmantoro. This was also in alignment with the disposition of the Javanese majority, who possess a certain level of knowledge, particularly regarding local matters that directly affect their livelihoods. These issues, which were often disregarded by the so-called national democracy elites, are of great significance to them. They are aware of who advocates for their interests and choose to remain silent until the opportune moment arises. In this instance, their voices were expressed through the act of voting, which largely accounts for Prabowo's overwhelming triumph in the election. The Javanese people are highly sensitive individuals. They closely observed the national presidential debates, as well as the numerous talk shows and reality shows that took place over the past 18 months, starting from late 2022. During these events, President Jokowi and, more significantly, Prabowo, were subjected to ridicule and insults on various matters. These included their alleged connections to the Suharto administration, particularly through marriage, accusations of human rights violations, and concerns about their advanced age and poor health. Although the general public remained silent, they sympathized with and supported Prabowo, while criticizing those who raised these issues, such as the Anies–Muhaimin and Ganjar–Mahfud teams.

The majority of people who did not express their opinions publicly were also displeased with the way the political elites in a democratic system, including presidential candidates like Ganjar and Anies, who were younger and less experienced in politics, attempted to mock and weaken Prabowo in order to gain political advantage. However, this strategy ultimately had a negative effect, as they were perceived as lacking in civility and manners. Ganjar and Anies, who previously supported many of Jokowi's programs and initiatives, chose to oppose them during the presidential debates, which gave the impression of insincerity and untrustworthiness. Significantly, the general population expressed support and satisfaction with the diverse projects implemented by Jokowi, which Prabowo had pledged to uphold during his tenure. Prabowo's decision not to respond by undermining his political opponents garnered significant admiration from the general population, showcasing his superior qualities as an individual, politician, and leader.

Furthermore, the common people were also perceiving the presidential competition through the lens of their own perspective and in the context of the Javanese wayang, a traditional shadow play. In this cultural tradition, although the actors hold significance, the puppet master, known as the dalang, holds even greater importance. In this scenario, the common Javanese people were observing not just Prabowo, Ganjar, and Anies but also the leaders supporting them, which significantly influenced their voting decisions. Among the Javanese population, Megawati was the puppet master behind Ganjar, Surya Paloh was the puppet master behind Anies, and Jokowi, Wiranto, Bambang Yudhoyono, Agum Gumelar, and several other influential politicians were the puppet masters behind Prabowo. Prabowo emerged as the winner of the *dalang* contest, largely because of the negative influence generated by Megawati and, to some extent, Surya Paloh over the past few years. Their opposition to Jokowi played a significant role in this. However, the public's approval of Jokowi remained very high until the presidential elections in February 2024. From this standpoint, the common people, in general, perceived Prabowo as the leader who would advocate for their interests and would carry on the legacies of Suharto and Jokowi. Therefore, if Suharto and Jokowi were considered their heroes, Prabowo was seen as a continuation of this tradition that would bring advantages to ordinary Indonesians, unlike the other two contenders for the presidency. The Prabowo–Gibran sweeping victories in West, Central, and East Java can be attributed, in part, to the demographic realities. The educated urban population, who were out of touch with the problems and challenges faced by the rural majority, had a significant role in this outcome. Simultaneously, there was apprehension that Ganjar was merely a surrogate and subordinate of Megawati, while Anies was solely proficient in verbal communication and lacked substance.

Kyai Hassan also argued that the most important Islamic mass organization, the Nahdatul Ulama, backed Prabowo as its members felt that its future was better assured under Prabowo than the other two candidates, with Ganjar seen as more aligned to the Muhammadiyah and Anies, of Arabic descent, least associated with the NU and parading more as a member of the HMI, the educated modernist Muslim intellectuals. As the two-term governor of Central Java, Ganjar was said to have done very little for and generally neglected the NU, in part due to his familial and extended family relations with the Muhammadiyah, while Anies was very remote from both the Islamic mass groups. Linked to this was also the split and distance between the student activists and urban activities that were not connected with a majority of Indonesians, especially the rural population.

Kyai Hassan asserted that the Javanese tradition and belief system made a clear difference in assuring the success of the Prabowo–Gibran team. This had to do with the notion that Prabowo and Gibran had been given the mandate to reign by the "Almighty" and that the Prabowo–Gibran combo had secured the "wahyu" to rule Indonesia. This is a belief system that may astound non-Javanese and non-Indonesians; however, the belief is strongly held in Java. According to Kyai Hassan, the manner in which the Prabowo–Gibran team conducted their campaign, behaved in what is said to be the "proper way" (*toto kromo*), and most importantly secured the backing of powerful individuals who are believed to have different degrees and levels of "*wahyus*" such as Jokowi and Wiranto swung the public in favor of a clear victory for the Prabowo–Gibran team. According to Kyai Hassan, the Javanese believe that the "wahyu" may be given to an individual in numerous ways, frequently through an heirloom, usually a keris, and this can lead an individual to be seen and acknowledged as a national leader, which was very much the case with Prabowo. According to Kyai Hassan, whether outsiders and non-Javanese believe it or not is unimportant since this is what the majority of Javanese and even Indonesians have come to accept as a political fact of leadership in the country. According to Kyai Hassan, Wiranto is linked by family ties to the "*Mankunegara Legion*," founded by the French under Napoleon Bonaparte, through his late uncle Troenosoeroko. This military force excelled in battle but also believed in "Javanism," leading to speculations that Wiranto undoubtedly was the owner of a heritage or heirlooms from his uncle, thereby explaining his greatness as a political and military leader in Indonesia, notably as a political strategist.[51] If Wiranto's *kerises* or heirlooms are tied to the Mangkunegara era, similarly, Jokowi's heirlooms are also associated with the region, especially Astana Mangadeg, the historical burial grounds of Solo monarchs such as Amangkurat I. As Jokowi comes from Solo and was its mayor two times, there is a strong conviction that he has gained from the spiritual realm which largely explains his political success all these years.[52]

Finally, Kyai Hassan said that most moderate Muslims, especially those connected with the NU, perceived the campaign in a strange manner with Prabowo seen as a "safe bet" compared to the other two presidential aspirants. Not only was Megawati perceived as proud and out of touch with modern-day realities but Ganjar's election team was also seen as being weak, fractured, and unable to reach out to the voters due to its lack of information technology capabilities. While Anies's team had significant information technology capabilities, it suffered from a fatal flaw, namely, of being linked with Islamist extremism and terrorism, as many of the extreme groups were considered to be supporting or even controlling Anies and his political campaign. This not only featured the PKS but also parties affiliated to the 212 Movement that installed Anies in office as governor against the challenge by the then ethnic Chinese Governor Basuki Tjaha Purnama or Ahok. Ahok was accused of blasphemy against Islam. The 212 Movement was renamed *Persaudaran Alumni 212* and comprised right-wing groups espousing Indonesia as an Islamic State. The new leader of PA 212 is Ahmad Shabri Lubis, who was

---

[51] *Ibid.*; also see Chris, A. and Nugroho, F. (2023). "Wiranto & Legiun Mangkunegaran, Pasukan Elite Ala Napoleon Bonaparte". *Intisari Online*, 10 April. See https://intisari.grid.id/read/033738027/wiranto-legiun-mangkunegaran-pasukan-elite-ala-napoleon-bonaparte?page=all.

[52] Interview with Erwin Endaryanta, a historical and cultural specialist from Yogyakarta, February 26, 2024, Yogyakarta.

appointed in January 2024, replacing Abdul Qohar.[53] These groups included the Salafist modernist network led by Bachtiar Nasir, conservative traditional groups such as the FPI led by Habib Rizieq, Hizbut Tahrir, and Wahdah Islamiyah. Radical groups such as *Majelis Mujahidin*, the successor of *Majelis Mujahidin* Indonesia, were also part of the group, which in the past, included leaders such as Abu Bakar Bashir and Abu Rushydan, emirs of the terrorist group Jemaah Islamiyyah. During the 2024 presidential election, Abu Bakar Bashyir supported Anies, as did Habib Rizieq, the leader of the FPI.

According to Kyai Hassan, what was interesting in the 2024 presidential race was the fact that while publicly there was often the narrative that the Anies–Muhaimin and Ganjar–Mahfud teams were cooperating to defeat the Prabowo–Gibran team, in reality there was often the concept of a "greater enemy" with the Anies–Muhaimin team seen as a greater danger. This led to the rise of a new phenomenon that was often not covered by the conventional media. This was the view that the Anies–Muhaimin team was a far greater danger to Indonesia in the medium to long run, and hence had to be defeated; Islamist radicalism and terrorism were viewed as a greater danger and Anies was seen as the "new Morsi," referring to the manner in which the Islamic Brotherhood captured the elections in Egypt. According to Kyai Hassan, this led to the birth of an intriguing view that "*daripada pelihara macan, lebih baik macan ompong.*"[54] Translated into English, it meant, "instead of raising or supporting a tiger, it is better to have a toothless tiger," with tiger alluding to Anies and "toothless tiger" referring to Prabowo, due to his old age. The belief was that Anies was a lot more dangerous than Prabowo.

---

[53] See Mawardi, I. (2024). "Ahmad Shabri Lubis Jadi Ketum Barau PAP 212". *DetikNews*, 11 February.

Author's interview with Kyai Mohammad Hassan at Pondok Pesantren Ar-Risalah, in Mlangi, Yogyakarta, central Java, February 29, 2024.

[54] Author's interview with Kyai Mohammad Hassan at Pondok Pesantren Ar-Risalah, in Mlangi, Yogyakarta, central Java, February 29, 2024. This view was confirmed in an interview with Erwin Endaryanta, a historical and cultural specialist from Yogyakarta, February 26, 2024, Yogyakarta.

Conclusion

By way of conclusion, an article by Ihsan Yilmaz, Hassan Bachtiar, Chloe Smith, and Kainat Shakil perfectly described the reasons and elements behind the Prabowo–Gibran triumph in the 2024 presidential elections in Indonesia. The article states the following: "Over the course of the previous decade alone, Prabowo has undergone substantial transformations in ideological views, rhetorical appeals, and electoral techniques. He has changed from an ultra-nationalist, chauvinist, and Islamist populist into a technocratic figure with a more affable attitude, carefully forging and altering coalitions in his efforts to guarantee electoral success."[55]

The writers highlighted that Prabowo "is a highly controversial former military officer with a past tarnished by a legacy of human rights abuses, the son-in-law of former dictator Suharto, and a prominent political actor and Presidential candidate over the past decade. Since 2009, Prabowo has constantly engaged in general elections, competing in consecutive races during each electoral cycle and ultimately earning victory in the most recent elections. Throughout the years, his image, attitudes, and storylines have experienced remarkable alterations, exhibiting a fascinating political fluidity and adaptivity."[56]

Moreover, "In past election campaigns, Prabowo was noted for exhibiting ultra-nationalist, strongly chauvinist, and Islamist populist characteristics. However, in the latest election, Prabowo has evolved, reemerging as a decidedly technocratic figure while still keeping some classic populist impulses. This alteration in his political character reflects fundamental strategic considerations, meaning to further his pursuit for power. Specifically, Prabowo now presents himself as the guardian of the people's *volonté générale* (general will) and adopts popular communication tactics that

---

[55] Yilmaz, I., Bachtiar, H., Smith, C., and Shakil, K. (2024). "The changing populist performances of Prabowo Subianto: Indonesia's incoming president". *European Center for Populism Studies*, 9 March.
[56] *Ibid.*

effectively involve Indonesia's youth. It has also been highlighted that his campaigning entailed simplifying complicated political problems and their remedies — such as his focus on a scheme for free meals and milk to fight hunger and food scarcity – a policy that has been criticized for being unrealistic."[57] "Prabowo's campaigning in 2024 also marked a notable departure from the more hostile parts of populism. Particularly notable was his renunciation of chauvinistic propaganda, which had earlier stoked religious-based conflicts, incited wrath against minorities, focused blame onto foreign powers, and scapegoated oligarchic elites to appeal to voters."[58]

The writers highlighted that "In this campaign, Prabowo refrained from emphasizing ideological issues that deepen social polarization and steered clear of his past narratives and rhetoric against Western neo-liberalism and the perceived greed of Chinese corporations. Additionally, he separated himself from religious right-wing groups, especially the civilizational populist Defenders Front of Islam (FPI), with whom he had previously allied himself in varied capacities during the 2019 election. Prabowo and his political campaign team also exploited internet culture and technologies to both appeal to Indonesia's youth and shake off his formerly violent and militant character. This entailed several techniques like rebranding to reflect a more modern and approachable attitude, participation through social media, employing platforms popular among youth, and providing compelling content."[59]

At the same time, "Prabowo has been newly portrayed as an adorable, friendly grandpa (*gemoy*). This rebranding exercise has been particularly effective among online and youth communities – Prabowo is represented in digital spaces with a cartoon photo generated by Artificial Intelligence (AI), and has become known for dancing the Korean Oppa style to disco music and the super hit song "*Oke Gas*" by the famous rapper, Richard Jersey. More than half of Indonesia's 204 million voters are millennials or younger and

---

[57] *Ibid.*
[58] *Ibid.*
[59] *Ibid.*

Prabowo's usage of social media has proved extremely popular amongst these people (*Economist*, 2024). This is a strong strategic move and displays a knowledge of the type of leader Indonesian millennials are seeking for. While numerous definitions challenge what is the 'ideal' or 'the hegemon' masculinity, there is a clear evidence that amongst Indonesian millennials and Gen-Zs, the traditional ideal of a 'strongman,' as Prabowo was before and generally regarded as being, does not garner their support. Prabowo's sensitivity to this development drove him to adjust his masculinity to become more acceptable in society. Being a dancing, friendly older man has garnered him the acceptance of young — unlike the extremely composed military man or conservative religious figure he has occupied in earlier election campaigns."[60]

In the end, through a robust system of political democracy, a peaceful election was conducted in Indonesia, with Prabowo being the fourth time lucky candidate, losing once as a vice presidential candidate and then after losing twice as a presidential candidate. On the third try as a presidential candidate, he eventually won the highest political office in Indonesia, the largest Muslim state and democracy and the third-largest democracy in the world.

---

[60] *Ibid.*

CHAPTER 12

WHAT THE 2024 INDONESIAN PRESIDENTIAL ELECTION MEANS FOR INDONESIA, THE REGION, AND THE WIDER WORLD?

Introduction

The 2024 election challenged and overcame many long-standing traditions and beliefs, both within Indonesia and internationally. An esteemed 72-year-old former general, renowned for his resilience and belonging to a prominent political dynasty, was elected as the leader of the largest state in Southeast Asia and the largest Muslim state globally. The controversies and cynicism surrounding Muslim-majority states and democracy in the Western world have been dispelled by Indonesia, which is regarded as a role model for practicing democracy. This is particularly significant given the current political, economic, and social crises faced by Western democracies. Indonesia's democratic practices involve the active participation of its citizens in electing leaders at all levels of government. The ramifications of the 2024 presidential elections in Indonesia are evident on a national, regional, and worldwide scale.

Implications for Indonesia

Whole-of-society support and endorsement

The magnitude of the Prabowo–Gibran triumph is truly remarkable. Litbang (research and development department) Kompas recently published intriguing statistics, which revealed that the Prabowo–Gibran duo achieved almost complete dominance over the voting population. The Prabowo–Gibran team received the support of 53.6% of males and 55.1% of females. The Prabowo–Gibran team received votes from 65.9% of individuals aged 17–25, 59.6% of individuals aged 26–33, and 54.1% of individuals aged 34–41. Regarding educational attainment, 55.6% of individuals with primary education and 57.4% of individuals with secondary education supported the Prabowo–Gibran team. Regarding social status, 55.9% of individuals in the lower and lower-middle class cast their votes for the Prabowo–Gibran combo.[1]

Operational democracy

Indonesia has successfully transitioned from an authoritarian political framework to a functioning democracy after the breakdown of the New Framework in May 1998. This was not only the sixth direct presidential election in Indonesia but it was also conducted simultaneously with the legislative elections, making it the largest single-day election in modern history.

Although many Western critics express skepticism about the viability of democracy in predominantly Muslim countries, Indonesia, as the largest Muslim nation, successfully conducted its election in a peaceful manner. Although it is customary for the losers to always

---

[1] "Prabowo-Gibran Unggul di Semua Gugus Pulau". Kompas.id, February 14, 2024; also see "2024 Indonesian general election", *Wikipedia*; "Indonesia election commission confirms Prabowo Subianto as new president". *Al Jazeera*, March 20, 2024, see https://www.aljazeera.com/news/2024/3/20/indonesia-election-commission-confirms-prabowo-subianto-wins-presidency.

complain about fraud and deceit, the winners, namely, the president and vice president, secured a resounding victory in the elections.

Furthermore, it indicated the development of a more advanced democracy, as well as a change in the political landscape with the younger generations, specifically Generation Z and Millennials, making up approximately 57% of the voting population. Furthermore, this indicated the emergence of a novel political custom, with Indonesia at the forefront as a newly established democratic system, spearheading the process of political transformation and reform through the implementation of impartial and unrestricted elections. Despite facing legal difficulties about charges of fraud and manipulation, these issues were being addressed by legal means rather than resorting to violent street politics.

Disputing the outcome

Curiously, it has become customary for the defeated parties to dispute the election results, claiming that the winners achieved victory by deceit and irregularities. This indicates that there is still a significant lack of political maturity, as the losers struggle to come to terms with the conclusion of the election. In both the 2014 and 2019 presidential elections, Prabowo Subianto said that Jokowi had secured victory by fraudulent means. During the 2014 presidential elections, Prabowo alleged that Jokowi secured victory through extensive fraudulent activities that were well-organized and methodical. He asserted that he and his running mate, Hatta, retained the prerogative to refuse the election outcomes on the grounds of their unconstitutionality.[2] In the 2019 presidential elections, Jokowi again emerged as the winner, while Prabowo again alleged extensive electoral fraud and asserted his victory. Both in the 2014 and 2019 instances, the KPU officially recognized Jokowi as the victor and the Constitutional Court dismissed any objections raised against the outcomes. After Prabowo contested Jokowi's victory in 2019,

---

[2] Bachelard, M. (2014). "Prabowo Subianto 'withdraws' from Indonesian presidential election on day vote was to be declared". *The Sydney Morning Herald*, 22 July.

Wiranto, who was the Security Affairs Minister at the time, dismissed the accusations by asserting that the KPU is an autonomous body whose members are selected by the House of Representatives. Wiranto contended that the government never considered intervening with the KPU and Bawaslu, nor did they engage in a deliberate, extensive, and organized plot to support a specific candidate.[3] He called the claims highly biased, untrue, defamatory, and unfounded, with their sole purpose being to undermine the legitimacy of the government, the KPU, and the Bawaslu as election organizers.[4]

Similarly, after the Prabowo–Gibran team's significant advantage in the Quick Count on February 14, 2024, the Anies–Muhaimin and Ganjar–Mahfud teams alleged that their defeat was a result of extensive and organized fraudulent activities. The former chief justice of the Constitutional Court, Hamdan Zoelva, who is currently a member of the Anies election team, asserted that there were compelling signs of planned, systematic, and extensive violations in the presidential election.[5] Lawyer Mulya Lubis, who represents the Ganjar-Mahfud team, contended that election irregularities took place before, during, and after the polls. However, he acknowledged that it is impossible to provide concrete evidence of these irregularities. Therefore, he argued that when discussing election disputes, it is important to consider not only the election outcome but also the pre-election process.[6]

Anies and Muhaimin have taken legal action by filing a court challenge. They argue that Gibran's candidature as a vice president was unfair because of the Constitutional Court's last-minute ruling about eligibility standards. Anies's legal representatives formally requested the Constitutional Court to mandate a repeat of the presidential election after excluding the President's son, Gibran, from

---

[3] "Indonesian elections: Prabowo alleges fraud, says he will reject official vote tally". *The Straits Times*, May 15, 2019.

[4] Firdaus, A., "Indonesian Minister: Allegations of Systematic Poll Fraud 'Baseless'". *Benar News*, April 24, 2019.

[5] Karmini, N. (2024). "Indonesian presidential rivals plan to contest official election results with allegations fraud". *Associated Press*, 14 March.

[6] *Ibid.*

participating in the campaign. Anies's legal team argued that excluding Gibran would diminish Jokowi's interference in the election. The team supporting Anies also asserted that the extensive distribution of social aid, including rice, fertilizer, and cash disbursements, in strategically important electoral regions had significantly impacted the election outcome, resulting in a resounding victory for Prabowo and Gibran.[7]

Despite the fact that both the Anies–Muhaimin and Ganjar–Mahfud teams were disputing the election outcomes, a noteworthy survey conducted by pollster Lingkaran Survei Indonesia Denny JA revealed that a majority of people who supported the unsuccessful presidential candidates accepted the election results and expressed a desire to move forward. LSI said that 89.9% of the participants acknowledged the final outcomes that confirmed Prabowo and Gibran as president and vice president, respectively. LSI reported that 90.3% of Ganjar's voters accepted the election outcome, 79.9% of Anies's supporters agreed with it, 93.8% of Prabowo's fans accepted it.[8] Additionally, it was disclosed that questioning the outcomes was perceived as an "impolite rejection of acknowledging loss." The conclusion was that while it is both lawful and constitutional to contest the election results, it is advised to refrain from using the Constitutional Court as a way to blame the winning candidates or their campaign teams for one's own defeat.[9]

Despite occasional protests against the election results, overall tranquilly has been maintained in major cities of the country. This might be attributed to the observance of the fasting month, during which large-scale rallies are deemed inappropriate. Significant protests are anticipated in the country following the conclusion of the Ramadhan month. Not only will the two main opposition parties, PDI-P and PKS, express their discontent with the election results but

---

[7] See "Anies files court challenge to election result, Ganjar to follow soon". *The Jakarta Post*, March 21, 2024.
[8] See Muhammad, D. (2024). "Anies and Ganjar supporters embrace 2024 election outcome: LSI Denny JA". *The Jakarta Globe*, 27 March.
[9] *Ibid.*

supporters of the Anies–Muhaimin and Ganjar–Mahfud teams, including members of the labor movement and potentially Islamic parties, are also expected to organize demonstrations against the victory of Prabowo–Gibran.

Continuation of Jokowi's policies

The presidential election revolved around the continuation of Jokowi's policies, including the establishment of a new capital in Kalimantan, the continuation of infrastructure projects, the promotion of economic growth through local raw material manufacturing, the efforts to build peace and confidence in Papua, and the positioning of Indonesia as a respected Middle Power on the global stage, particularly in relation to major powers like China and the United States. Regardless of whether the incoming government is considered Jokowi 2.0 or Suharto 2.0, it will exhibit a significant level of continuity. Prabowo positioned himself as the candidate who would maintain the existing political, economic, and international policies of Jokowi during his election campaign. In acknowledgment of Prabowo's dedication to maintaining political stability, on February 28, 2024, just two weeks after winning the elections in the Quick Count, Jokowi elevated the three-star general Prabowo to the honorary status of a "four-star" general.

Shift toward more socialist policies at home

Ideologically, under the Prabowo leadership, there may be a shift toward a more socialist approach in domestic issues, such as providing free food and milk for children. While the previous two administrations led by Jokowi were recognized for their efforts in providing public services in education and health, it is evident that the upcoming administration under Prabowo is anticipated to enhance these services through the implementation of new policies that prioritize social well-being in areas such as education, health, and overall societal welfare. Prabowo has been advocating for the "white revolution," which aims to ensure that Indonesian youngsters receive fresh milk on a daily basis. Since 2017, he has been advocating for the implementation of this initiative. Once again, in preparation for the 2024 election campaign, the program grew to include a complimentary breakfast. The primary objective was to promote the physical and intellectual development of children through proper nutrition. Prabowo also prioritizes the development of a robust agricultural industry in Indonesia.[10]

Cabinet formation

An important part of the Prabowo government's trajectory is the makeup of his cabinet. Historically, successful presidents have established cabinets comprising members of coalition parties that backed the winning candidate, specifically Gerindra, Golkar, PAN, Democratic Party, PBB, Gelora Party, Garuda Party, and the Indonesian Solidarity Party. In the present case, it is anticipated that these coalition members will be compensated in some manner. Another cohort of individuals anticipated to join the cabinet are accomplished and competent professionals and specialists to head specialized ministries such as the Ministry of Finance and Ministry of Trade. Ultimately, it is anticipated that supporters of both Prabowo and Jokowi–Gibran would also be included as members of the upcoming cabinet.

One important topic that may arise during the cabinet formation is if Prabowo will approach potential "opposition" parties such as the PDI-P, PKS, and the historical Islamic party, PPP, with the offer of cabinet positions in order to share political power, similar to the time when Jokowi proposed the role of Minister of Defense to Prabowo. It is uncertain whether the leaders of the PDI-P, PKS, and PPP would agree to the proposition of establishing a collaborative and nationally unified cabinet.

---

[10] See Moestafa, B. and Chatterjee, N. (2014). "Jakarta governor to run for Indonesia president in July election". Bloomberg.Com, 24 March; Toriq, A. (2017). "Begini Penjelasan soal Gerakan 'Revolusi Putih' Prabowo". *DetikNews*, 26 October; "Prabowo-Gibran to create new ministry to manage free food program". *The Indonesian Business Post*, February 22, 2024.

Is there a need for political opposition?

Since the rapid-count results, which were later confirmed by the Real Count figures, proved the Prabowo–Gibran team's victory in mid-February, there has been a continuous debate regarding the necessity for political opposition during the Prabowo administration.[11] The question at hand pertains to the expectation that Prabowo will assume a leadership role characterized by strong and authoritative governance. In order to uphold democratic principles and provide a system of checks and balances, it is deemed necessary to have a capable opposition that can effectively scrutinize and counterbalance a powerful administration. Although the PDI-P and PKB, supported the losing presidential candidates Ganjar and Mahfud, and the Nasdem, PKB, and PKS backed Anies and Muhaimin, it is anticipated that all parties except the PDI-P and PKB will likely be assimilated into the government by Prabowo.[12] The Secretary-General of the PDI-P, Hasto Kristiyanto, contended that the PDI-P has robust qualifications to serve as a deserving opposition political party under the forthcoming Prabowo–Gibran administration. This is partially attributed to its expertise as a successful opposition from 2004 to 2014, aimed at enhancing the caliber of democracy, and its sense of obligation to safeguard the welfare of the people. However, the PDI-P has expressed its intention to wait for the official results before making a decision regarding its position in parliament.

The political parties associated with Prabowo managed to secure approximately 42–43% of the overall parliamentary influence. As a result, political leaders aligned with Prabowo have expressed their intention to be receptive to other political parties. Therefore, the objective would be to extend an invitation to all political parties, including the PDI-P and PKS, to participate in the government.

---

[11] Idrus, P. G. and Latif, N. (2024). "Prabowo presidency may face a hostile, opposition-controlled parliament, analysts say", and "Who can stand being in the opposition when Prabowo is president?" *Benar News*, 16 February.
[12] *Ibid.*

This strategy, known as "*sapu bersih semua competitor dirangkul*" or creating a limited coalition, aims to provide Prabowo with a parliamentary majority. The PKB, PPP, and Nasdem are the three political parties currently under consideration for a potential partnership. One contributing factor is the lack of experience of these political parties in being in the opposition. However, there is a concern that if Prabowo manages to convince these parties to join the government, it could lead to an unhealthy democracy where the cabinet is not subject to parliamentary checks, as was the situation under Jokowi since 2019. There are suggestions that the PDI-P, due to personality differences with leaders like Megawati, Bambang Yudhoyono, and Jokowi, may choose to be in the opposition. This is similar to the PKS, which has had difficulties in forming closer relationships with the Prabowo–Gibran team and other coalition members due to ideological reasons.[13]

Despite the absence of official presidential results, there is already speculation that Prabowo would likely secure a significant majority in parliament by co-option once he assumes the presidency in October 2024. According to the rapid-count results, there is a likelihood that the Prabowo–Gibran coalition might include the following political parties: Golkar with a percentage of 15.18%, Gerindra with 13.34%, Democratic Party with 7.41%, PAN with 7.27%, Nasdem with 9.24%, PKB with 10.89%, and PPP with 3.84%. This would be 67.17% of the overall vote share in parliament. The PDI-P has a remaining percentage of 16.64% and the PKS has a remaining percentage of 8.17%, which adds up to a total of 24.81%.[14]

Arya Budi, the Director of Research at Poltracking Indonesia, indicated that the PDI-P is hesitant to support Prabowo's administration because of Gibran's candidacy as his running mate. He further contended that it is difficult to envision PKS aligning with the administration due to ideological reasons, as PKS wishes to retain its

---

[13] *Ibid.*

[14] Paat, Y. (2024). "PDI-P and PKS identified as opposition forces against Prabowo's dominant coalition: Poltracking". *The Jakarta Globe*, 1 March.

supporters who are opposed to both Jokowi and Prabowo. Conversely, other political parties such as the PPP, PAN, and Nasdem have a high likelihood of joining the Prabowo–Gibran government.

Issues arising from the Prabowo–Gibran leadership

Prabowo's health

The main concern surrounding Prabowo's leadership is his health as he is 72 years old and has reportedly experienced a minor stroke in the past. He has also been seen limping due to poor health. The question arises whether Prabowo will be able to complete his 5-year term or if he will pass on power to the younger Gibran due to health reasons. As someone who has always aspired to hold the highest political position in the country, Prabowo may find additional motivation to maintain good health and effectively govern the country until the end of his term in 2029. He may draw inspiration from other elder leaders such as Dr. Mahathir Mohammad, Joe Biden, Donald Trump, and Lee Kuan Yew.

Sustainability of the "Tidar Compact"

The Indonesian military generals who support Prabowo are known as the "Tidar Alumni." In addition to some senior police generals like Sutarman, Sutanto, Idham Azis, Ari Dono Sukmanto, Condro Kirono, and M. Iriawan, there is also a group of prominent military generals supporting Prabowo. This group includes Wiranto, Bambang Yudhoyono, Agum Gumelar, Luhut Panjaitan, Evert Ernest Mangidaan, Sjafrie Syamsoedin, Admiral Widodo Adi Sutjipto (former Chief of the Armed Forces), and Air Marshall Iman Sufaat. The term "Tidar Alumni" is significant, particularly for Javanese people, as it refers to the Indonesian military academy located near Mount Tidar in the city of Magelang, which is considered the heart of Java.

According to Javanese mythology, Mount Tidar is linked to several legends. One story suggests that the mountain was created by a divine being who used a nail to secure it to the ground. In Javanese folklore, Java was originally a floating island in the ocean until it was anchored by a nail sent from the heavens. This nail is believed to be located at Mount Tidar, which resembles the head of a nail. The mountain is often referred to as the "head of the nail of Java." Additionally, Mount Tidar is associated with ancient graves, including one believed to belong to Syeikh Subakir, an Islamic propagator from Turkey who supposedly battled and defeated a Genie king.

Mount Tidar has become associated with various aspects of leadership, such as defending the homeland, happiness, high rank, and education. As a result, the Indonesian Military Academy was established there, and its former students are known as the "Tidar Alumni." With Prabowo's victory in the presidential elections, a significant question arises regarding the sustainability of the unity among the "Tidar alumni." Many of them had a strained relationship with Prabowo until around 2023 when they began supporting his presidential bid. The crucial question is how long this unity among the former generals will last and what implications it will have for Prabowo and the stability of his government after October 2024.

Elections and the Future of Islamic Political Parties in Indonesia

Indonesia's Islamic political parties have consistently struggled to perform well in elections. Despite being in the largest Muslim state in the world, these parties have faced difficulties since they were forced to unite under the PPP label during the New Order. In the 2009 elections, the leading Islamic political parties were the PPP, PKB, and PKNU, receiving 5.32%, 4.94%, and 1.47% of the total votes, respectively. In the 2014 elections, the PKS, PPP, and PBB won 6.79%, 6.53%, and 1.46% of the total votes, respectively. In the 2019 elections, the PKB, PPP, and PBB won 9.69%, 4.52%, and 0.79% of the total votes, respectively. This trend of poor performance continued in the 2024 elections, with the PKB receiving 10.62%, PKS 8.42%, PAN 7.42%, PPP 3.87%, Ummah Party 0.42%, and PBB 0.32% of the votes.[15]

The decline of Islamic political parties in Indonesia can be attributed to several factors. Firstly, non-Islamic political parties such as the PDI-P, Golkar, and Gerindra have gained popularity due to their strong leadership and well-defined programs. Secondly, most Islamic political parties have a narrow focus on religious issues, which may not resonate with a broader voter base. Additionally, the vague programs of Islamic political parties and the general preference of voters to separate religion and politics have contributed to their decline. According to a report, the combined vote share of Islamic parties in the 2024 legislative election was 26%, down from 30% a decade ago and 35% two decades ago. Notably, the oldest Islamic political party, the PPP, failed to meet the 4% minimum threshold to enter parliament in the 2024 elections.

The Indonesian Economy under the Prabowo Leadership

Indonesia is a significant global economy, ranking 16th in terms of GDP and 7th in terms of PPP in 2024. It has the fourth-largest population in the world and is a crucial center of resources, making it an important economic hub, particularly in the context of the growing economic power of China, India, Japan, South Korea, and other Southeast Asian economies. Therefore, Prabowo's commitment to continue Jokowi's growth-oriented economic policies is significant in determining the economic direction of the country. Consequently, after the KPU's announcement of the Prabowo–Gibran victory on March 20, 2024, the president-elect expressed his intention to utilize the solid foundation established by Jokowi, particularly in the economic sector, to work diligently and efficiently in order to deliver prompt results to the Indonesian people. He forecasted that

---

[15] See Soerjaatmadja, W. (2024). "Indonesia's Islamic parties facing falling support from voters". *The Straits Times*, 25 March.

within the next four to five years, the nation's economy will experience a growth rate of approximately 8%, which is an exceedingly ambitious goal.[16]

Historically, Prabowo, renowned for his fervent nationalism, has advocated for non-liberal economic policies, particularly emphasizing greater government involvement in the economy. He also emphasized the importance of reducing Indonesia's reliance on being solely a provider of resources and raw materials. Lately, particularly since assuming the position of Jokowi's defense minister in 2019, he has been advocating for "hilirisasi," which refers to Jokowi's policies aimed at enhancing the industrial framework of the agricultural, mining, and oil-based chemical industries. The primary motivation is to enhance the worth of Indonesia's natural resources prior to their exportation, consequently advancing the prosperity and welfare of farmers and augmenting state revenue. As a result of "hilirisasi," the exports of valuable resources like gold, oil, gas, and nickel have been limited in order to attract processing and manufacturing firms to the country. This policy was initiated by Jokowi. Therefore, it is widely anticipated that Prabowo's administration will prioritize a state-led growth approach, diverging from Jokowi's emphasis on market-oriented policies, particularly those implemented by Sri Mulyani, Jokowi's finance minister. Prabowo rejects the idea of relying on divine intervention in economic matters and instead advocates for active intervention to stimulate the economy, particularly in specific industries. The goal is to foster growth and establish powerful national enterprises that can compete on a global scale, similar to the success of South Korea, and generate substantial foreign currency.[17]

---

[16] Oshikiri, T. (2024). "Prabowo set to keep Indonesia on Jokowi's growth-focused path". *Nikkei Asia Review*, 22 March; Yuniar, R. W. (2024). "Is Prabowo's growth target for Indonesia realistic? 'Delusional' plan could be costly for economy, analysts say". *The Jakarta Post*, 10 March.

[17] See Heilson, J., Pemadi, D., and Dwiartama, A. (2018). "Hilirisasi: Resource-based industrialization and Global Production Networks in the Indonesian coffee and cocoa sectors". Conference paper, September 2018. See https://www.researchgate.net/publication/327764501_Hilirisasi_Resource-based_industrialisation_and_Global_Production_Networks_in_the_Indonesian_coffee_and_cocoa_sectors.

Possible Impact on the Forthcoming Regional Elections in November 2024

After the national elections for the President, Vice President, and members of the DPR and DPD on February 14, 2024, there will be elections for regional legislatures and local councils. In 2016, a law was enacted mandating that all regional elections would take place concurrently on a single date. The regional leaders elected in 2017 and 2018 would serve until the end of their tenure, at which point they would be appointed by authorities until the November 2024 polls. The schedule for the regional and local elections is as follows: candidate registrations will take place from August 27–29, 2024, formal candidate confirmation will occur on September 22, the campaigning period will run from September 25 to November 23, polling day will be on November 27, and vote counting will take place from November 27 to December 16, 2024.

An issue of great concern among observers is the potential impact of the 2024 presidential, vice presidential, and legislative elections on the regional elections. Will the outcome of the regional elections adhere to the pattern set by the legislative elections, or will new alignments and coalitions alter the ultimate result? The major political parties in the legislative elections were the PDI-P with a vote share of 16.72%, Golkar with 15.29%, Gerindra with 13.22%, PKB with 10.62%, Nasdem with 9.66%, PKS with 8.42%, Democratic Party with 7.43%, and PAN with 7.42%. Two interconnected issues can influence the regional elections in November.

If the Prabowo–Gibran leadership manages to form alliances with existing political parties such as Gerindra, Golkar, Democratic, and PAN, and potentially Nasdem and PPP, these parties will likely benefit from the advantages of being in power. The PDI-P and PKS, two political parties that have consistently and strongly criticized Jokowi, as well as Prabowo and Gibran, may face a disadvantage in regional elections. This is because voters are more likely to choose the benefits provided by the central government and its allies, rather than risk being deprived of services and local investments due to their affiliation with the opposition. Furthermore, the government's approach of temporarily appointing regional leaders, such as Governors and Bupatis, since 2022, may result in the selection of individuals who are both direct and indirect supporters of the president. This could potentially influence local voters to back the central government and, in this specific scenario, endorse Jokowi and his allies, including those who initially voted for Prabowo–Gibran in the presidential and vice presidential elections. This can be a disadvantage for political parties that are considered opponents of the president and his allies, such as Gerindra, Golkar, Democratic Party, and PAN. It may also affect parties that could potentially join to support the Prabowo Gibran combo in the upcoming months.[18]

Significance for the Southeast Asian Region

Active foreign policy presence

Indonesia under Jokowi's leadership experienced a period of relative stability and progress, which has had positive effects on the surrounding area. Nevertheless, Jokowi had chosen to maintain a predominantly inconspicuous presence in the region, prioritizing his attention on internal affairs. Prabowo, in contrast, possesses a higher level of assertiveness, linguistic proficiency, and geopolitical understanding due to his background as a military commander. He demonstrates a strong interest in the broader Asian area and global affairs. It is anticipated that he will have a more proactive approach on the international stage in contrast to Jokowi.

An Indonesia that is more assertive

Prabowo's presidency, supported by his family background and extensive expertise, may indicate the emergence of a leader who strengthens the nation, as evidenced by his reputation as a prominent leader and former defense minister. Simultaneously, it is

---

[18] See Wilson, I. (2023). "Indonesia's appointed leaders and the future of regional elections". *The Fulcrum*, 16 August.

anticipated that he will display more engagement in ASEAN and advocate for a larger ASEAN presence in addressing many matters, including the South China Sea dispute, managing relations with major global powers, and even addressing remote situations such as the present Gaza war. He likely wants to enhance ASEAN's assertiveness and influence on the global stage.

The Global Ramifications of a Prabowo–Gibran Victory

Prabowo's strong character and extensive international background, including his military leadership and his role as defense minister under Jokowi from 2019 to 2024, position him favorably to assert Indonesia's presence on the global stage with more impact. He is renowned for his exceptional communication skills, as he is fluent in English and several other non-Indonesian languages, including French, German, and Dutch. This proficiency allows him to effortlessly interact with global leaders, particularly those in North America and Western Europe. Furthermore, he is expected to have a more proactive role in advancing Jokowi's foreign policy agenda, while also emphasizing Indonesia's growing influence as a prominent middle power.

The World Congratulates Prabowo and Gibran

Shortly after the Quick-Count results were announced, Prabowo and Gibran received congratulations for their triumph in the presidential elections and their upcoming roles as leaders of Indonesia from several countries, including China, India, Iran, Japan, Jordan, Malaysia, Singapore, Australia, Saudi Arabia, Palestine, France, Germany, United Kingdom, Russia, Netherlands, and Spain. Among those who extended their congratulations is Xi Jinping, the leader of China.

A US State Department spokesman expressed cautious congratulations to the Indonesian people for their strong voter turnout in the election. The spokesman praised the Indonesian people's unwavering commitment to the democratic process and electoral institutions, highlighting their resilience and determination.[19] Nevertheless, the United States refrained from promptly extending congratulations to Prabowo, as the US National Security Council announced that a statement would be issued at a suitable moment to honor the wishes of the Indonesian populace. President Biden conveyed his congratulations to Prabowo for his election triumph on March 12, 2024 through the US Ambassador to ASEAN, Yohannes Abraham. On March 22, 2024, after the official results were announced, Biden personally contacted Prabowo to extend his congratulations for the victory, with US Secretary of State, Antony Blinken, doing the same.[20]

Prabowo's Policy Orientation

Prabowo's electoral success can largely be attributed to his close association with Jokowi and his portrayal as a relatable and experienced leader who will continue to guide the economy and the nation, much like Jokowi did. Consequently, Prabowo was obligated to implement similar popular policies as his predecessor. Due to this factor, Prabowo will have limited flexibility in his policy formulation. If economic development stagnates or if the state's budgetary health deteriorates, Prabowo may face less leniency from the electorate compared to the current situation.

Considering the possibility of a substantial coalition being established, Prabowo is also expected to encounter substantial difficulties in shaping policies. In contrast to Jokowi, who successfully

---

[19] *Election in Indonesia Press Statement.* United States Department of State, February 14, 2024.

[20] See Jati, H. (2024, March 23). "Joe Biden Akhirnya Telepon Presiden Terpilih Indonesia Prabowo untuk Beri Selamat, Ini Katanya". *Kompas TV* (in Indonesian); ^ Blinken, Antony [@SecBlinken] (March 20, 2024). "Congratulations to President-elect @Prabowo Subianto on his victory in Indonesia's Presidential Election. We look forward to partnering closely with the President-elect and his Administration when they take office in October" (Tweet).

established a substantial coalition that enabled him to enact his most ambitious programs, Prabowo will need to exert more initial effort in assembling his coalition partners for an administration and garnering support for his plans. This situation is expected to get more intricate due to the endorsement of Prabowo by Jokowi, who is his main supporter. By supporting Prabowo instead of the PDI-P's nominee Ganjar, Jokowi caused a significant portion of parliament to become estranged from Prabowo. As a consequence, Prabowo must form a heterogeneous alliance involving numerous minor political groups. He may encounter difficulties in effectively handling the varied interests within his coalition, as he strives to maintain a delicate equilibrium among different parties and factions using a "big-tent" strategy. This situation is further complicated by the strong likelihood of an "ongoing shadow government" where Jokowi, despite formally resigning, continues to exert substantial influence behind the scenes. This role has been suggested due to his continued participation in forming alliances on behalf of Prabowo. This might potentially lead to conflicts between the visions of Jokowi and Prabowo, similar to the growing divide between President Ferdinand "Bongbong" Marcos Jr and Vice President Sara Duterte in the Philippines. In addition, Jokowi's estrangement from the PDI-P and their anticipated hesitance to join Prabowo's cabinet could lead to the emergence of a strong opposition coalition consisting of various prominent parties, such as the PDI-P, the Prosperous Justice Party (PKS), and the National Awakening Party (PKB). Prabowo may encounter a more formidable opposition to his legislative ambitions, as compared to his predecessor. Previously, only the PKS opposed and contested his agenda.[21]

However, Prabowo is expected to depend on precarious populist strategies to strengthen domestic backing, such as his proposal to expand subsidized lunches in schools throughout Indonesia.

---

[21] Mathai, A. and Sood, A. (2024). With Prabowo set to be president, what 'surprises' are in store for Indonesia?" *South China Morning Post*, 15 February. See https://www.scmp.com/week-asia/politics/article/3252003/indonesia-2024-election-prabowo-subianto-wild-card-nationalistic-agenda.

Prabowo's proposed program, estimated to cost up to IDR400 trillion rupiah (US$25.5 billion) every year, is expected to create financial pressure on Indonesia's budget and increase the country's fiscal imbalance, ultimately resulting in long-term inflation.[22]

It is important to mention that Prabowo has indicated a tendency toward a more nationalistic approach when it comes to developing policies for both internal and foreign matters. Prabowo's election manifesto outlined his intention to prioritize the transformation of Indonesia into a robust and powerful nation. The manifesto outlines Indonesia's goal of becoming a nation that is highly regarded in its international dealings. It also emphasizes the importance of having a well-organized defense and security system that can safeguard the country and maintain peace within its borders. Due to his military experience, Prabowo is anticipated to have ambitions of enhancing Indonesia's might, both economically and militarily, according to experts. Given his current role as defense minister and his military background, it is probable that Prabowo will allocate a significant portion of his budget to defense spending. This will aim to strengthen the Indonesian military, making it one of the largest armies in the region.[23]

Foreign Policy

Prabowo is expected to exhibit significant differences in his approach as a president on the global stage compared to his predecessor. Jokowi had a strong aversion to the formalities of diplomatic summits and consistently refrained from visiting a UN General Assembly in person. He firmly believed that foreign policy should

---

[22] Armandhanu, D. & Haizan, R. Y. A. (2024, February 28). *Prabowo awarded four-star general rank by Jokowi, who fends off talk of a political transaction.* CNA. https://www.channelnewsasia.com/asia/indonesia-jokowi-prabowo-military-general-four-star-rank-free-lunch-politics-4156271.

[23] Mathai, A. and Sood, A. (2024). "With Prabowo set to be president, what 'surprises' are in store for Indonesia?" *South China Morning Post*, 15 February. See https://www.scmp.com/week-asia/politics/article/3252003/indonesia-2024-election-prabowo-subianto-wild-card-nationalistic-agenda.

prioritize the advancement of trade and investment. Prabowo, who is proficient in English, enjoys being in the spotlight and is expected to take on a more assertive global role compared to his predecessor. Prabowo frequently demonstrates his strong nationalism through his speeches, and he is likely to be quite sensitive to any perceived disrespect from foreign countries. Although it is improbable that Prabowo will reverse Indonesia's enduring dedication to an autonomous and non-aligned foreign policy, he will introduce his own fervent yet unpredictable approach, as demonstrated by his impromptu peace proposal for Ukraine that he revealed at a significant regional defense conference in June of last year, during the Shangri-la Dialogue in Singapore.[24] However, it is highly improbable that Prabowo will deviate from Indonesia's approach of refraining from aligning with either China or the US, the two competing major powers. Instead, Indonesia will continue to pursue a neutral stance and avoid becoming embroiled in geopolitical competition. During a speech at the Centre for Strategic and International Studies think tank in Jakarta in November 2023, Prabowo explicitly stated his dedication to non-alignment in his foreign policy. He emphasized that Indonesia would maintain its independent foreign policy and would not align itself with any military or geopolitical bloc. Prabowo also emphasized the importance of maintaining positive relations with all neighboring countries.[25]

Prabowo is expected to continue Jokowi's pragmatic stance toward Beijing, despite his tendency to use nationalistic rhetoric. This is partly because Chinese investments have played a significant role in Indonesia's rapid infrastructure development over the past decade, and Prabowo would not want to jeopardize this relationship. Prabowo has made a clear promise to maintain a balanced foreign

---

[24] Bland, B. (2024, February 15). "'Continuity' Prabowo means change for Indonesia". Chatham House – International Affairs Think Tank. https://www.chathamhouse.org/2024/02/continuity-prabowo-means-change-indonesia.

[25] Sood, A., Yuniar, R. W., and Mathai, A. (2024, February 16). "Prabowo's presidency: New chapter in Indonesia–China ties or business as usual?" *South China Morning Post.* https://www.scmp.com/week-asia/politics/article/3252127/indonesia-china-ties-will-president-elect-prabowo-confront-beijing-or-maintain-widodos-economic.

policy position between China and the United States. He also plans to continue implementing Jokowi's economic strategy, which focuses on strengthening business relations with China. Jokowi's business-friendly policies have resulted in a significant increase in Chinese foreign investments, which have played a crucial role in Indonesia's economy, growing more than eightfold during his 10-year tenure.[26] Despite Indonesia's economic reliance on China, it has managed to maintain a robust relationship with Western countries. This was evident when the United States lifted its ban on Prabowo in 2019, allowing him to become the defense minister. Since then, Prabowo has strengthened military connections that were initially established through joint infantry training in the 1980s. Additionally, he has overseen a continuous acquisition of Western weaponry to modernize the armed forces, which has garnered favor from Western arms suppliers.[27] Indications of this moderate stance in the US–China geopolitical rivalry can also be observed during his time as defense minister, where he always pursued a balanced approach between the two nations, characterizing them as "good friends."

Nevertheless, this attitude differs significantly from that of other Southeast Asian countries. These countries have skillfully managed their economic reliance on China while also considering security concerns. As a result, they have adopted a more balanced approach toward both Beijing and Western countries. Indonesia perceives itself as an emerging middle power with the ability to properly handle this dichotomy. As a result, China has emerged as one of the primary contributors of foreign direct investment to Indonesia, amounting to a substantial sum of US$7.4 billion in 2023. In comparison, investments from the United States only reached US$3.28 billion. Part of the reason for this is Jokowi's ambitious economic

---

[26] "Chinese firms to benefit if front-runner Prabowo seals Indonesian election win". South China Morning Post, 2024, February 11. https://www.scmp.com/business/china-business/article/3251669/chinese-companies-set-benefit-if-front-runner-prabowo-subianto-seals-victory-indonesian-presidential.

[27] "What will Prabowo Subianto's foreign policy look like?" *The Economist*. https://www.economist.com/asia/2024/02/29/what-will-prabowo-subiantos-foreign-policy-look-like.

and infrastructure plans, with China's investments playing a crucial role in the construction of Indonesia's inaugural high-speed rail line as part of the Belt and Road Initiative. One viewpoint suggests that Prabowo could leverage Indonesia's non-aligned stance to capitalize on the competing interests of the two superpowers in the country. In doing so, he would utilize China as a significant player to balance the power of the US, while also aiming to maximize the advantages of existing security assurances.[28]

Prabowo's forthright, confrontational, and gradually tempering irritable demeanor is expected to influence his approach to foreign affairs. Considering his election manifesto, it can be inferred that he will prioritize projecting Indonesia as a powerful nation on the world stage, one that is esteemed in international relations and has a proficient defense and security system to safeguard its territory and maintain peace.[29] Unlike Jokowi, who is known for being kind and popular among the people, Prabowo has a confrontational demeanor that suggests he would not hesitate to lecture Western powers. This is a behavior he has exhibited on numerous occasions in the past.[30] Prabowo, for instance, has expressed that Indonesia does not require instruction in democracy from external sources. He has also reacted strongly to criticism from European nations on Jakarta's dependence on palm oil exports, citing the historical context of colonialism. Prabowo criticized the EU's deforestation policies during the presidential campaign, stating that Europeans "compelled us to cultivate tea, coffee, rubber, and chocolate. Are you suggesting that we are currently causing the destruction of our

---

[28] Sood, A., Yuniar, R. W., and Mathai, A. (2024, February 16). "Prabowo's presidency: New chapter in Indonesia-China ties or business as usual?" *South China Morning Post.* https://www.scmp.com/week-asia/politics/article/3252127/indonesia-china-ties-will-president-elect-prabowo-confront-beijing-or-maintain-widodos-economic.

[29] Sood, A. (2024, February 26). "Will Indonesia's unpredictable president-elect continue Jokowi's China approach?" *South China Morning Post.* https://www.scmp.com/economy/article/3253175/global-impact-cuddly-grandpa-prabowo-subianto-claims-victory-all-indonesians-defence-minister.

[30] Tripathi, S. (2024, March 8). "How will Prabowo lead Indonesia?" *Foreign Policy.* https://foreignpolicy.com/2024/02/28/indonesia-elections-prabowo-leader-human-rights-jokowi/.

forests? You were the ones who initially decimated our forests." Prabowo has also stated his willingness to adopt a strong stance when dealing with Western countries. During a discussion on foreign policy at CSIS Indonesia, he expressed his belief that Europe had lost its "moral leadership" and highlighted the discrepancy between the West's teachings on democracy and human rights and their actual standards. There is a global transformation taking place. Now Europe is no longer necessary.[31]

In a world characterized by multiple centers of power and constantly changing coalitions driven by a limited set of goals, Prabowo may perceive himself as Suharto and want to establish an autonomous stance. Despite Indonesia and China both being claimants of disputed islands in the South China Sea, Prabowo has sought favor with Beijing due to its investments being less restrictive compared to those of European businesses. At the same time, bearing the US–Russian conflict over Ukraine, during the Shangri-La Dialogue in Singapore in June 2023, Prabowo shocked regional analysts, the Indonesian government, and Indonesian media by presenting a peace plan for Russia's conflict in Ukraine that strongly benefitted Russia.

An imminent challenge for Prabowo is the South China Sea dispute, where Beijing asserts its near complete ownership.[32] Nevertheless, as defense minister, Prabowo had indicated a predilection for the use diplomacy as a means to address the territorial conflicts between China and ASEAN nations in the waters abundant with natural resources. Prabowo, in a statement after the 2021 ASEAN–China Defense Ministers' meeting, expressed that engaging in dialogue and consultations founded on mutual trust could

---

[31] Yuniar, R. W. (2023b, November 14). "Indonesia's Prabowo slams West for double standards, lack of moral leadership: 'We don't really need Europe'" *South China Morning Post.* https://www-scmp-com.libproxy1.nus.edu.sg/week-asia/politics/article/3241398/indonesias-prabowo-slams-west-double-standards-lack-moral-leadership-we-dont-really-need-europe?module=inline&pgtype=article.

[32] Wang, O. and Chen, A. (2023, December 8). "Is Beijing warming to South China Sea code of conduct?" *South China Morning Post.* https://www-scmp-com.libproxy1.nus.edu.sg/news/china/diplomacy/article/3245375/beijing-warming-south-china-sea-code-conduct?module=inline&pgtype=article.

effectively address all conflicts in the contested waterway. He also expressed his endorsement for ongoing negotiations on a South China Sea Code of Conduct, which would establish clear boundaries and rights regarding territorial claims among all involved parties. During a presidential debate in January, Prabowo highlighted the importance for Indonesia to strengthen its marine defense capabilities in order to protect itself in the North Natuna Sea when the South China Sea issue was discussed. China has unilaterally claimed the nine-dash line intersects within Indonesia's exclusive economic zone in the Natuna Islands. China has asserted fishing rights within these seas, resulting in multiple clashes in the past. Prabowo's mention of enhanced marine defense implies that he may be more assertive in upholding Indonesia's sovereignty in that specific area of the ocean. Prabowo's campaign manifesto acknowledges that the South China Sea is a geopolitical challenge for Jakarta. It also suggests that Indonesia should foresee future conflicts between the United States and China over the disputed waterway in order to limit potential hazards.

President Xi extended a formal invitation to president-elect Prabowo to visit China from March 31 to April 2, 2024, which was noteworthy. In addition to his role as Indonesia's Defense Minister, Chinese officials have claimed that Prabowo was invited to China in his capacity as Indonesia's president-elect. This visit marks Prabowo's first official trip overseas following his victory in the presidential elections. During the significant diplomatic visit, Prabowo had the opportunity to meet with President Xi and was also slated to have a meeting with Prime Minister Li Qiang. The purpose of the visit was primarily to establish contact between the newly elected president of Indonesia and Chinese political officials, while also indicating the ongoing strong political, economic, and strategic connections between the two countries that were initially formed during President Jokowi's tenure in 2014. Prabowo expressed his belief that China is an important partner in maintaining peace and stability in the region. President Xi emphasized China's commitment to contribute positively to regional and global peace, highlighting the significance of cooperation between China and Indonesia in safeguarding maritime security in Southeast Asia.[33] Aligning with China's stance, Prabowo emphasized the importance of strengthening the current economic and security connections between the two nations. Prabowo stated that there is an existing cooperative connection and he intends to enhance it in the future. After his trip to China, Prabowo traveled to Japan where he had meetings with Japanese Prime Minister Fumio Kishida and the country's defense minister, Minoru Kihara.

Undoubtedly, Prabowo's travel to China and Japan, the dominant economic forces in Asia, has emphasized the significance of foreign policy under the new leader and the proactive approach that can be anticipated throughout his tenure. Additionally, the purpose was to showcase to China the dependability of Indonesia as a strategic ally, despite Prabowo's reputation for being aligned with Western countries and advocating for economic nationalism. Prabowo's visit to Japan, following his visit to China, served as a clear indication of Indonesia's proactive foreign policy in the future. It also highlighted the significance of geopolitics for the upcoming Prabowo administration, considering the unresolved issues that continue to impact states in the region, particularly in terms of maritime security.

Democratic Backsliding

The concerns about democratic regression in a country that has struggled to achieve democratic reforms in the post-Suharto era arise from two factors: firstly, the gradual weakening of democracy under Jokowi's leadership and, secondly, the question of whether democracy can withstand Prabowo's authoritarian inclinations. Jokowi's tenure witnessed a gradual erosion of democratic checks and balances. The authority of the Corruption Eradication Commission was reduced and the requirement of a minimum age of 40 years for presidential and vice presidential candidates was

---

[33] See Zhang, L. M. (2024). "Beijing willing to deepen cooperation with Jakarta, Xi says". *The Straits Times*, 2 April.

revoked, enabling Gibran to become eligible for the position of vice president.

The oligarchic dominance centered around Jokowi has exerted significant pressure on democracy. Contemporary oligarchy in Indonesia emerged as a consequence of the implementation of market capitalist policies in the Suharto regime. These policies not only facilitated economic growth and expansion but also facilitated the consolidation of wealth and power by the collaboration of influential bureaucrats and large corporations.[34] During Jokowi's tenure, the oligarchy made repeated attempts to weaken Indonesia's democratic institutions. In 2019, the Indonesian parliament, which had significant financial support from the oligarchs, enacted legislation that significantly curtailed the authority of its anti-corruption institution, as the oligarchs saw the institution as a challenge to their own interests. The anti-corruption body was created following the downfall of Suharto in 1998 and played a crucial role in achieving democratic advancement. Additional democratic elements implemented were the decentralization of authority to regional administrations, but this was largely reversed as Jokowi sought to centralize power in the capital.

In 2020, the legislature passed a comprehensive law on job creation that reversed the legal progress made by advocates of the reform movement, partly due to the influential backing of mining oligarchs, some of whom hold positions in Jokowi's cabinet.[35]

---

[34] Hermawan, A. (2024, February 27). "The biggest threat to Indonesia's democracy? It's not Prabowo, it's the oligarchy." The Conversation. http://theconversation.com/the-biggest-threat-to-indonesias-democracy-its-not-prabowo-its-the-oligarchy-223974.

[35] Hamid, U. and Hermawan, A. (2020, October 9). "Indonesia's omnibus law is a bust for human rights". *New Mandala.* https://www.newmandala.org/indonesias-omnibus-law-is-a-bust-for-human-rights/; Hermawan, A. (2024, February 27). "The biggest threat to Indonesia's democracy? It's not Prabowo, it's the oligarchy." The Conversation. http://theconversation.com/the-biggest-threat-to-indonesias-democracy-its-not-prabowo-its-the-oligarchy-223974; Jong, H. N. (2020, October 26). Indonesian officials linked to mining and 'dirty energy' firms benefiting from deregulation law. *Mongabay Environmental News.* https://news.mongabay.com/2020/10/indonesia-

This has led to criticism of the decline of democracy and a shift toward illiberalism. Jokowi's emphasis on economic growth enabled oligarchs to exert their political and economic influence, straining Indonesia's democratic institutions. The oligarchs played a crucial role in Prabowo's electoral triumph by supporting him due to Jokowi's endorsement and because they believed he was the most suitable candidate to serve their interests. Prabowo received significant backing from the oligarchy, as evidenced by his initial campaign expense of Rp 31.4 billion (US$2 million), which was 31 times larger than that of his primary challenger, Anies.[36]

The strain has been exacerbated by Jokowi's political machinations prior to the elections. Specifically, Jokowi has been accused of meddling in the election to guarantee Prabowo and Gibran's victory in a single round. In 2023, the Constitutional Court, headed by Jokowi's brother-in-law, issued a contentious decision to grant Gibran an exemption from the required age limit for standing for the positions of president or vice president. Jokowi's brother-in-law was subsequently convicted of an ethical violation for failing to abstain from involvement in the case, despite having an evident conflict of interest.[37] Jokowi has faced criticism for using social aid as a means to gain support for the Prabowo–Gibran ticket. Additionally, he has been accused of leveraging state resources, including the police, military, and government officials, to exert pressure on village heads to endorse the pair. The erosion of democratic safeguards is further demonstrated by the fact that Jokowi was unable to

---

coal-mining-energy-omnibus-deregulation-law-oligarch/; Suroyo, G. and Sulaiman, S. (2022, June 9). "Explainer: What's at stake with Indonesia's controversial jobs creation law?" *Reuters.* https://www.reuters.com/world/asia-pacific/whats-stake-with-indonesias-controversial-jobs-creation-law-2022-06-09/.

[36] Lamb, K. and Teresia, A. (2023, October 16). "Jokowi, Indonesia's kingmaker, works to keep influence after election". *Reuters.* https://www.reuters.com/world/asia-pacific/jokowi-indonesias-kingmaker-works-keep-influence-after-election-2023-10-14/.

[37] Janti, N. (2023, November 7). "BREAKING: Ethics council removes chief justice Anwar – Politics". *The Jakarta Post.* https://www.thejakartapost.com/indonesia/2023/11/07/breaking-ethics-council-removes-chief-justice-anwar.html.

secure a third term due to constitutional limitations, which could not be amended due to the opposition of Megawati Sukarnoputri. This highlights an internal power struggle rather than the institutional democratic safeguards that were intended to uphold democracy.[38]

Furthermore, there are apprehensions that Jokowi's participation in the 2024 elections indicates a regression in the hard-won democratic advancements established during the Reformasi era, specifically a resurgence of dynastic politics.[39] The elite's control over power relied heavily on dynastic succession, a practice that was eliminated during the democratization process in the post-Suharto era, when democratic elections were introduced. Suharto's peaceful abdication of authority, however, enabled numerous individuals within his close circle to superficially transform themselves into democratic politicians and rise to positions of power, all while preserving the traditional practices of behind-the-scenes political maneuvering. Jokowi's initial electoral victory in 2009 was met with widespread optimism due to his perceived departure from the long-standing lineage of leaders from the Suharto era. Unlike his predecessors who hailed from the Jakarta elite, Jokowi came from the provinces and had earned his reputation as a trustworthy and efficient local administrator, which further enhanced his national standing. However, in order to solidify his position against potential resistance from the established political leaders, Jokowi employed the same tactics as those in power: A survey conducted by Indonesian media outlet Kompas, after the contentious court decision that permitted Gibran to run for vice president, revealed that nearly two-thirds of the participants viewed this action as an attempt to establish a political dynasty.

---

[38] Lai, Y. (2022, March 21). "PDI-P puts brakes on plan to amend Constitution". *The Jakarta Post*, March 21, 2024. See https://www.thejakartapost.com/paper/2022/03/21/pdi-p-puts-brakes-on-plan-to-amend-constitution.html.

[39] Basorie, W. D. (2023, October 29). "Commentary: His son's election run could tarnish Jokowi's legacy". *CNA*. https://www.channelnewsasia.com/commentary/indonesia-jokowi-son-gibran-legacy-election-3877661.

Rather than altering the system, the system itself influenced him, as indicated by his previously described activities that undermine democracy.[40] These actions are unlikely to be undone and are more likely to worsen under Prabowo's leadership. Observers consider Jokowi's appointment of his son as vice president as the ultimate indication of his integration into the elite and the success of dynastic politics, which includes Kaesang's ascent as the leader of the PSI. A potential tacit collaboration between Prabowo and Jokowi could serve as a means to suppress political rivalry and establish the customary practice of hereditary succession. Prabowo's victory, although appearing democratic, is said to have solidified a government system that undermines the democratic principles established during the Reformasi era.[41]

Given the recent decline in democratic practices, Prabowo's rise to the presidency is especially concerning. Prabowo has already expressed strong opposition to the excessive cost and intricacy of Indonesian democracy, causing concern among rights groups regarding his potential actions once he assumes control of the system. However, the democratic protections that were put in place after the downfall of Suharto's autocratic government in the late 1990s, known as the reform era, have been weakened. Nevertheless, experts predict that these safeguards will still be strong enough to prevent Prabowo from becoming an autocratic leader. This is primarily due to three factors: Firstly, Prabowo lacks the same level of popularity as Jokowi. Jokowi's significant approval ratings have granted him considerable latitude and immunity to push the boundaries of his authority. In contrast, Prabowo's lack of popularity is evident from the election results. Prabowo routinely ranked second with approximately 20% of the vote until Jokowi indirectly supported him. It is highly improbable that Prabowo could have

---

[40] Kurlantzick, J. (2024). "Prabowo wins. Does Indonesian democracy lose?" *Blog Post*, 14 February.
[41] Sherlock, S. (2024, February 19). "What Indonesia's election means for its democracy". Australian Institute of International Affairs. https://www.internationalaffairs.org.au/australianoutlook/what-indonesias-election-means-for-its-democracy/.

attained even the second-place position in the election if it had taken place a year ago. Based on the Quick Count results of the parliamentary elections, Prabowo's political party Gerindra ranked third, trailing behind the PDI-P and Golkar. This indicates that his party lacks sufficient popularity to maintain the level of support he has previously had.

Secondly, although Prabowo's image as a powerful leader may have garnered support from several individuals, it also implies that many voters would be cautious of him. Although political parties typically grant their members a certain level of flexibility, it is improbable that they would grant the same level of flexibility when it comes to relinquishing the hard-earned power they acquired following Suharto's tyranny to Prabowo. Thirdly, it is possible that the military may not offer their support to Prabowo, despite his strong military background. The military institution has consistently valued adherence to the rule of law and constitution, particularly throughout the reform era. Consequently, the military has strong internal motivations to avoid jeopardizing its well-established reputation and public confidence by endorsing any actions that Prabowo might take to undermine democracy. Moreover, the proximity of Myanmar, which is currently experiencing a civil war and where the military is on the losing side, is likely to make the Indonesian military (and democratic watchdogs) particularly aware of any potential role in undermining democracy.[42]

Jokowi's Continued Influence

Jokowi's involvement in Prabowo's win, along with his actions immediately following the election, strongly indicates that he intends to retain his political power even after stepping down from office. This could be achieved through his role as a kingmaker, by taking on an

---

[42] Sulaiman, Y. (2024, February 16). "Commentary: Prabowo's likely victory will be a test for Indonesia's democracy". *CNA*. https://www.channelnewsasia.com/commentary/prabowo-subianto-indonesia-presidential-election-democracy-jokowidodo-influence-4125806.

official position in the presidential advisory council, or by becoming the chairman of a political party. Following Prabowo's announcement of victory on February 14, Jokowi invited Surya Paloh, the leader of the National Democratic (Nasdem) Party, which supported Anies, for a dinner at the presidential palace on February 18, 2024. When interrogated by journalists, Jokowi minimized the significance of the meeting, referring to it as "routine," and conveyed his aim to serve as a "bridge."[43] Following the dinner with Paloh, Jokowi designated Agus Harimurti Yudhoyono, the leader of the Democratic Party and the son of former president Susilo Bambang Yudhoyono, as the Minister of Agrarian Affairs and Spatial Planning three days later. This strategic maneuver effectively included the Democrats into Jokowi's cabinet. The objective was to enhance the connection between Nasdem and both Jokowi and Prabowo. Despite supporting Anies in the presidential contest, Nasdem remains a component of Jokowi's coalition. Significantly, Jokowi's action may be an endeavor to hinder the establishment of a cohesive alliance between Nasdem and Megawati's PDI-P in opposition to Prabowo.

Analysts have suggested that Jokowi is strategically working to strengthen the support for his probable successor in the 580-member House of Representatives. This is particularly important because Prabowo's coalition of parties does not have a majority in parliament, which could result in a deadlock in the legislative process. Prabowo's coalition, consisting of his Great Indonesia Movement Party (Gerindra), Golkar, Democratic Party, and National Mandate Party, is projected to have control over only 43% of parliamentary seats. However, in order to achieve the desired political stability sought by Jokowi, the next government coalition would need to have a wide majority. Indonesia's political environment is dynamic, with political parties often forming new alliances after elections to ensure they can continue to benefit from government support and

---

[43] Ericssen. (2024, February 25). "Indonesian President Jokowi makes power play to bolster Prabowo's coalition – and wield political influence after stepping down". *CNA*. https://www.channelnewsasia.com/asia/indonesia-jokowi-smooth-transition-power-prabowo-coalition-political-influence-4144611.

resources. As an illustration, the Golkar party, which was not successful in the election, formed an alliance with the Democratic Party and the PDI-P in 2009 and 2014, respectively. In 2019, Gerindra, led by Prabowo, unexpectedly decided to join Jokowi's cabinet despite losing the election and facing a tough presidential race. This means that Jokowi's attempt to strengthen Prabowo's political alliance in parliament might still be successful. Once Prabowo becomes president, the PDI-P may become the only opposition party. However, its capacity to successfully challenge the government may be restricted due to its control of fewer than 20% of parliamentary seats, in contrast to the administration's anticipated supermajority coalition. The PDI-P was in the lead among the 18 parties in the parliamentary elections, having received 16.78% of the vote. This was based on nearly 62% of the official ballots that had been counted before the official results were declared.

It is important to mention that Jokowi made efforts to prevent a parliamentary inquiry, known as Hak Angket, regarding the alleged electoral fraud. Ganjar and the ruling PDI-P have called for this inquiry against Jokowi due to the alleged irregularities in the election. In order to conduct this inquiry, it is necessary to have the backing of a minimum of 25 members of the House of Representatives and several party groups in parliament, as specified in Law No. 17 of 2015. The implementation of a parliamentary inquiry has the potential to result in the impeachment of the president. This could cause political unrest that may destabilize the current administration and hinder the smooth transition to Prabowo's presidency. However, Jokowi's actions effectively eliminated this risk by reducing the chances of any requests for a parliamentary inquiry gaining enough support in parliament to be initiated. However, Jokowi's actions following the presidential election have been perceived as an attempt not only to ensure a smooth transition for the next eight months of his term but also to preserve his political influence whenever he steps down from office.

Nevertheless, Jokowi's impact, if it exists, is likely to be diminished, partly due to Prabowo's authoritative nature. Although

Prabowo's independent spirit was less prominent in the 2024 presidential elections, it was evident in his previous campaigns, particularly in his unwavering confidence in fate. Prabowo has specifically conveyed his conviction in the existence of a structured and organized universe, where the powerful take care of the vulnerable and an authentic leader possesses wahyu, which signifies "divine revelation." According to Prabowo, both Sukarno and Suharto possessed wahyu, and he believes that he also possesses wahyu, which means he is destined to govern the country. It is highly improbable that Jokowi will be able to exert political influence through his son Gibran, mostly due to the limited power of the vice presidential post in Indonesia and the clear dominance of Prabowo's personality over Gibran's during their combined rallies.

Establishment of Jokowi's "Political Dynasty"

Jokowi's persistent use of power in the 2024 presidential election indicates his role as a decisive force in determining the outcome. Observers have stated that Jokowi's involvement in Prabowo's election, as well as Gibran's acceptance of the vice president job alongside Prabowo, suggests that Jokowi will have the greatest ability to influence the administration for the next 5 years. Jokowi has demonstrated his ability to effectively create a stable political environment and promote economic growth through his pragmatic approach. As a result, he has gained significant influence over the electorate, surpassing Indonesia's previous influential figures, including his former political mentor, Megawati Sukarnoputri, who is the chairwoman of the ruling PDI-P party. This is evident in Prabowo's significant victory over Ganjar, who was supported by Megawati. Despite the various controversies surrounding Jokowi during the elections, such as the Constitutional Court's ruling, which was overseen by Jokowi's brother-in-law, to make an exception to the 40 years of age minimum requirement for Gibran to run, Widodo's statements about intervening in the election to ensure continuity, and a sitting president's ability to campaign for a specific candidate if desired, these did not seem to have negatively affected Jokowi's standing, including his support for Prabowo. Jokowi has faced allegations of utilizing state resources to advance Prabowo's campaign, such as the aforementioned manipulation of welfare benefits for the underprivileged. However, Jokowi's immense popularity was influential enough for the majority of voters to disregard these concerns.[44]

There is speculation that Prabowo's failing health may prevent him from completing the entire electoral term. Therefore, if Prabowo resigns as president, Gibran would assume the presidency, ultimately restoring control to Jokowi. Some analysts have suggested that Jokowi may request Prabowo to appoint certain individuals from his close circle in order to maintain consistency with his own administration. These individuals include Luhut Pandjaitan, a former military general who had previously clashed with Prabowo during their time in the army, and Erick Thohir, the Minister of State-Owned Enterprises, who strongly supported Prabowo in the recent election.

An important point to consider is that Jokowi's efforts to strengthen his ongoing influence in Indonesian politics have diminished his reputation as a populist leader. The criticism of Jokowi's actions in suppressing and undermining democracy in order to strengthen his authority has caused significant division within the country. Similarly, Jokowi's attempts to include those who would have opposed his agenda in his cabinet have also contributed to this division. However, Jokowi's strategic and deliberate actions have effectively created what is now seen as a budding political dynasty. His oldest son, Gibran, is the vice president-elect, while his other son, Kaesang Pangarep, 29, serves as the chairman of the Indonesia Solidarity Party. Although this party did not meet the vote threshold to secure parliamentary seats in the February 14 election, it has gained popularity among the country's young voters due to its

---

[44]Yuniar, R. W. (2024b, February 7). "Indonesia election 2024: Will Gibran be hurt by poll body's scanda?" *South China Morning Post.* https://www.scmp.com/week-asia/politics/article/3251181/indonesia-election-2024-will-gibrans-chances-be-hurt-election-bodys-ethics-scandal.

progressive policy agenda. Bobby Nasution, who is the son-in-law of Jokowi, is apparently aspiring to participate in the upcoming gubernatorial race in North Sumatra. This would be a significant advancement for him, considering his current role as the mayor of Medan. Observers have hypothesized that Jokowi is expected to request "concessions" from Prabowo in order to place one of his sons in a leadership position in Jakarta, thus strengthening his authority in the future.

CONCLUSION

Due to the geographical and demographic size and character, its strategic location and treasure house of resources, Indonesia's presidential election in February 2024 was important as whoever led the country would impact the country's policies and directions, with the big question being, will they change fundamentally from the pathways set by Jokowi who ran the country from 2014 to 2024.

Eventually, despite various predictions to the contrary, the Prabowo–Gibran team won the election in a single round without the need for a runoff, something that had not transpired since 2004 when direct presidential elections were first introduced in Indonesia. The reasons for the victory of the Prabowo–Gibran team were manifold, but largely stemmed from the immense strengths and attractions of the team compared to their two competitors, the Anies–Muhaimin and Ganjar–Mahfud teams. From a Javanese perspective, the Prabowo–Gibran team had financial resources, the support of strong personalities, a powerful political coalition, the support of Jokowi's incumbency, and potent forces that believed that the Prabowo–Gibran team was chosen by the Almighty, with Divine Mandate, and, hence, in possession of the all-important *wahyu*. In the main, the Prabowo–Gibran team won resoundingly due to the following factors:

The strengths and competencies of the Prabowo–Gibran team

- Support of pro-Jokowi Millennial and Generation Z first-time voters.
- Won the support of those who were antithetical to Megawati and Anies.
- Promised to continue Jokowi's policies that were popular with the voters.
- Prabowo's image "makeover" as a cuddly grandpa, including dancing in public, resonated with the youth;
- Prabowo apologized for past mistakes, including alleged human rights abuses, of which many younger voters were unaware.
- Presidential Bansos (*Bantuan Sosial* or Social Assistance programs) policies of providing social assistance and rise in civil servant salaries before the elections.
- Use of famous celebrities and influencers in party campaigns.
- Public's belief that the Prabowo–Gibran team would be good for national stability, unity, and economic development.
- Success in riding on the Jokowi factor as since mid-2023, the president made it clear that he favored Prabowo as his successor and not Ganjar, a candidate from his party, the PDI-P. With Jokowi enjoying an astounding high public approval rating of nearly 80%, there was little chance that Prabowo would lose.

At the same time, Prabowo's competitors suffered from various weaknesses.

Weaknesses of Ganjar Pranowo and Mahfud MD

- Suffered from the rising anti-PDI-P sentiments, a party that appeared out of touch with the masses.
- Lost out due to negative sentiments toward Megawati who started dynastic politics by placing Puan as the DPR leader and even

wanted her as the PDI-P presidential candidate, and yet had the temerity to accuse Jokowi of political dynasticism.
- Megawati's condescending attitude toward President Jokowi, greatly angered his supporters and the public at large.
- Ganjar triggered anti-PDI-P sentiments by calling for the cancellation of FIFA World Cup U-21 tournament in Indonesia even through Jokowi wanted it.
- The public was also tired and bored with Megawati and PDI-P, especially its Secretary-General, Hasto, consistently lecturing others about "Sukarnoism" and the weaknesses of other leaders such as Jokowi and Prabowo.

Weaknesses of Anies Baswedan and Muhaimin Iskandar

- Anies was only relevant to a niche group of voters, namely, urban Muslims, educated people, and mainly city voters.
- People continued to be traumatized by the Jakarta gubernatorial elections in 2016 where Anies was a key player in harnessing identity politics to defeat the then Governor Ahok, with Anies seen as being supported and linked to "Islamist radicals."
- Pilpres Ahok stated that he supported the Ganjar–Mahfud team, which might have reduced the already small number of supporters for Anies.
- Anies's campaign tactics and strategies were different and ineffective, using small and organic public discussions called *Desak Anies*, held in big cities only.
- Anies's campaign strategy used limited banners, invested little in the campaign due to limited funds.
- Anies and Muhaimin's policies and narratives were largely irrelevant to non-city and less educated voters.
- Anies and Muhaimin's call to change Jokowi's policies if elected, including the new national capital, lost them much support from pro-JW supporters, especially in Kalimantan.

In the end, for most voters, the most important "enemy" to emerge was Megawati, who was leading the charge against a popular and populist president, Jokowi, with Anies, who was largely irrelevant to the masses, especially the poor and lowly educated rural folks, leaving them with the only option of backing Prabowo and Gibran. The link between Anies and what was seen as "Islamist radicals" also weakened Anies and Muhaimin and led most voters to support what appeared to be the truly nationalist team, the Prabowo–Gibran team.

The Road Ahead

With the presidential elections over and the Prabowo–Gibran team being declared as the official winners over the challenge by the Anies–Muhaimin and Ganjar–Mahfud teams, the next order of things would be the kind of Indonesia that would emerge in the coming months, once Prabowo and Gibran are sworn in on October 20, 2024. Here, the big questions include the following:

- Will there be change or continuity? Will "Jokowoism" continue through Prabowo, especially the investments in infrastructure projects, Jokowi's peace policies in Papua, the building of a new capital, and Jokowi's foreign policy, including the policy of strengthening Indonesia's military power that was initiated by Prabowo as a Defense Minister?
- What will be the role of Jokowi in the next constellation of power? Will Prabowo, after successfully using Jokowi as part of his "electoral strategy" abandon Jokowi when it comes to governing the country after October 2024?
- What will Prabowo and his running mate Gibran signify as far as Indonesian politics is concerned? Will there be a backsliding of democracy and a stronger policy toward his political opponents and critics? Most importantly, for the outside world, what will be the direction of Indonesia's foreign and defense policy under Prabowo in the coming years?

Here, the overpowering question that has preoccupied many would be the role Jokowi will play in the Prabowo government.

There has been much speculation since February 2024 as to whether Jokowi will join the Presidential Advisory Council alongside Wiranto and Bambang Yudhoyono or even take over as the chairman of Golkar, PDI-P, or even Gerindra. Will he play the role of uniting and leading various political parties into a mega political structure as a machinery of support for the Prabowo–Gibran government? Or even more sinister, will the Jokowi–Prabowo "*entente cordiale*" collapse due to conflicting interests and priorities? These are critical questions that will have implications for the future of Indonesian politics once President-elect Prabowo is sworn in.

Still, the sun would continue to shine on Prabowo and the type of leader he would emerge as president of the country. The one important factor that cannot be ignored is the character and will power of Prabowo Subianto as an individual, even as he has the backing of a powerful historical family. It is very rare to witness an individual, a senior officer at that, who has been dismissed from the military on disciplinary grounds, return to mainstream politics, first as a losing vice presidential candidate, then losing twice in the presidential race, and finally triumphing in his third presidential contest. This is indeed a rare accomplishment that demonstrates the strong-willed persona of Prabowo. Clearly, the February 2024 presidential elections have fully vindicated and rehabilitated Prabowo in toto, and he can be expected to be his own man despite paying deference to Jokowi and Wiranto, two key figures who were instrumental in his victory. The author still recalls a discussion with Prabowo when he was still a Major-General in the TNI more than twenty years ago about certain developments in Indonesia, with Prabowo finally narrowing down the reason for whatever happened on the grounds that "*dia tak kuat dradjat*," that is, "he is not of a strong character and will." This is something that needs to be understood and will define and determine the presidency under Prabowo, and most probably the directions of the country's domestic and foreign policy.

In the meantime, the spiritual world that defines most Javanese has continued "to spin" with various predictions of how Prabowo would rule and administer the country. One of these emerged in the aftermath of the Prabowo–Gibran massive lead in the Quick Count following the February 14, 2024 election mentioning eight major developments that would take place under Prabowo's presidency. This was said to be in line with Ronggowarsita's predictions of the seven leaders who would rule Indonesia, changing one after the other, in what was referred to as the "cycle of change" or "*cokro Manggilingan*," which all Javanese are destined to go through, whatever their positions in life. In this regard, Ronggo Warsita predicted seven types of leaders who would rule Indonesia, each with a specific type of leadership quality.

The seven leadership types were (1) *Satrio Kinunjoro Murwo Kuncoro*; (2) *Satrio Mukti Wibowo Kesandung Kesampar*; (3) *Satrio Jinumput Sumela Atur*; (4) *Satrio Lelono Tapa Ngrame*; (5) *Satrio Hamong Tuwuh*; (6) *Satrio Boyong Pambukaning Gapuro*; and (7) *Satrio Pinandito Sinisihan Wahyu*. In this regard, when Prabowo is finally sworn in as the country's president in October 2024, then Prabowo is said, according to these predictions, to qualify under leadership character number two, namely, *Satrio Mukti Wibowo Kesandung Kesampar*, meaning one who has wealth and leadership but will suffer as a result of mistakes made. However, as Prabowo has already suffered in different ways, including being divorced, dismissed from the military, and losing elections in the past, these mistakes would now be overcome as a result of having paid the price in the past [*sudah menebus dosa*, or has repented for his sins]. In short, Prabowo has already atoned for all the sins and mistakes committed in the past, and hence will be able to restart on a clean slate, something that Wiranto hinted in his speech in support of Prabowo when he said that the new president will now be living not for himself but for the people of Indonesia with God's blessings.

According to this school of thought, under Prabowo's leadership, there will be eight major developments in the coming years. First, Prabowo will be able to unite the big opposing forces in the country, best expressed in terms of the conflict between the "old and new orders," clearly evident in the post-1998 era. Prabowo's ability to unite these forces will be due to the presence of two key leaders, namely, Prabowo representing the "new order" and Jokowi representing the "old order." Their unity will have a profound impact on the country's progress. Second, the new-found unity will bring much prosperity and strength to the country, and that will make it difficult for external forces and Indonesia's enemies to weaken Indonesia through division and exploit its resources. Third, in the early period of the Prabowo–Gibran leadership, there will be attempts by those who oppose the new leadership to topple the government, especially by those who are influenced by or even proxies of external forces who mean to do harm to Indonesia. These external forces and groups will try to use local proxies and agents of influence to weaken the country but this will be neutralized and overcome.

Fourth, the enemies of the nation will be decisively defeated, especially those who have been determined to undermine and weaken Indonesia from within, often through the aid of external forces. These external agents will be defeated decisively once and for all. Fifth, in the early period of the Prabowo government, there will be much progress and prosperity for the nation as a whole due largely to the leader's credibility and leadership qualities. Sixth, many people in the country who have been unable to progress or climb up the socio-economic ladder will be able to do so, with groups such as the farmers and the poor in general benefiting greatly. Seventh, there will be a determined effort to run the country through laws in order to ensure justice for all, and those violating the country's law will be duly punished. Finally, through the strong leadership experience of Prabowo, the country will be safeguarded from external threats and the nation will be well regarded internationally due to the all-round strengths it will acquire under the new leadership.[1]

Whether the eight predictions — namely, unity of the old and new political forces, especially of the old and new orders; the close cooperation and harmony of political elites, especially Jokowi and Prabowo; the initial challenges of the Prabowo government, especially from the losers of the presidential elections; overcoming the

---

[1] See "8 peristiwa Besar ini akan terjadi setelah Prabowo-Gibran dilantik", YouTube. https://www.youtube.com/watch?v=i5XVNj1Vh0I; "Semakin Ditakuti Negara Tetangga! 8 Peristiwa Besar Akan Terjadi Setelah Prabowo Gibran Dilantik". See https://www.youtube.com/watch?v=dLqSTKxFmr4.

state's enemies, especially from within; the early prosperity of the nation; the rise of respect, honor, and dignity of the populace; improvement in the system of laws; and the bravery in overcoming external threats — will be actualized or not remains to be seen. For many, these predictions and scenarios are based on non-scientific concepts and belief systems that cannot be proven or verified; still, what is critical is that the Javanese people believe in them and to that extent would even hold the Prabowo–Gibran team to account as part of the transactional contract between the Prabowo–Gibran team and the citizens who voted them overwhelmingly to power in the hope of a new and powerful Indonesia.

Similarly, there are also those who believe that while Prabowo won the presidency, he did not qualify according to the traditional Javanese and spiritual dictum. Hence, there may be dangers ahead for him and his presidency. According to past predictions of 'NOTONOGORO', Prabowo did not qualify in the present spiritual circumstances as there is no 'GO' in his name, his reign may be short-lived or short-circuited, in line with past presidents such as Habibie, Abdurrahman Wahid and Megawati. Hence, from the Javanese spiritual world, there may be uncertainties ahead and Prabowo's hold to power remains to be seen, all the more, due to Prabowo's age, where he would be 73 years and 3 weeks old when he is sworn in on October 20, 2024. This is not to mention of his medical health. Hence, 'Prabowo watching' would be politically important to ascertain the future of the country in the coming years.

In this regard, what will determine the success of the Prabowo–Gibran team and government as a whole in the coming months and even years will be a number of key developments and deliverables. The following are some important questions:

(a) How would the legal or constitutional challenge by the losers, namely, Ganjar–Mahfud and Anies–Muhaimin, now supported by some elements of civil society groups, be handled and concluded by the Prabowo–Gibran team, especially in light of the fact that the victory was too strong and overwhelming and such challenges had never succeeded in the past? Clearly, with strong international recognition of the Prabowo–Gibran leadership and victory, and with plans and programs being laid out for the public to see, these challenges are unlikely to make any serious impact on the Prabowo–Gibran leadership, all the more with Jokowi still strongly entrenched in power till October 2024. Still, how these legal challenges are handled and dealt with will signal the type of democracy Indonesia will adopt in the coming years. With the Constitutional Court already dismissing these challenges by April 2024, Prabowo has emerged stronger, with his mandate even more enhanced and consolidated. Prabowo's legitimacy and credibility have been strengthened by his one-round victory on February 14, 2024 being confirmed by Quick and Real Counts that was endorsed by the KPU, the victory being reaffirmed by the Constitutional Court that dismissed challenges to the presidential election results and where the public believed, through various surveys that the win by the Prabowo-Gibran team was final and the country should move on with preparing for the post-Jokowi era.

(b) Will the PDI-P withdraw its ministers from the Jokowi cabinet before the president's term ends in October 2024, thereby destabilizing the country's politics and governance, even though Megawati had said that she will not do so? While this cannot be ignored, to do so would also be politically foolhardy as the PDI-P would lose critical access to resources and not be part of the political decision-making machinery of which it is a key player today. Yet, since the defeat of the PDI-P's candidate, Ganjar, in the presidential elections, the PDI-P as a whole and especially its Secretary-General, Hasto, have been increasingly belligerent and hostile toward President Jokowi, among others, accusing him of wanting to take over the PDI-P's leadership from Megawati and even accusing him of become the "Second Suharto" in the country. In short, the PDI-P–Jokowi relationship can be expected to deteriorate, and how this will impact the incoming Prabowo–Gibran government remains to be seen, especially if the PDI-P becomes a key opposition party in parliament.

(c) How will Prabowo construct a "national unity" political coalition (*koalisi besar*) in support of the Prabowo–Gibran government that can have an overwhelming majority in parliament along the lines that were established by Bambang Yudhoyono and Jokowi from the period 2004 to 2024? This will be critical to ensure the power and sustainability of the Prabowo–Gibran government and its ability to carry out the various programs it had promised in the election campaigns, especially in the economic arenas and social programs such as free milk and food for students.

(d) Who will form the members of the Prabowo–Gibran cabinet and how will power be shared between the initial members and supporters of the Prabowo coalition, new coalition members, and professionals and specialists needed to head the more technical ministries such as finance, technology, justice, and environment? This may involve not just political parties that crossed the parliamentary threshold of 4% but also political parties that did not, but that supported the Prabowo-Gibran coalition such as PBB, PSI, Gelora and Garuda as well as political parties that did not back the Prabowo-Gibran team such as PPP, Hanura, Perindo, among others.

(e) What are the likely roles of the key players behind Prabowo, such as Jokowi, Wiranto, Bambang Yudhoyono, and Agum Gumelar in the new power structure that is likely to emerge after October 2024? Will fractures emerge between these key players and Prabowo in the coming months and years?

(f) How will the Prabowo government deliver its campaign promises to uplift the well-being and welfare of Indonesians, including various programs for the farmers, students, and older Indonesians? How will resources be deployed for these purposes?

(g) What will be the foreign and defense policies of Indonesia and how will the Prabowo–Gibran team want to project its power in the region and beyond, all the more in view of the overwhelming public endorsement of a strongman style of leadership backed by Jokowi, Wiranto, Bambang Yudhoyono, and Agum Gumelar? A key issue in this regard will be Indonesia's policies toward China and the United States, which will set the tone for a foreign policy of "*bebas and aktif*," free and active, which is the time-honored foreign policy *mantra* of Indonesia. Here, Indonesia's policies toward ASEAN; its Oceanic neighbors of Australia, New Zealand, and the South Pacific; its Northeast Asian neighbors of Japan, South and North Korea, and even Taiwan; South Asia, especially India; and key Middle East states such as Iran, Saudi Arabia, Egypt, and the UAE will be important to watch as these will have serious implications at the national, regional, and global levels.

A Strongman Prabowo-Centric Government

Whatever the specific shape and character of the policies the Prabowo–Gibran government will adopt at home and abroad after October 2024, what is explicitly clear is that the coming five years will have a strongman Prabowo-centric government, with the new leader's energy, self-confidence, broad knowledge of global affairs, and iron-clad vision of what is needed for Indonesia leading the country. Prabowo will probably follow the lead of similar strong leaders elsewhere, regardless of their political systems, such as Vladimir Putin, Xi Jinping, Recep Tayyip Erdoğan, Narendra Modi, Mahathir Mohammad, and Lee Kuan Yew. Such leaders tend to be highly proactive due to their knowledge and competence of the subject matter in domestic and foreign policies, tend to be mission-driven, wanting to achieve certain short- to medium-term goals for their countries and people, and eventually aim to place their country on the world map. Prabowo clearly fits the bill and, hence, his entry into the new political ecosystem of a new type of leader in the largest Southeast Asian state and the biggest Muslim state that is not just strategically located but also strongly endowed with resources in the 17,000 island-wide archipelago that controls key sea lanes of communications adjoining the Pacific and Indian Oceans. Even more critical will be the strong mandate the Prabowo–Gibran team received from the Indonesia public that was largely made up of Gen Z and Millennial voters. Clearly, the 2024 Indonesian presidential elections have catapulted into power an individual who due to his age will probably only serve one term but who will be bent on making a difference at home and abroad, partly due to the powerful family he comes from, the experiences he has been through, and the drive he possesses, all the more having been dismissed from the military and lost key elections since 2009.

Conclusion

Political changes in big states anywhere in the world tend to have domestic, regional, and international impacts. For Indonesia, there are bound to be implications for domestic politics in the arena of governance, economic and social policies, and coalition building. Regionally, Indonesia can be expected to act with a stronger voice in addressing regional issues of direct concern, such as the South China Sea conflict, or indirect concern, in terms of bilateral tensions in the region. With one of the largest emerging economies in the region and world, the Prabowo–Gibran economic policies will have wide-ranging implications, especially in the context of rising economic competition between the West and China. Geopolitically, Indonesia's policies toward national, regional, and global Islamist politics will also be important, especially in terms of managing what is viewed as the rising threat of extremism and terrorism. Finally, due to Indonesia's critical strategic position that straddles the Indian and Pacific Oceans and controls key sea lanes of communications, it will play a vital role in the rising geopolitical balance, with key powers such as the United States, China, and India trying to develop close ties with Indonesia, hence improving its standing in the global balance of power.

Since the decolonization of states in Asia and Africa, elections have become an important means of peacefully transferring power from one group to another. While many countries were planning to hold their elections in 2024, some of the more critical ones were in the United States, India, Russia, and Indonesia, as the leaderships in these countries will have important consequences for national, regional, and global politics. As the largest state in Southeast Asia and the largest Muslim state that is also bountiful in natural resources and strategically located, what the Prabowo–Gibran leadership will mean for Indonesia and the outside world, remains to be seen. Still, there is much promise ahead of a strong leadership that will navigate in a complex set of political, economic, and strategic variables, and where the new leaders are strongly equipped and endowed to lead such a powerful and historical state. There is also the expectations of many positive spillovers, including the emergence of a strong ASEAN addressing regional issues and standing tall in international politics in the midst of the intensifying US–China rivalry and other issues such as in Ukraine, Gaza and elsewhere that may surface.

SELECT BIBLIOGRAPHY

Adams, C. (1965). *Bung Karno, My Friend*. New York: Bobbs-Merrill.
Aditya, A., Sipahutar, T., and Rahadiana, R. (2019). "Indonesia picks Borneo for new capital amid Jakarta gridlock". Bloomberg. Retrieved August 15, 2022, from https://www.bloomberg.com/news/articles/2019-08-26/jokowi-picks-borneo-for-new-capital-as-jakarta-nears-gridlock.
Adyatama, E. (2024). "A clandestine operation for Gibran", *Tempo*, 11 February. https://magz.tempo.co/read/cover-story/41561/a-clandestine-operation-for-gibran.
Aglionby, J. (2002). "Indonesia takes a giant step down the road to democracy". *The Guardian*. Retrieved August 15, 2022, from https://www.theguardian.com/world/2002/aug/11/indonesia.johnaglionby.
Al-Hamdi, R. (ed.) (2023). *Dinamika Jelang Pemilu Serentak 2024*. Yogyakarta: Penerbit Samudra Biru.
Amalia, L. S., Haris, S., Romli, L., Nuryanti, S., Ichwanuddin, W., and Budiatri, A. P. (eds.) (2016). *Evaluasi Pemilihan Presiden Lansung di Indonesia*. Yogyakarta: Pustaka Pelajar.
Amar, A. (2021). *Tak Tumbang Dicerca Tak Terbang Dipuja: Anies Baswedan dan Kerja-Kerja Terukurnya*. Surabaya: Ikon Teralitera.
Amindoni, A. (2017). "Apa yang perlu Anda ketahui tentang UU Pemilu". *BBC News Indonesia*. Retrieved August 15, 2022, from https://www.bbc.com/indonesia/indonesia-40678216.
Anggrainy, F. (2022). "Simulasi Pilpres 2024 Charta: Ganjar Menang Siapa Pun Cawapresnya". *DetikNews*. Retrieved August 15, 2022, from https://news.detik.com/berita/d-6050146/simulasi-pilpres-2024-charta-ganjar-menang-siapa-pun-cawapresnya.

Aqil, A. (2022). "Majority of Indonesians reject extending presidential terms: SMRC". *The Jakarta Post.* Retrieved August 15, 2022, from https://www.thejakartapost.com/paper/2022/04/04/majority-of-indonesians-reject-extending-presidential-terms-smrc.html.

Arifianto, A. (2024). "Prabowo owes his landslide victory to Jokowi's endorsement". *East Asia Forum.* https://doi.org/10.59425/eabc.1708182000.

Armandhanu, D. and Haizan, R. Y. A. (2024, February 28). "Prabowo awarded four-star general rank by Jokowi, who fends off talk of a political transaction." *CNA.* https://www.channelnewsasia.com/asia/indonesia-jokowi-prabowo-military-general-four-star-rank-free-lunch-politics-4156271.

Arshad, A. (2020). "Indonesia's new omnibus law can make or break Jokowi's legacy." *The Straits Times.* Retrieved August 15, 2022, from https://www.straitstimes.com/asia/se-asia/indonesias-new-omnibus-law-can-make-or-break-jokowis-legacy.

Aspinall, E., Klinken, G., and Feith, H. (1999). *The Last Days of President Suharto.* Melbourne: Monash Asia Institute, University of Monash.

Aspinall, E. and Mietzner, M. (2019). "Indonesia's democratic paradox: Competitive elections amidst rising illiberalism". *Bulletin of Indonesian Economic Studies,* 55(3), 295–317.

Bartlett, C. (2022, November 30). "Oligarchs weaken Indonesia's fight against corruption". 360. https://360info.org/oligarchs-weaken-indonesias-fight-against-corruption/.

Barton, G. (2002). *Abdurrahman Wahid: Muslim Democrat, Indonesian President.* Sydney: University of New South Wales Press.

Basorie, W. D. (2023, October 29). "Commentary: His son's election run could tarnish Jokowi's legacy". *CNA.* https://www.channelnewsasia.com/commentary/indonesia-jokowi-son-gibran-legacy-election-3877661.

Bland, B. (2021). *Man of Contradictions: Joko Widodo and the Struggle to Remake Indonesia.* Penguin Random House Australia.

Bland, B. (2024, February 15). "'Continuity' Prabowo means change for Indonesia". Chatham House – International Affairs Think Tank. https://www.chathamhouse.org/2024/02/continuity-prabowo-means-change-indonesia

Business Enabling Environment (BEE). The World Bank. Retrieved August 15, 2022, from https://www.worldbank.org/en/programs/business-enabling-environment.

"Chinese firms to benefit if front-runner Prabowo seals Indonesian election win". (2024, February 11). *South China Morning Post.* https://www.scmp.com/business/china-business/article/3251669/chinese-companies-set-benefit-if-front-runner-prabowo-subianto-seals-victory-indonesian-presidential.

Dwipayana, G. and Ramadhan, K. (1989). *Soeharto: My Thoughts, Words, and Deeds: An Autobiography.* Jakarta: Citra Lamtoro Gung Persada Publishers.

Endrasawara, S. (2006). *Filsafat Kejawen Dalam Aksara Jawa.* Yogyakarta: Gelombang Pasang.

Endrasawara, S. (2013). *Falsafah Kepemimpinan Jawa: Butir-butir Nilai yang Membangun Karakter Seorang Pemimpin Menurut Budaya Jawa.* Yogyakarta: Penerbit Narasi.

Elson, R. (2001). *Suharto: A Political Biography.* Cambridge, England: Cambridge University Press.

Ericssen. (2024, February 25). "Indonesian President Jokowi makes power play to bolster Prabowo's coalition – and wield political influence after stepping down". *CNA.* https://www.channelnewsasia.com/asia/indonesia-jokowi-smooth-transition-power-prabowo-coalition-political-influence-4144611.

Fealy, G. (2020). "Jokowi in the Covid-19 era: Repressive pluralism, dynasticism and the overbearing state". *Bulletin of Indonesian Economic Studies,* 56(3), 301–323.

Ghaliya, G. (2020). "Intimidation of government critics raises concerns about freedom of speech". *The Jakarta Post.* Retrieved August 15, 2022, from https://www.thejakartapost.com/news/2020/06/02/intimidation-of-government-critics-raises-concerns-about-freedom-of-speech.html.

"Gini index – Indonesia". *The World Bank Data.* Retrieved August 15, 2022, from https://data.worldbank.org/indicator/SI.POV.GINI?locations=ID.

Gouda, F. (2002). *American Visions of the Netherlands East Indies/Indonesia: US Foreign Policy and Indonesian Nationalism, 1920–1949.* Amsterdam: Amsterdam University Press, Amsterdam University.

Guild, J. (2021). "How Jokowi solved Indonesia's toll road dilemma. Sort of". *The Diplomat.* Retrieved August 15, 2022, from https://thediplomat.com/2021/05/how-jokowi-solved-indonesias-toll-road-dilemma-sort-of/.

Guild, J. J. (2024, February 7). "How Prabowo Subianto Is Closing In on the Indonesian Presidency". *RSIS IP24012.* https://www.rsis.edu.sg/rsis-publication/idss/ip24012-how-prabowo-subianto-is-closing-in-on-the-indonesian-presidency/.

Hamid, U. and Hermawan, A. (2020, October 9). "Indonesia's omnibus law is a bust for human rights". *New Mandala.* https://www.newmandala. org/indonesias-omnibus-law-is-a-bust-for-human-rights/.

Hermansyah, A. (2018). "New regulation on foreign workers part of administrative reform: Jokowi". *The Jakarta Post.* Retrieved August 15, 2022, from https://www.thejakartapost.com/news/2018/04/25/new-regulation-on-foreign-workers-part-of-administrative-reform-jokowi. html.

Hermawan, A. (2020). "Fight for your freedom: Indonesian online civic space under siege". *The Jakarta Post.* Retrieved August 15, 2022, from https://www.thejakartapost.com/academia/2020/08/25/fight-for-your-freedom-indonesian-online-civic-space-under-siege.html.

"Highlights: Indonesia elections 2024 results – Prabowo Subianto claims presidential victory based on early counts". (2024, February 14). *CNA.* https://www.channelnewsasia.com/asia/indonesia-elections-2024-live-results-anies-baswedan-prabowo-subianto-ganjar-pranowo-4119676.

Hermawan, A. (2024, February 27). "The biggest threat to Indonesia's democracy? It's not Prabowo, it's the oligarchy". *The Conversation.* http://theconversation.com/the-biggest-threat-to-indonesias-democracy-its-not-prabowo-its-the-oligarchy-223974.

Hughes, J. (2002). *The End of Sukarno – A Coup that Misfired: A Purge that Ran Wild.* Singapore: Archipelago Press.

"Indonesia government debt to GDP." *Trading Economics.* Retrieved August 15, 2022, from https://tradingeconomics.com/indonesia/government-debt-to-gdp.

"Indonesian politicians are giving the armed forces a big role in government". (2019). *The Economist.* Retrieved August 15, 2022, from https://www.economist.com/asia/2019/10/31/indonesian-politicians-are-giving-the-armed-forces-a-big-role-in-government.

Isdiyanto, Isman, B., and Solikun (eds.) (2016). *Kontroversi Ganjar.* Jakarta: Penerbit Kompas.

Ismail, S. (2024, February 13). "Indonesia Elections 2024: How the "Jokowi effect" has influenced the electoral landscape". *CNA.* https://www.channelnewsasia.com/asia/indonesia-elections-joko-widodo-jokowi-effect-kingmaker-influence-4118726.

Ismawan, I., Felecianus, J., Putra, W. W., and Darmaputra, W. (eds.) (2022). *Ganjar Perkasa: 'Duet Maut' Sipil-Militer Menjaga Keutuhan NKRI.* Yogyakarta: Medpress.

Janti, N. (2023, November 7). "BREAKING: Ethics council removes chief justice Anwar – Politics". *The Jakarta Post.* https://www.thejakartapost.com/indonesia/2023/11/07/breaking-ethics-council-removes-chief-justice-anwar.html.

"Joko Widodo is considering extending his term in office". (2022). *The Economist.* Retrieved 15 August 2022, from https://www.economist.com/asia/2022/03/26/joko-widodo-is-considering-extending-his-term-in-office.

Jong, H. N. (2020, October 26). "Indonesian officials linked to mining and 'dirty energy' firms benefiting from deregulation law". *Mongabay Environmental News.* https://news.mongabay.com/2020/10/indonesia-coal-mining-energy-omnibus-deregulation-law-oligarch/.

Kurlantzick, J. (2020). "How Jokowi failed the test of COVID-19 in Indonesia". *World Politics Review.* Retrieved August 15, 2022, from https://www.worldpoliticsreview.com/amid-lackluster-response-by-jokowi-indonesia-reels-from-covid-19/.

Kusuma, A. (2022). *The Birth of the 1945 Constitution: Including Copies of the Authentic Documents of the Investigating Committee for Preparatory Work for Independence* (in Indonesian). Jakarta: University of Indonesia, Badan Penerbit Fakultas Hukum Universitas Indonesia.

Lai, Y. (2022, March 21). "PDI-P puts brakes on plan to amend Constitution". *The Jakarta Post.* https://www.thejakartapost.com/paper/2022/03/21/pdi-p-puts-brakes-on-plan-to-amend-constitution.html.

Lamb, K. (2022). "Explainer: Talk of extended Jokowi term puts Indonesia democratic resilience under spotlight". *Reuters.* Retrieved August 15, 2022, from https://www.reuters.com/world/asia-pacific/talk-extended-jokowi-term-puts-indonesia-democratic-resilience-under-spotlight-2022-03-17/.

Lamb, K. and Teresia, A. (2023, October 16). "Jokowi, Indonesia's kingmaker, works to keep influence after election". *Reuters.* https://www.reuters.com/world/asia-pacific/jokowi-indonesias-kingmaker-works-keep-influence-after-election-2023-10-14/.

Langit, R. (2002). "Indonesia's Military: Business as usual". *Asia Times Online.* Retrieved 9 June 2009.

Lee, S. (2022). "Anies Baswedan: Potential kingmaker in Indonesia's 2024 presidential race?". *Fulcrum.* Retrieved August 15, 2022, from https://fulcrum.sg/anies-baswedan-potential-kingmaker-in-indonesias-2024-presidential-race/.

Legge, J. (2003). *Sukarno: A Political Biography*. Singapore: Archipelago Press.

Mahbubani, K. (2021). "The Genius of Jokowi". *Project Syndicate*. Retrieved August 15, 2022, from https://www.project-syndicate.org/commentary/indonesia-president-jokowi-effective-democratic-governance-model-by-kishore-mahbubani-2021-10.

Mathai, A. and Sood, A. (2024, February 15). "With Prabowo set to be president, what 'surprises' are in store for Indonesia?" *South China Morning Post*. https://www.scmp.com/week-asia/politics/article/3252003/indonesia-2024-election-prabowo-subianto-wild-card-nationalistic-agenda.

Moedjanto, G. (1993). *The Concept of Power in Javanese Culture*, Third Printing. Yogyakarta: Gadjah Mada University Press.

Mortimer, R. (2006). *Indonesian Communism under Sukarno*. Singapore: Equinox Publishers.

Nugroho, J. (2021). "Will Jokowi pull off a three-peat?" Lowy Institute. Retrieved August 15, 2022, from https://www.lowyinstitute.org/the-interpreter/will-jokowi-pull-three-peat.

Nugroho, R. (2022), *Kebijakan Pemilihan Umum: Sebuah Literasi Politik*. Yogyakarta: Pustaka Pelajar.

Ompusunggu, M. (2018). "Opposition questions Jokowi's policy on foreign workers". *The Jakarta Post*. Retrieved August 15, 2022, from https://www.thejakartapost.com/news/2018/04/20/opposition-questions-jokowis-policy-on-foreign-workers.html.

Ovier, A. (2019). "Publik Cenderung Dukung Presiden Jokowi 3 Periode". *Berita Satu*. Retrieved August 15, 2022, from https://www.beritasatu.com/politik/789663/publik-cenderung-dukung-presiden-jokowi-3-periode.

Paddock, R. and Sijabat, D. (2020). "Indonesia has no reported coronavirus cases. Is that the whole picture?". *The New York Times*. Retrieved August 15, 2022, from https://www.nytimes.com/2020/02/11/world/asia/coronavirus-indonesia-bali.html.

"President Jokowi denies politicizing social assistance—Politics". (2024, February 5). *The Jakarta Post*. https://www.thejakartapost.com/indonesia/2024/02/05/president-jokowi-denies-politicizing-social-assistance.html.

Purdey, J. (2006). *Anti-Chinese violence in Indonesia, 1996–1999*. Honolulu: University of Hawaii Press.

Purwadi, (2003). *Sosiologi Mistik R. Ng. Ronggowarsito: Membaca Sasmita Jaman Edan.* Yogyakarta: Persada.

Purwadi, (2006). *Jongko Joyoboyo: Jongko Jangkah Jangkaning Jaman.* Yogyakarta: Gelombang Pasang.

Rachman, M. F. (2024). *Indonesia Memilih Presiden.* Jakarta: Kepustakan Populer Gramedia.

Ratcliffe, R. and Mulyanto, R. (2024, January 9). "From military leader to 'harmless grandpa': The rebranding of Indonesia's Prabowo". *The Guardian.* https://www.theguardian.com/world/2024/jan/09/indonesia-election-prabowo-subianto-rebranding-kidnapping-accusations.

Rayda, N. (2024, February 16). "A controversial former general is set to become Indonesia's new president. How did Prabowo Subianto pull it off?" *CNA.* https://www.channelnewsasia.com/asia/indonesia-presidential-election-prabowo-subianto-4127931.

Ressa, M. A. (2014, July 16). "Indonesia: Prabowo and the divine revelation". *Al Jazeera.* https://www.aljazeera.com/opinions/2014/7/16/indonesia-elections-prabowo-and-the-divine-revelation.

Ricklefs, M. (1991). *A History of Modern Indonesia since c. 1300,* 2nd ed. Stanford: Stanford University Press.

Romli, L. (2019). *Sistem Presidential Indonesia: Dinamika, Problematik dan Penguatan Pelembagaan.* Malang, Setara Press.

Salna, K. (2018). "Indonesia needs $157 billion for infrastructure plan". *Bloomberg.* Retrieved 15 August 2022, from https://www.bloomberg.com/news/articles/2018-01-25/indonesia-seeks-to-plug-157-billion-gap-in-nation-building-plan.

Sambhi, N. (2021). "Generals gaining ground: Civil-military relations and democracy in Indonesia". *Brookings.* Retrieved August 15, 2022, from https://www.brookings.edu/articles/generals-gaining-ground-civil-military-relations-and-democracy-in-indonesia/.

Sartono, F. W. (2023). *Ganjar Pranowo: 8 Tahun Mengabdi Dengan Hati.* Bogor: Naratama.

Schwarz, A. (1994). *A Nation in Waiting: Indonesia in the 1990s.* Boulder, Colorado: Westview Press.

Sekretariat Negara Republik Indonesia. (1985). *30 Tahun Indonesia Merdeka (30 Years of Indonesian Independence) 1965–1973.* Jakarta: Sekretariat Negara.

Sherlock, S. (2024, February 19). "What Indonesia's election means for its democracy". Australian Institute of International Affairs. https://www.internationalaffairs.org.au/australianoutlook/what-indonesias-election-means-for-its-democracy/.

Simandjuntak, D. (2022). "Looking ahead to Indonesia's 2024 elections". *East Asia Forum.* Retrieved August 15, 2022, from https://www.eastasiaforum.org/2022/06/10/looking-ahead-to-indonesias-2024-elections/.

Sindunata. (2024). *Ratu Adil: Ramalan Jayabaya & Sejarah Perlawanan Wong Cilik.* Jakarta: Kompas Gramedia.

Siregar, K. (2022). "Discussions intensify over potential presidential candidates for Indonesia's 2024 general election". *Channel News Asia.* Retrieved August 15, 2022, from https://www.channelnewsasia.com/asia/indonesia-elections-2024-presidential-candidate-pdip-golkar-gerindra-2760381.

Smith, R. (1974). *Southeast Asia: Documents of Political Development and Change.* Ithaca, New York: Cornell University Press.

Sood, A. (2023a, July 23). "Indonesia's Prabowo casts himself as 'Jokowi's man' in third bid for presidency." *South China Morning Post.* https://www.scmp.com/week-asia/politics/article/3228519/indonesias-prabowo-subianto-sheds-strongman-image-he-guns-top-job-being-jokowis-man.

Sood, A. (2023b, October 16). "Fears for Indonesia democracy as Jokowi's son could run as VP after court ruling". *South China Morning Post.* https://www.scmp.com/week-asia/politics/article/3238124/fears-indonesia-democracy-jokowis-son-gets-vp-election-pathway-plot-twist-move-court.

Sood, A. (2024, February 26). "Will Indonesia's unpredictable president-elect continue Jokowi's China approach?" *South China Morning Post.* https://www.scmp.com/economy/article/3253175/global-impact-cuddly-grandpa-prabowo-subianto-claims-victory-all-indonesians-defence-minister.

Sood, A., Yuniar, R. W., and Mathai, A. (2024, February 16). "Prabowo's presidency: New chapter in Indonesia-China ties or business as usual?" *South China Morning Post.* https://www.scmp.com/week-asia/politics/article/3252127/indonesia-china-ties-will-president-elect-prabowo-confront-beijing-or-maintain-widodos-economic.

Sri Wintala Achmad. (2014). *Satria Peningit: Menyingkap Tabir Falsafah Kepimpinan Ratu Adil.* Yogyakarta: Koreksi Aksara.

Stefanie, C. (2017). "Jokowi Tegaskan UU Ormas untuk Lindungi Pancasila". *CNN Indonesia*. Retrieved August 15, 2022, from https://www.cnnindonesia.com/nasional/20171026105856-20-251210/jokowi-tegaskan-uu-ormas-untuk-lindungi-pancasila.

"Suharto tops corruption rankings". (2004). *BBC News*. Retrieved August 15, 2022, from http://news.bbc.co.uk/2/hi/business/3567745.stm.

Suhenda, D. (2022). "Luhut says most people want longer term for Jokowi. But experts, surveys beg to differ". *The Jakarta Post*. Retrieved August 15, 2022, from https://www.thejakartapost.com/indonesia/2022/03/15/luhut-says-most-people-want-longer-term-for-jokowi-but-experts-surveys-beg-to-differ.html.

Sulaiman, Y. (2024, February 16). "Commentary: Prabowo's likely victory will be a test for Indonesia's democracy". *CNA*. https://www.channelnewsasia.com/commentary/prabowo-subianto-indonesia-presidential-election-democracy-joko-widodo-influence-4125806.

Sunano, A. S. (2023). *Lucunya Prabowo: Tegas, Santuy, Ikhlas and Senyumin Aja*. Jakarta: PT Kompas Media Nusantara.

Suroyo, G. and Sulaiman, S. (2022, June 9). "Explainer: What's at stake with Indonesia's controversial jobs creation law?" *Reuters*. https://www.reuters.com/world/asia-pacific/whats-stake-with-indonesias-controversial-jobs-creation-law-2022-06-09/.

Suryaningty, M. T. (2024, January 23). "Social assistance, from state aid to politicization". *kompas.id*. https://www.kompas.id/baca/english/2024/01/22/en-bansos-dari-bantuan-negara-hingga-politisasi.

Susetya, W. *Pemimpin Masa Kini & Budaya Jawa: Menghidupkan Kembali Nilai-Nilai Kepribadian dan Kepemimpinan dalam Perspektif Jawa*. Jakarta: Percetakan Gramedia.

The Jakarta Post. (2023, November 8). "A judicial disgrace—Editorial". *The Jakarta Post*. https://www.thejakartapost.com/opinion/2023/11/08/a-judicial-disgrace.html.

The Word Bank. (2014). *Doing Business 2014: Economy Profile Indonesia*. Retrieved August 15, 2022, from https://openknowledge.worldbank.org/bitstream/handle/10986/18499/828630Indonesia0IDN0Box0382099B00PUBLIC0.pdf?sequence=1&isAllowed=y.

Transparency International. (2007). *Global Corruption Report 2007* [Ebook]. Retrieved August 15, 2022, from https://images.transparencycdn.org/images/2007_GCR_EN.pdf.

Tripathi, S. (2024, March 8). "How will Prabowo lead Indonesia?" *Foreign Policy*. https://foreignpolicy.com/2024/02/28/indonesia-elections-prabowo-leader-human-rights-jokowi/.

Undang-Undang RI No 2 Tahun 1999 Tentang Partai Politik. (2006). Detik.

Undang-Undang RI No 22 Tahun 1999 Tentang Pemerintahan Daerah. (2006). Tumotou.

Vickers, A. (2005). *A History of Modern Indonesia*. Cambridge: Cambridge University Press.

Vickers, A. (2012). *Bali – A Paradise Created*. Sydney: Tuttle Publishing.

Wanandi, J. (2012). *Shades of Grey: A Political Memoir of Modern Indonesia 1965–1998*. Singapore: Equinox Publishing.

Wang, O. and Chen, A. (2023, December 8). "Is Beijing warming to South China Sea code of conduct?". *South China Morning Post*. https://www-scmp-com.libproxy1.nus.edu.sg/news/china/diplomacy/article/3245375/beijing-warming-south-china-sea-code-conduct?module=inline&pgtype=article.

Warburton, E. (2016). "Jokowi and the new developmentalism". *Bulletin of Indonesian Economic Studies*, 52(3), 297–320. https://doi.org/10.1080/00074918.2016.1249262.

Warburton, E. and Aspinall, E. (2019). "Explaining Indonesia's democratic regression: structure, agency and popular opinion". *Contemporary Southeast Asia*, 41(2), 255–285.

Ward, K. (2022). Soeharto's Javanese Pancasila. In E. Aspinall and G. Fealy (eds.), *Soeharto's New Order and Its Legacy: Essays in Honour of Harold Crouch*. Canberra: The ANU E-Press.

Wulan, M. K., Martiar, N. A. D., and Salam, H. (2024, January 7). Sinyal Jokowi Dukung Prabowo Kian Kasat Mata. *kompas.id*. https://www.kompas.id/baca/polhuk/2024/01/06/sinyal-jokowi-dukung-prabowo-kian-kuat

"What will Prabowo Subianto's foreign policy look like?" (2024, February 29). *The Economist*. https://www.economist.com/asia/2024/02/29/what-will-prabowo-subiantos-foreign-policy-look-like.

Yuniar, R. W. (2023a, March 30). "Indonesians angry, sad as Fifa pulls U20 World Cup over its Israel stance". *South China Morning Post*. https://www.scmp.com/week-asia/politics/article/3215447/indonesias-jokowi-sad-football-fans-angry-fifa-pulls-u20-world-cup-over-israels-participation.

Yuniar, R. W. (2023b, November 14). "Indonesia's Prabowo slams West for double standards, lack of moral leadership: 'We don't really need

Europe'". *South China Morning Post.* https://www-scmp-com.libproxy1. nus.edu.sg/week-asia/politics/article/3241398/indonesias-prabowo-slams-west-double-standards-lack-moral-leadership-we-dont-really-need-europe?module=inline&pgtype=article.

Yuniar, R. W. (2024a, January 25). "Jokowi under renewed fire for saying presidents 'can take sides' in election". *South China Morning Post.* https://www.scmp.com/week-asia/politics/article/3249793/indonesias-jokowi-stokes-further-controversy-declaring-presidents-can-take-sides-elections.

Yuniar, R. W. (2024b, February 7). "Indonesia election 2024: Will Gibran be hurt by poll body's scandal?" *South China Morning Post.* https://www.scmp.com/week-asia/politics/article/3251181/indonesia-election 2024-will-gibrans-chances-be-hurt-election-bodys-ethics-scandal.

Yuniar, R. W. (2024c, February 15). "'Very popular' Joko Widodo to continue political dynasty with Prabowo win". *South China Morning Post.* https://www.scmp.com/week-asia/politics/article/3252080/indonesias-kingmaker-joko-widodo-leaves-indelible-mark-nation-prabowo-subianto-win.

INDEX

A

ABRI (Indonesian armed forces), 41–42, 60, 83, 109

Amin, M., 29, 32, 55–56, 64, 67, 87, 96, 126, 144–145, 152

B

Baswedan, A., xxvi, 67, 71, 87, 93, 97–98, 114, 128, 134, 142–143, 145, 153, 160, 172, 177, 190, 226, 228

Boediono, 29, 32, 55, 71, 74, 77, 80–81, 87, 111

D

Dewan Perwakilan Rakyat Republik Indonesia (DPR), 10

Djojohadikusomo, H., 202

Djojohadikusomo, M., 142, 200

Djojohadikusomo, S., 142

DPRD, 104–105, 188

G

Garuda Party, 197–198, 204–205, 253

Gerindra, xxviii, 67–71, 93, 111–112, 131, 142, 144–145, 147–148, 150, 153, 155, 170, 173–174, 190, 196–200, 203–205, 224, 255, 258, 260–261, 276–278

Golkar, xxviii, 20, 25–26, 32, 38, 42–43, 46, 48, 55–64, 67, 82, 85, 94–95, 111, 113, 120, 144, 148, 153, 155, 160, 166–167, 173–174, 190, 196, 198, 203–205, 224, 232, 253, 255, 260–261, 271

Gumelar, A., xxix, xxvii, 85, 87, 170, 206, 208, 229, 239, 256, 292

H

Hamengkubuwono IX, S., 32, 38

Hanura, 96, 155, 163, 174, 197–198, 236, 292

Hartarto, A., 48, 64, 113–114, 120, 141, 143, 150, 162, 176, 217, 232–233

Hasan, Z., 77, 148, 185, 217

Hatta, M., 32–33

Haz, H., 21, 27, 32, 43, 78, 84, 86–87, 270
Hidayat, D. S., 116, 134, 145, 163, 173

I
Indian Ocean, 3, 46, 72, 293
Indonesia, xxvii, xxx, 2–5, 7, 10, 17–21, 23, 32, 34, 36, 38, 40–41, 45, 47–48, 52–55, 57, 59, 61, 65, 67, 69, 72–73, 76, 78, 80, 82, 84, 90, 94, 101, 103, 107–108, 113, 115–116, 118, 120, 124–125, 129–131, 135–136, 139–141, 144, 147, 149, 154, 157–158, 162, 164, 170, 178, 181, 187, 189, 197, 201, 203, 207, 212, 217, 222, 228, 231, 234, 236, 242, 247–281, 283, 287–289, 291, 293–295
Iskandar, M., 67, 71, 74, 97, 120, 141, 144, 155, 176, 183, 190, 285–286

J
Java, xxiii, 56, 68, 70, 86, 100, 104–107, 127, 129, 143, 150, 170, 177, 192–193, 196, 213, 215, 226, 240
Jayabaya, 149

K
Kaesang, P., xxvi, 5, 94, 167, 179, 181, 223, 234, 280
Kalla, J., 29, 32, 45–46, 55–56, 63–64, 67, 77, 79, 81, 147–149, 154
Kamil, R., 131, 143–144, 173, 176
Khofifah, 129, 142, 176, 224
Kim, S. Y., 158, 164, 224

Komite Nasional Indonesia Pusat (KNIP), 17
Kopassus, 108–109, 202, 229
Kostrad, 43, 89, 108–109, 202
KPU (General Election Commission), xxi, xxviii, 30, 66, 111, 153, 183, 188, 190, 192, 199, 226, 250, 291
Kristiyanto, H., 147, 254

L
Labour Party, 141, 197–198
Lahadalia, B., 120, 185

M
Machmudin, B., 149
Maharani, P., 5, 99–101, 133, 142–143, 145, 165, 180
Mahfud, M. D., 56, 96, 142–143, 148, 176, 183, 190, 213–214, 254
Majapahit, 2, 151
Majelis Permusyawaratan Rakyat Republik Indonesia (MPR), 13
Malik, A., 32
Masjumi Party, 98
Mataram, 2
MPRS (Provisional People's Consultative Assembly), 18–20, 22, 43
Mulyono, 118, 150

N
Nasdem, 48, 65–67, 115, 155, 160–161, 174, 176, 197, 254–255, 260, 277
Nasution, B., xxvi, 179, 181, 281
Nusantara Awakening Party, 141, 197

P

Pacific Ocean, 294
Paloh, S., 48, 63, 65–66, 97, 148, 156, 160, 176, 239, 277
PAN (National Mandate Party), 65, 75–77, 95, 148, 197, 204, 232, 277
Panjaitan, L., xxvii, xxix, 170, 208, 256
Papua, 52, 56, 109, 154, 180, 184, 191, 195, 216, 252, 286
Pareira, A., 163
Parmusi, 25, 82
Partai Keadilan Sejahtera (PKS), 72, 103
Partai Nasional Indonesia (PNI), 32
Partai Persatuan Pembangunan (PPP), 38, 81
PBB (Crescent Star Party), 80, 141, 197–198, 253, 257–258, 292
PD, 32, 146, 173
PDI-P, xxv–xxvi, xxviii, 32, 42, 46, 49, 53–56, 63, 84–85, 95, 100, 102–103, 105, 143, 145–147, 153, 155, 160, 163–166, 168–170, 173, 175, 179–183, 196, 205, 211, 232, 253–255, 260, 264, 276, 278, 285, 291
Perindo, 96, 141, 155, 174, 197, 292
Perkasa, A., 89, 103, 117–118, 144, 163
Plate, J., 160–161
Pranowo, G., 56, 96, 103–107, 143, 159–160, 164, 172, 174, 196, 284–285
Projo, xxiii, 95, 170, 233
PSI (Indonesian Solidarity Party), xxvi, 108, 167, 181, 197, 223, 234, 275, 292
Purnama, B. T. (Ahok), 116, 124, 134, 143–145, 162, 241

R

Raka, G., 93, 167, 183, 217, 232
Razi, F., 50
Rismaharini, T., 143, 145
Rizieq, H., 124, 177–178, 242
Ronggowarsita, 149, 151–153, 223

S

Setiadi, B. A., 95, 170
Srivijaya, 2, 235
Straits of Lombok, 5
Straits of Makassar, 5
Straits of Malacca, 5
Straits of Sunda, 5, 157
Subianto, P., xxvi, 5, 29, 48, 55, 57, 63–64, 69, 74, 77, 81, 93, 101, 108–110, 142, 153, 200, 226, 249, 287
Sudharmono, 26, 32, 64, 83
Sudjatmiko, B., 166
Suharto, xxv, 19–20, 24, 36–39, 44, 52–53, 58–59, 61, 73, 82–83, 89, 108, 110, 121, 142, 150, 152, 179, 202, 217, 229, 237, 239, 252, 272, 274, 276, 291
Sukarno, 17–19, 24, 31, 33–36, 52, 57, 100, 147, 150–152, 163, 201–202, 279
Sukarnoputri, M., 5, 21, 27, 29, 32, 42, 44–45, 53, 56, 69, 76, 80, 100, 103–104, 111, 140, 148, 231, 274, 279
Sutrisno, T., 32

T

Tentara Nasional Indonesia (TNI), 10, 87
Thohir, E., 48, 143, 148, 280
Tidar, xxiii, 110, 256–257
Tjahjanto, H., 117–118, 191, 207

U

Ummah Party, 141, 198, 205, 258
Uno, S., 5, 29, 69, 74, 81, 86, 116, 134, 142–143, 145, 148, 173, 176, 204
Usman, A., 94, 167, 181

W

Widodo, J., 1, 29, 46–51, 55–56, 63, 65–67, 71, 93, 96, 101, 112–113, 115, 117–118, 121, 192, 206, 218, 222, 227, 256, 279
Wirahadikusumah, A., 43
Wirahadikusuma, U., 32
Wiranto, xxvii, 43, 63–64, 109–111, 206–208, 224, 239–241, 250, 256, 287–288, 292, xxix

Y

Yudhoyono, B., xxvii, 1, 29, 45–46, 54, 57, 63, 77–81, 85–86, 97, 115, 124, 132, 145, 149–150, 152, 154, 156, 192, 204, 208, 222, 224–225, 228, 230, 239, 255–256, 277, 287, 292
Yudhoyono, H., 176, 228, 277
Yusuf, S., 185